The Complete Virtual Guide To Pricing Your Morgan Silver Dollars (1878-1921)

By Michael S. Fey, Ph.D.

Stamping coins at the U.S. Mint in New Orleans, La., in 1897.

ISBN: 979-8-9919648-1-4

Editing and design by Mary Jo Meade
Cover photos by Tom Mulvaney

CONTENTS

Title Page......1

PREFACE......6

What's included......7

My background......8

Critical steps in the process of valuing your Morgan silver dollars......9

Two kinds of value......9

Finding your coins' value......10

Start by looking up the spot price of silver......12

Selling your coins......15

A word about supply and demand......17

Getting started......18

Careful handling protects value......19

Proper handling......20

Safe Storage......21

Problem coins and culls......22

The right way to view a Morgan dollar......25

Step 1: Your coin's date and mintmark......27

Dates, mintmarks and rarity......29

Morgan dollar design changes over time......30

Step 2: Grading Morgan silver dollars......34

Grading criteria......36

Strength of strike......38

Contact marks......39

Luster......41

DMPL Relativity Scale......43

Toning......45

Overall eye appeal......47

Grading coins on a numerical scale......48

Grading circulated coins......49

A visual guide......51

Grading mint state coins......55

Uncirculated......56

Select Uncirculated (MS-63)......57

Choice Uncirculated......58

Gem Uncirculated......59

High-end Gem Morgan silver dollars......60

Superb Gem Uncirculated......61

Perfect Uncirculated......62

Grading PL/DMPL coins, proofs and specialty strikes......63

Step 3: Is your coin a proof, specimen or pattern?......65

Proof coins......66

Specimen coins and Branch Mint proofs......68

Pattern Morgan dollars......69

Step 4: Spotting valuable VAM die varieties......70

Step 5: Does your coin have a special provenance?......72

Step 6: Do you have an error coin?......75

Kinds of minting errors......76

Striking errors......77

Heavy-premium errors......79

Step 7: Is your silver dollar genuine or a counterfeit?......81

Has it been altered?......83

A final word about pricing your Morgan silver dollars......84

Value charts......86

Appendix: Top 100 Morgan Silver Dollars, The VAM Keys......97

Preface

If you have Morgan silver dollars you want to sell — and you want to get the best possible price for them — this book is designed for you. It's a fast read, rich with photos instead of text so you can quickly identify your coins' value drivers and evaluate their potential for sale to collectors or for their melt value plus a small premium based on the spot silver market.

You can use this knowledge to determine whether you are being offered a fair price by a potential buyer or, if you don't want to sell your coins, you will be able to establish the approximate value of your collection for insurance purposes.

George T. Morgan (seated, third from left) and other Mint engravers.

What's included

• Tips for protecting coins from value loss through mishandling

• Explanations of the lingo you will encounter in evaluating and selling your coins

• How to determine the approximate grade of your coins, from 1 (poor) to 70 (an utterly flawless coin)

A Poor-1, left, and an MS-67 Gem.

• How to spot detriments that can affect sale price

• Value drivers most in demand by Morgan dollar collectors, from the most common to the ultra-rare

• How to identify "error coins," highly collectible Morgan dollars that have mint-produced manufacturing flaws

• When it makes sense to have a coin professionally graded

• Ways to spot altered or counterfeit Morgan dollars

My background

I've been buying, selling, grading and consulting on silver dollars for more than 30 years, and...

• Served as Senior Instructor for Silver Dollars for the American Numismatic Association's (ANA) Summer Seminar class "Collecting and Investing in Morgan Silver Dollars." (Numismatics is the study of coins, paper money, medals, etc.)

Michael Fey

• Served on the ANA Board of Governors, received the ANA Glenn B. Smedley Memorial Award and three ANA Presidential Awards

• Discovered more than 50 new Morgan silver dollar varieties

• Co-authored *The Top 100 Morgan Dollar Varieties: The VAM Keys*

• Published *A Decade of Top 100 Insights for the Advanced Morgan Dollar Collector*

• Published the *Top 100 Insights and Value Guide* quarterly newsletter

• I am a frequent contributor to numismatic journals and other publications

For more information, visit rcicoins.com, and for a more complete listing of my credentials, refer to my curriculum vitae.

Thank you for purchasing *The Complete Virtual Guide to Pricing Your Morgan Silver Dollars (1878-1921)!* — Michael S. Fey, Ph.D.

Critical steps in the process of valuing your Morgan silver dollars

Two kinds of value

Morgan dollars are 90% silver and 10% copper. A new or **uncirculated (mint state)** Morgan contains 0.77344 troy ounce of silver, or 31.1034768 grams (an individual dollar's silver value will decrease slightly as it wears down over time in circulation). The value of silver fluctuates, but at, say, $17 a troy ounce, the silver in your coin would be worth about $13.15. Because smelters usually charge about 20% to melt silver, your coin might have a $10.52 **melt value**. To track the spot price of silver, just check the internet. Kitco.com is a good resource.

However... because your Morgan silver dollars are old, and may be in poor or better condition, they will likely have collector value, trading for a **numismatic premium** above the value of the silver they contain — perhaps $16 or more. In Gem Mint State 65 condition (see Grading, below), even a common silver dollar might trade for $100 or more.

Finding your coins' value

As you follow the steps below, you will learn to spot the value drivers that determine each coin's collector — or numismatic — value. You will find deeper information in each of the steps as you work through the guide. Once you know your coins' general value in the marketplace, you can choose the best way to sell them to get the highest return.

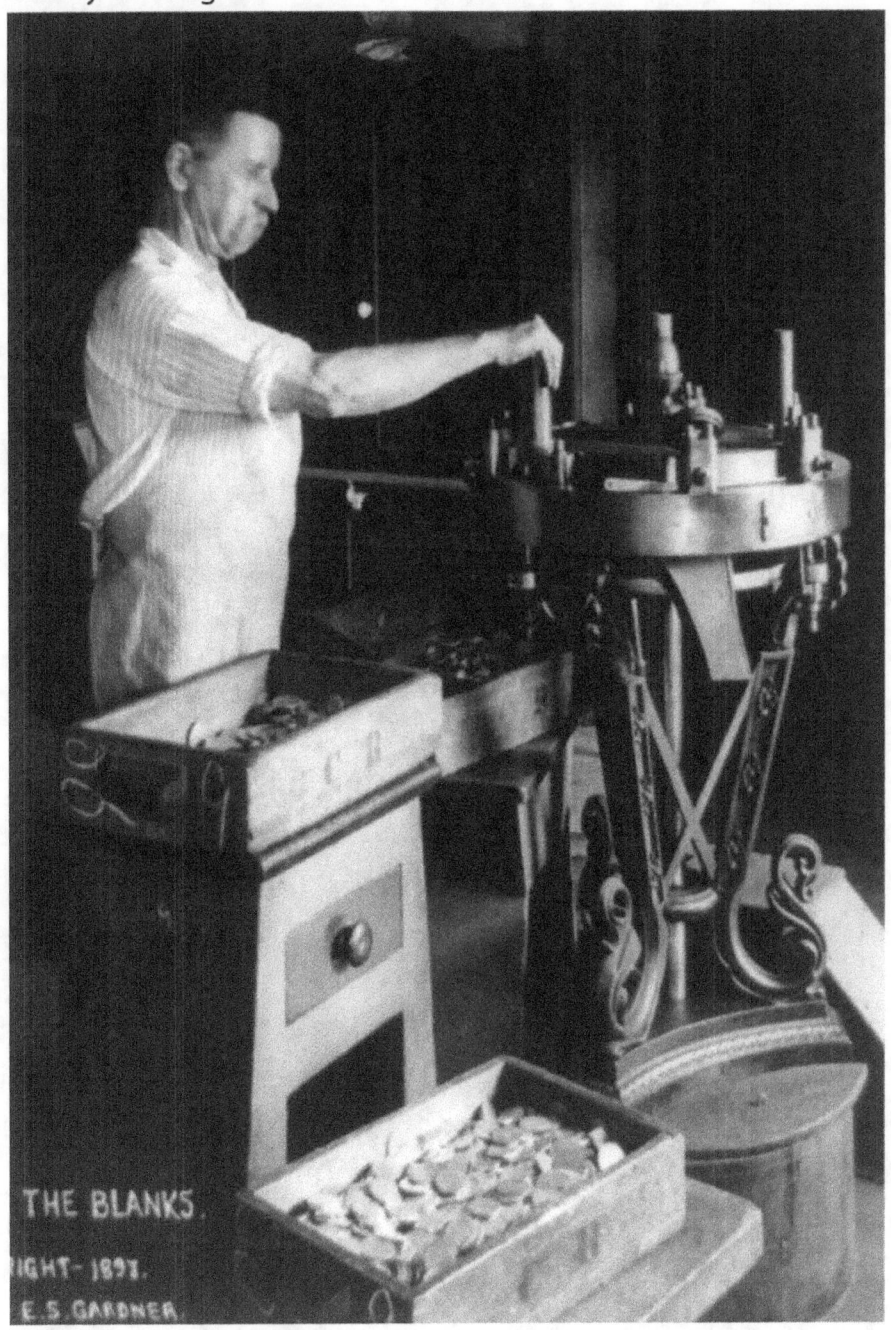

A New Orleans Mint worker mills coin blanks, which reduces their diameter slightly. The resulting excess metal becomes rims on the obverse and reverse, turning blanks into planchets (1897).

Start by looking up the spot price of silver

This is expressed in dollars per troy ounce and changes throughout the five-day workweek. You can follow the price of silver at kitco.com.

Then work through these seven steps to determine whether your coin is worth more for its collector value than just the value of the silver it contains.

Step 1

Look up your coin's date and mintmark

A collection of the entire Morgan dollar series — sometimes the work of a lifetime — most likely included all **dates** and **mintmarks**, totaling more than 90 coins. The year your coin was manufactured and the U.S. Mint facility where it was struck are important factors in determining value.

Step 2

Determine an approximate grade for your coin

A coin's **grade**, or degree of preservation, has a direct effect on its value. Grade hinges on a number of factors, including strength of strike, number of contact marks, degree of luster, toning and overall eye appeal. This guide will teach you grading basics, but the more coins you grade, the stronger your skills will become.

Step 3

Is your coin a proof, specimen or pattern?

The Mint struck **proof** or **specimen** coins specifically for the collector market or as presentation pieces, and **pattern** coins are design prototypes. All of these coins are rare and desirable and worth a significant premium to collectors.

Step 4

Determine whether your coin is a rare VAM die variety

Some collectors also focus on Morgan die varieties, known as VAMs, named after Leroy **V**an **A**llen and A. George **M**allis, who wrote "the Big VAM encyclopedia" on the subject. VAMs include design variations or imperfections that result from an obverse/reverse pair of dies being altered, damaged (e.g., die cracks or die scratches), or different from normal die pairs each year.

To learn more about the history and production of Morgan silver dollars, including all the known varieties, I would highly recommend obtaining a copy of *The Comprehensive Catalog and Encyclopedia of Morgan and Peace Dollar Varieties*, fourth edition, by Van Allen and Mallis (1991; Bob Paul Inc., 648 South St., Philadelphia, PA 19147).

You may also visit vamworld.com to learn more about Morgan dollar VAM varieties.

Step 5

Determine whether your coin has a special provenance

Some silver dollars have a unique history and are therefore worth an extra premium. They may have been collected by a famous person or are part of an important hoard of coins. You will learn more about provenance later in the guide, but if you suspect your coins have a special history, look them up online.

Step 6

Is your silver dollar an error coin?

Some Morgan silver dollars show manufacturing errors, perhaps with dies out of 180-degree alignment, struck off-center or double-struck. Some were not struck at all and left the Mint as **planchets** (coin **blanks** with flat or raised rims), or were struck through various materials like thread or wire. Silver dollars bearing significant errors can command additional premiums.

Step 7

Is your silver dollar genuine or a counterfeit?

This is difficult to determine, even for experienced numismatists. Tiny dots or lumps on the coin's surface, or die spikes going from the rim into the field are good signs that a coin may be counterfeit. A ring test — comparing the sound of a genuine silver dollar when tapped lightly on a table versus the sound of a suspected counterfeit is a good way to determine if one is a counterfeit. Better dates and mintmarks are typically chosen to counterfeit. When in doubt, if the coin's potential value exceeds $300, send your coin to Numismatic Guaranty Corporation (NGC, NGCCoin.com) or Professional Coin Grading Service (PCGS, PCGS.com) for authentication and certification.

Selling your coins

After evaluating your Morgan silver dollars using the instructions in this guide, you may find that some have very little or no collector value. If you want to simply sell them for a bit over the value of the silver they contain, you can contact the author of this guide, or search the American Numismatic Association's database (see below) of member dealers in your neighborhood. You need not be afraid to mail your coins via the United States Postal Service. Registered, insured mail using a flat rate "Priority Box" is the least expensive and safest way to mail your coins.

If you determine that your silver dollars have collector value you can sell them retail, perhaps to a friend or direct to a collector, or wholesale to a dealer. Or you may consign them to a coin shop or auction house. Heritagecoin.com or Stacksbowers.com coin auctions are for high-end coins, and they may require that your coins be certified. There are smaller auction houses, and you can do an internet search to find those located near you.

Auction houses charge anywhere from 15% to 20% of the selling price, but prefer to deal with coins valued at $300 to $500 and up. They typically require a minimum value of $5,000 for a collection.

For lower-value coins, eBay.com is a good auction site. Dealers typically charge a discount of 10% to 20% from wholesale prices, whereas eBay charges about 10% of the selling price.

You will find potential buyers among dealers at local coin shows where you can show your coins to several different dealers at one time and accept the best offer.

Contact the author of this guide at (201) 859-2337 or feyms@aol.com, or go to the American Numismatic Association website to find trusted ANA dealers in your area. These dealers and auction houses are bound by the ANA Code of Ethics. You can mail your coins to them — **always by registered, insured mail** — and expect to be treated fairly.

I can help you, too. If you have a large collection you want to sell and need professional assistance, please feel free to contact me at: Michael S. Fey, Rare Coin Investments, P.O. Box C, Ironia, NJ 07845; (201) 859-2337 or FAX (973) 252-0481; feyms@aol.com.

A word about supply and demand

Coin collecting is all about supply and demand, which can change over time. The balance can shift as numismatists (or their estates) sell off huge collections, flooding the market and sometimes turning "rare" into "common." The market took a huge jolt in the 1960s and '70s when the Government Services Administration dispersed more than 3 million Morgan silver dollars that had been in storage. Some of the coins in this "GSA Hoard" were Carson City-minted dollars, a few of which had previously been considered rare.

In general, as a result of the economic downturn of 2007 and the aging of the Boomer generation, the supply of Morgan silver dollars in the marketplace has increased as older numismatists who collected during the hobby's heyday convert their silver dollars to cash. The result is a slow decline in Morgan values that I expect will continue.

Getting started

Below is a list of the equipment you'll need, and some background information that will help you as you use this guide to evaluate your coins.

You will need...

• A good light source! A halogen light is best, but an incandescent lamp will do.

• A good 10X triplet magnification loupe

• A soft cloth to lay your coins on

• The included date and mintmark "Value Guide"

• The included *Top 100 Morgan Dollar* variety guide (Appendix)

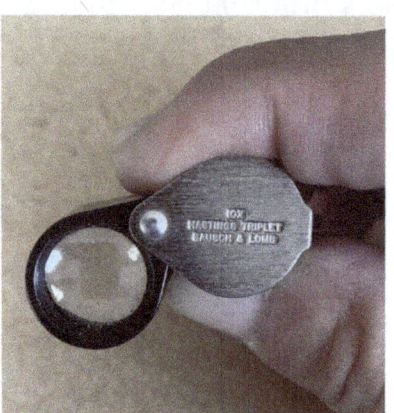

A 10X loupe is great for viewing fine details of varieties on Morgan silver dollars.

Careful handling protects value

Holding, handling and storing your Morgan silver dollars incorrectly can severely reduce their value. Here are some tips that will help you protect your coins.

Perhaps the best advice I can give you is **DO NOT EVER CLEAN YOUR COINS!**

Morgan dollars were minted between 1878 and 1921. Coin dealers and collectors can easily spot attempts to clean old coins to make them look better. These clues include, but are not limited to hairline scratches, residue from cleaning agents, eraser marks and unnatural-looking bright spots, or broken luster affecting the reflective quality or sheen on a coin's flat areas **(fields)** that are produced during the minting process.

The safest way to hold a coin.

Proper handling

Uncirculated coins — those that were set aside and never used as money, will be worth more if they are in high grade. Collectors look for pristine coins with original surfaces that can easily be destroyed through improper handling. Even circulated coins that have been mixed in pocket change and handled frequently in commerce will be worth more if you don't add to the wear they already have. Below are some tips for safe handling and storage.

• **Don't touch the faces** of your coins — the front (**obverse**/heads) and back (**reverse**/tails) — which can leave behind fingerprints, oil, dirt and moisture from your skin.

• **Use hand sanitizer** to remove skin oils from your hands, especially your fingertips, before examining coins, or wear latex gloves.

• **Don't slide coins** on any hard surface, which can leave hairline scratches on the high points of the design.

• **Examine coins over a soft surface** in case you accidentally drop one. Dings and scratches reduce value.

• **Don't sneeze on**, eat around or otherwise get contaminants on them. Be careful talking over your coins as tiny aerosol droplets of saliva can cause damage to the fragile surfaces.

Safe storage

People often end up dealing with a shoebox, purse or drawer full of coins collected by a relative. They may be taped to cardboard, sorted into sandwich bags, stored in soft flips or remain loose and take on more contact marks when moved. These are fine for storing low-value silver dollars that might sell for near silver value, but could cause damage to more valuable silver dollars you may have.

• Keep your coins in a cool, dry place away from direct contact with sulfur sources (i.e., paper, wood, heater or boiler) along with a desiccant, such as silica gel to help keep moisture from damaging your coin.

• Don't store Morgan silver dollars in soft, see-through 2-by-2-inch flips or other holders made of PVC (including some old coin album pages) for long periods of time. Polyvinylchloride (PVC) tends to interact with heat and silver, and can cause irreversible damage. PVC has a greenish tinge and is highly carcinogenic, so avoid touching greenish PVC-caused deposits you find on your coins.

• For short-term storage — six months or less — you can use tissue paper, aluminum foil, soft flips or albums to store your coins.

• For long-term storage — more than six months — 2x2 Mylar flips, good quality coin albums as well as Airtight™ and similar hard plastic holders are best.

Problem coins and culls

If you have a large number of coins to work through, especially if they were collected by someone else, you may want to look through them and set aside any **culls**, **potential counterfeits**, or **altered** coins, which are common silver dollars that may have been altered to look like higher-value coins.

Morgan silver dollars that are not deemed collectible are considered culls, coins that:

• have been polished or "whizzed" (using a fine wire brush to remove scratches, giving the fields a fake luster)
• have a rim ding or nick approaching 1/16 of an inch, depending on how noticeable it is (two rim dings will just about always be a cull)
• have obvious dings or dents
• lack a full rim on both sides, or have filed rims
• are extremely weakly struck, so that circulation has made the lettering unreadable
• have severe, uneven toning (half bright, half black), or heavy black toning
• have a hole or a hole that has been plugged
• have been bent, burnt or disfigured by heat
• have been heavily cleaned
• have pitting from environmental damage
• have rust, or heavy mineral deposits (brown or green), or white calcium build-up from exposure to water
• have been painted, enameled, colorized or have nail polish on them
• have heavy tape residue, glue, heavy PVC gum, or solder from mounting

Some culls can saved by a knowledgeable coin dealer.

MORGAN DOLLAR OBVERSE

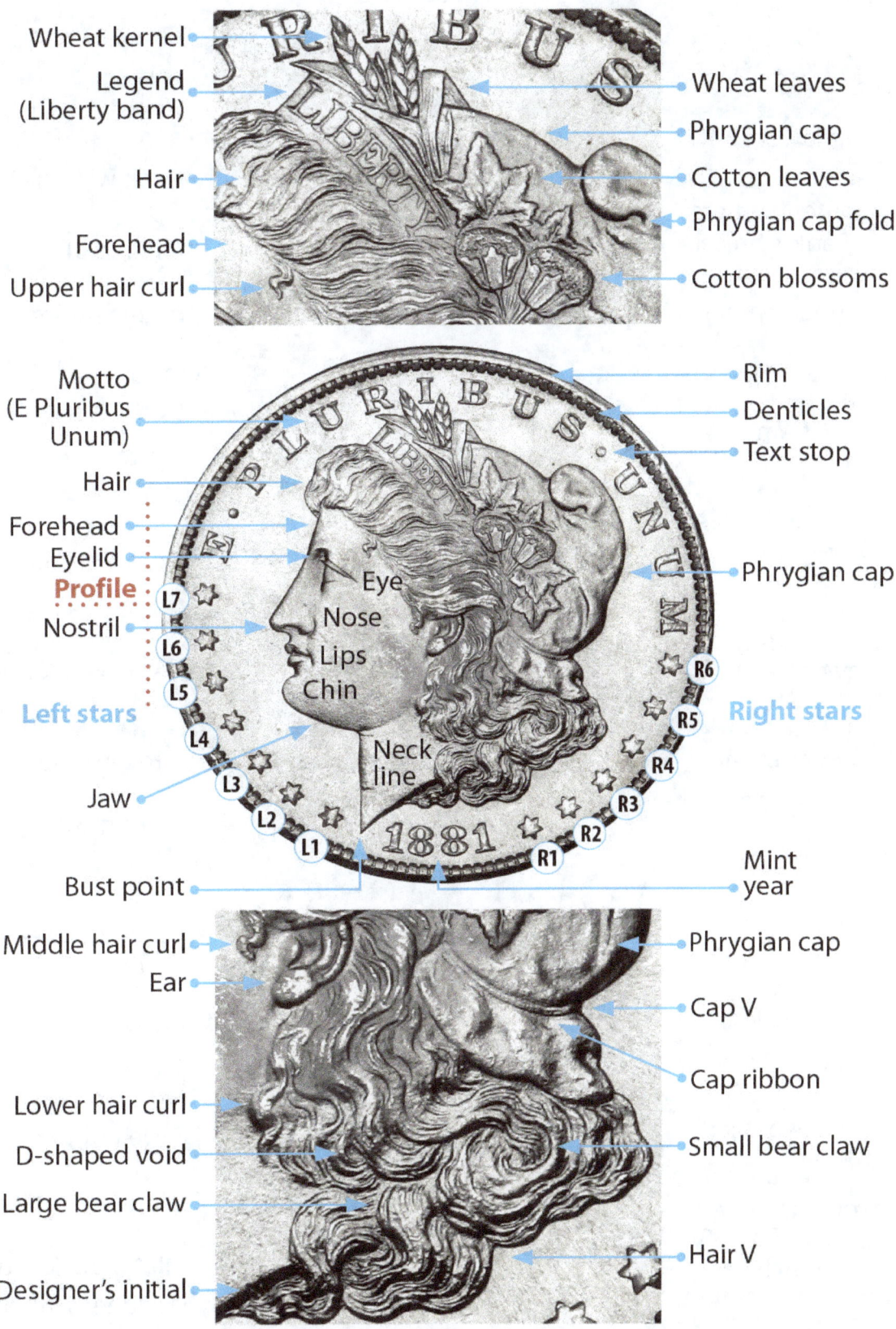

Wheat kernel

Legend (Liberty band)

Hair

Forehead

Upper hair curl

Wheat leaves

Phrygian cap

Cotton leaves

Phrygian cap fold

Cotton blossoms

Motto (E Pluribus Unum)

Hair

Forehead

Eyelid

Profile

Nostril

Left stars

Jaw

Rim

Denticles

Text stop

Phrygian cap

Right stars

Eye

Nose

Lips

Chin

Neck line

L7 L6 L5 L4 L3 L2 L1

R6 R5 R4 R3 R2 R1

Bust point

Mint year

1881

Middle hair curl

Ear

Lower hair curl

D-shaped void

Large bear claw

Designer's initial

Phrygian cap

Cap V

Cap ribbon

Small bear claw

Hair V

23

MORGAN DOLLAR REVERSE

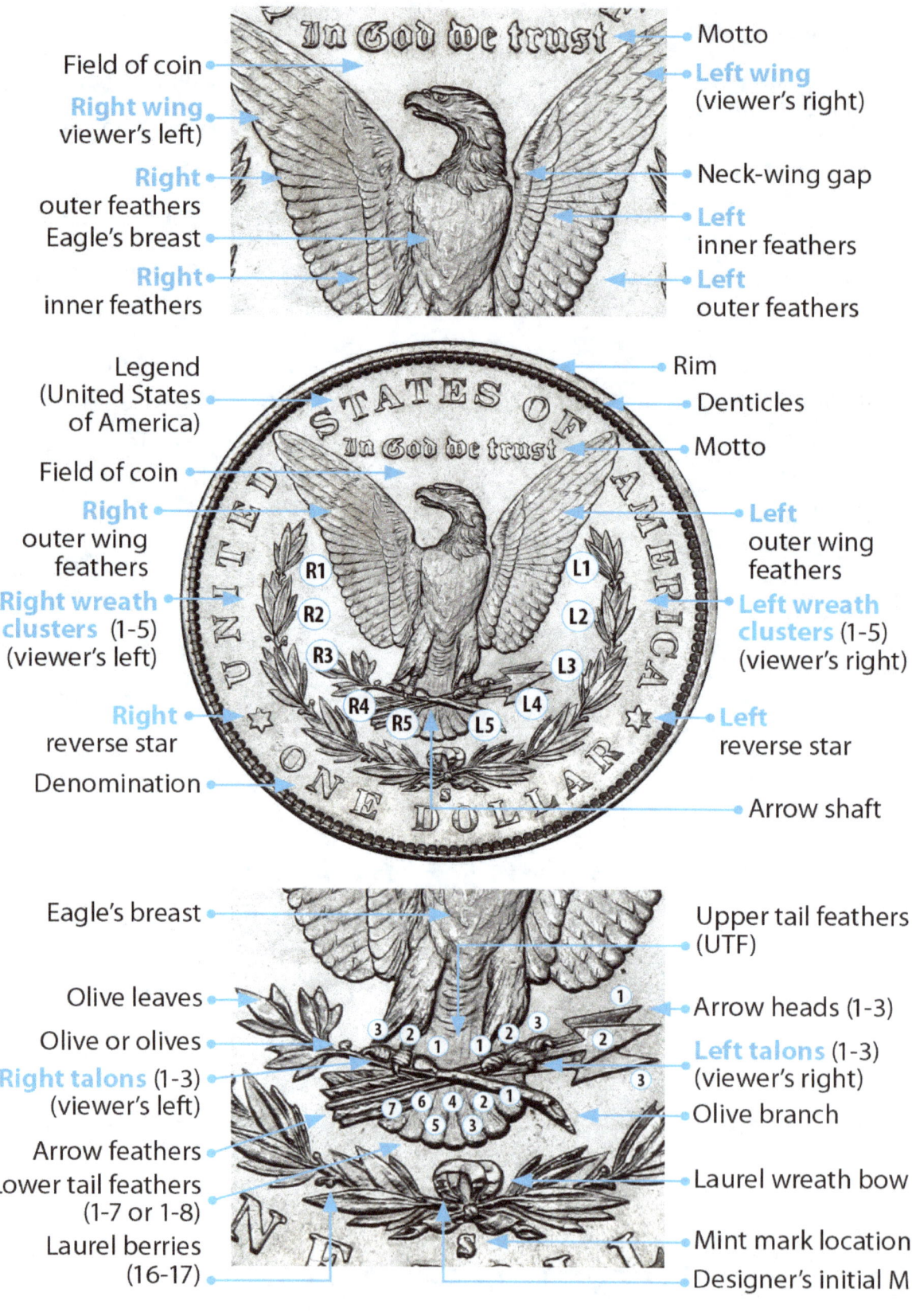

Motto

Field of coin

Left wing
(viewer's right)

Right wing
viewer's left)

Neck-wing gap

Right
outer feathers
Eagle's breast

Left
inner feathers

Right
inner feathers

Left
outer feathers

Legend
(United States
of America)

Rim

Denticles

Motto

Field of coin

Right
outer wing
feathers

Left
outer wing
feathers

Right wreath
clusters (1-5)
(viewer's left)

Left wreath
clusters (1-5)
(viewer's right)

R1 L1
R2 L2
R3 L3
R4 L4
R5 L5

Right
reverse star

Left
reverse star

Denomination

Arrow shaft

Eagle's breast

Upper tail feathers
(UTF)

Olive leaves

Arrow heads (1-3)

Olive or olives

Left talons (1-3)
(viewer's right)

Right talons (1-3)
(viewer's left)

Olive branch

Arrow feathers

Lower tail feathers
(1-7 or 1-8)

Laurel wreath bow

Laurel berries
(16-17)

Mint mark location

Designer's initial M

The right way to view a Morgan dollar

Because you need to see the tiniest details on your coins, you will need proper magnification and a good light source. I recommend a 10X Hastings Triplet magnifier, made by Bausch & Lomb. You can find one relatively inexpensively on eBay or at your local coin or jewelry store.

The best way to view a coin is by twisting and turning it under a halogen light source.

I use a halogen light and hold the coin at sharp angles to the light to spot minute damage and examine design features. (Some dealers and collectors use 100-watt incandescent light bulb about 3 feet away from the coin or a 50-watt bulb about a foot away.)

In teaching my "Collecting and Investing in Morgan Dollar" class at the American Numismatic Association, I show students how to look at a silver dollar. First, hold the coin with your index finger and thumb on the outside edges of the coin while twisting and twirling it under a halogen light. Notice the date, the portrait, the legend and anything that looks peculiar — die cracks, die breaks, scratches, etc.

On a Morgan silver dollar that has been struck properly, the obverse design will be aligned exactly upside down if you turn the coin left or right. Flip the coin carefully from top to bottom. The eagle on the reverse side should appear perfectly straight up. If not, the dies that struck it may have been rotated relative to one another. If that rotation is more than 20%, you have an error coin that would command a numismatic premium (see error coins below).

Next, look at the mintmark, the condition of the design features, fields and letters to see if you spot anything unusual. Use your 10X triplet to see features under magnification.

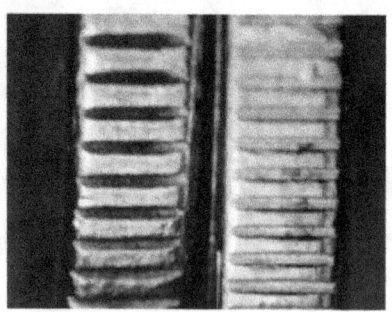

Different reed sizes and
counts may occur on the
outside edge.

STEP 1: Your coin's date and mintmark

George T. Morgan's new design for the silver dollar was minted continuously from 1878 until 1904 and again in 1921, with slight design modifications **(varieties)** over the years. Look for dates on the obverse under Ms. Liberty's head.

A workman punches out coin blanks at the New Orleans Mint, c. 1897.

  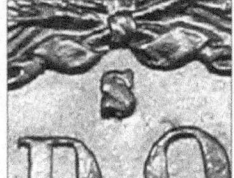 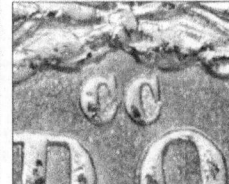 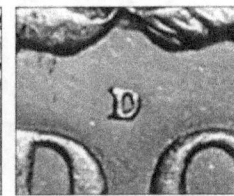

Philadelphia   New Orleans   San Francisco   Carson City   Denver

Morgan silver dollars were struck at five mint facilities across the country; look for the mint of origin just above the DO in DOLLAR on the reverse. Morgan dollars struck at the main U.S. Mint in Philadelphia **do not have a mintmark**, but those from branch mints do: San Francisco (S), Carson City, Nevada (CC), New Orleans (O), and Denver (D). Morgans from 1921 were struck only in Philadelphia, San Francisco and Denver, and coins from the latter two display very small **"micro"** S and D mintmarks.

Look up current values in the "Value Guide" included with this book or go to eBay.com and look up **Completed Auction Prices** by using the "advanced" button to the right of the search criteria and then check completed auctions for comparably graded coins. Then subtract about 10%, the amount eBay.com charges to sell.

Dates, mintmarks and rarity

Business strikes are coins for use in commerce. **Proof** coins were specially struck for collectors. Mintages of business strikes and proofs varied widely over the years (check the internet for these figures), and the current availability of any given date-mintmark combination is controlled by the market. The supply of and demand for various silver dollars by date, mintmark, grade, variety, appearance and provenance results in their trading price.

The rarest dates and mintmarks in the series, those that command the highest premiums in all grades are:
- **1893-S**
- **1894**
- **1889-CC**

However, some silver dollars that are difficult to find in mint state — including 1884-S, 1892-S, 1895-O, 1901, 1903-S and others — all command significant premiums.

Because the Government Services Administration released about a million mint state silver dollars in the 1960s and '70s, many date-mintmark combinations from 1878 to 1921 are considered common today.

Morgan dollar design changes over time

Design modifications made between March and June of 1878, the Morgan dollar's first production year, are important to variety collectors. There were four slightly different designs used for business strikes (8TF, 7/8TF, 7TF reverse of 1878, and 7TF Reverse of 1879) and four for proof coins (1878 8TF VAMs 14.3 and 14.8, 7TF Reverse of 1878 VAM-131, and 7TF Reverse of 1879 VAM-215 — **see Step 4 below for information on VAMs**) all initially minted at Philadelphia.

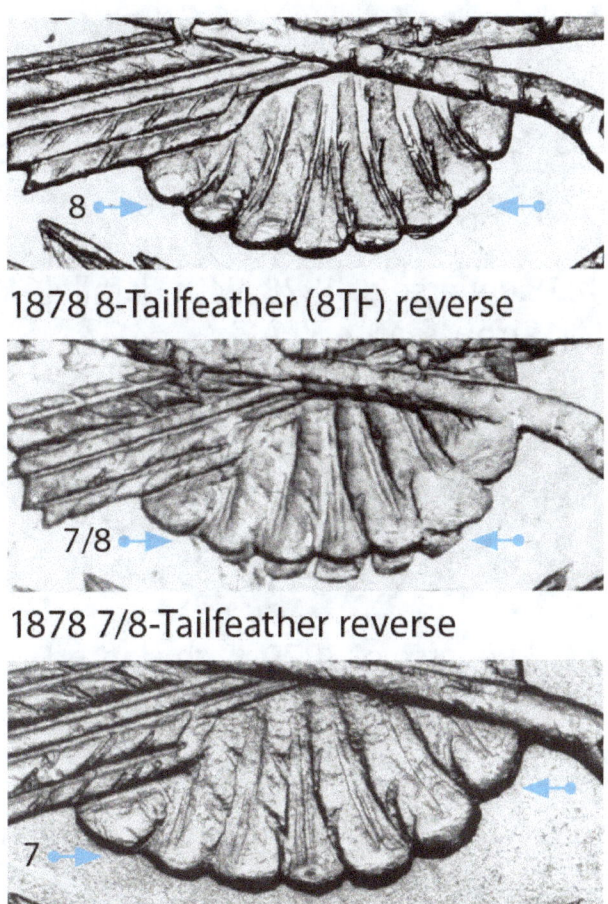

1878 8-Tailfeather (8TF) reverse

1878 7/8-Tailfeather reverse

1878 7-Tailfeather reverse

The reverse of the first business-strike design included a round-breasted eagle with 8 tailfeathers (1878 8TF). This design was used only for a few weeks.

It is believed that eagles depicted on previous U.S. coins had always had an odd number of tailfeathers, the feathers on the Morgan dollar's reverse, so they were reduced to seven. Rather than waste otherwise usable eight-feather dies, it is also believed that seven feathers were engraved right over the existing design, resulting in 7/8TF dollars.

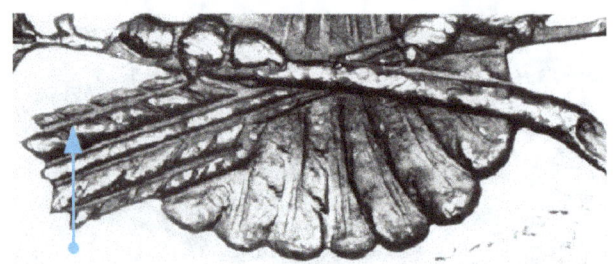

1878 Reverse of 1878, with parallel
top arrow feather (PAF)

1878 Reverse of 1879, with slanted
top arrow feather (SAF)

New dies show seven tailfeathers but retain the eagle's flat breast. On the 8TF, 7/8TF and these new 7TF dollars, the feather (fletching) on the top arrow in the eagle's right talon (viewer's left) sits parallel to the rest (parallel top arrow feather, or PAF).

Finally, in June, the flat eagle's breast gave way to a somewhat rounder version. The feather (fletching) on the top arrow in the eagle's right talon (viewer's left) now sits at an angle to the rest. (slanted top arrow feather, or SAF).

Silver dollars were also struck in San Francisco (S) and Carson City (CC) in 1878, some with the PAF design, and some with the SAF design. In 1879, silver dollars were struck in Philadelphia (no mintmark), San Francisco (S) and Carson City (CC), as well as New Orleans (O). While the SAF reverse design was adopted for normal business strikes, some old PAF dies from 1878 were used, resulting in the 1879-S Reverse of 1878 variety. About 20 varieties of these 1879-S Reverse of 1878 varieties exist and all bring a numismatic premium. A few are very rare (see Appendix).

In 1880, Philadelphia (without a mintmark), S and O coins were minted, with CC coins struck only from 1878 to 1885 and from 1889 to 1893. All

CC-minted coins carry a premium over common dates and mintmarks, the rarest being the 1889-CC.

Morgan silver dollar production, which had ceased from 1905 through 1920, resumed in 1921 with obverse and reverse designs slightly different from those of earlier coins. These carry no mintmark if struck in Philadelphia, or an S or D if struck in San Francisco or Denver.

STEP 2: Grading Morgan silver dollars

Morgan silver dollars are graded on a scale of 1 to 70, where 1 represents a poor, nearly completely worn example, and 70 represents a coin in perfect condition. Grades 60 to 70 are reserved for uncirculated Mint State (MS) or specially minted Proof (PF) coins that were never in circulation.

There are a number of independent grading services, but silver dollars graded by Numismatic Guaranty Corporation (NGC, NGCCoin.com) and Professional Coin Grading Service (PCGS, PCGS.com) tend to command the highest prices when sold. Independent Coin Graders (ICG, ICGcoin.com) and ANACS (ANACS.com) also serve collectors.

It is important to mention that the final arbiter in grading is agreement between a buyer and a seller, or alternatively having coins independently authenticated, graded and certified by an impartial third party such as NGC or PCGS. Since the cost of grading in many cases is considerable, it is often impractical and a waste of money (a minimum of $15 to $20 and up, depending on the estimated value of your coin) to have your coins certified. A good general rule: Unless your coin is in the $300 price range, spending about 10% of its value on grading may not be warranted. Many silver dollars fit into this lesser-value category.

There are many resources you can use to build your grading skills. *The Official American Numismatic Association Grading Standards for United States Coins*, edited by Ken Bressett (Whitman Publishing, LLC) is one of the best. *Coin World's Making the Grade* (Amos Press, Inc.) is another good reference.

An 1878 silver dollar graded and "slabbed" by PCGS.

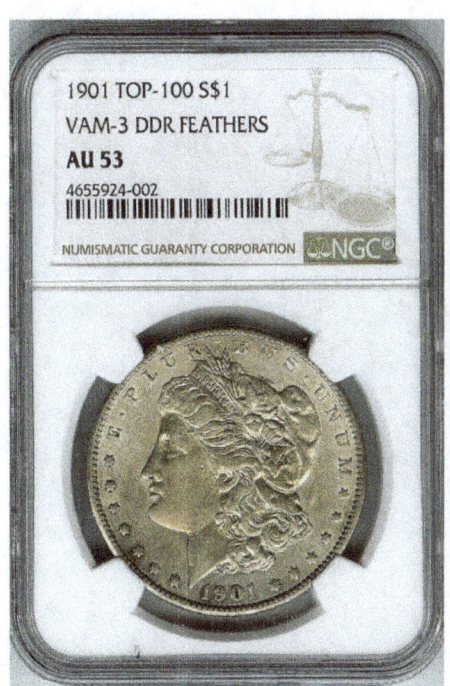

A 1901 VAM-3 silver dollar graded by NGC.

Grading criteria

The five main factors taken into account when assigning a grade include:

• Strength of strike
• Quantity of contact marks
• Degree of luster: Satiny, Prooflike (PL) and Deep Mirror Prooflike (DMPL)
• Toning
• Overall eye appeal

1878 Morgan dollar struck at Philadelphia

1878 proof Morgan dollar struck at Philadelphia

Strength of strike

One of the factors in grading Morgan silver dollars is the strength of the strike — the pressure the Mint used to stamp the design on both sides and the rim of the planchet to create a strong, clear image. Strike is generally categorized as **weak**, **average** or **strong**. These are relative terms, most useful in evaluating mint state coins struck at the various mints.

From experience, I can tell you that the San Francisco Mint made coins with the strongest strikes. For example, the 1879-S, 1880-S and 1881-S coins have a needle-sharp appearance. Whereas New Orleans typically struck coins with weak pressure, resulting in weak strikes. In some cases, coins from the New Orleans Mint have a pancake or flattened look, which is especially evident in the hair over Ms. Liberty's ear — instead of individual strands, the hair looks flat and blended together. The eagle on the reverse often has a flattened chest. For coins to grade above MS-64, the strike needs to be sharp and above average for that mint.

Contact marks

It was Kenneth Bressett the well-known numismatist and longtime editor of *A Guide Book of United States Coins*, "The Red Book," who said (and I'm paraphrasing here): Grading is easy. All it takes is a good loupe, a good light, and experience from looking at about 100,000 coins.

When you're new to grading coins, you might miss seeing tiny contact marks or hairline scratches from coins sliding against hard surfaces or from abrasive cleaning, but your observation skills will improve as you grade more coins.

Imagine a newly minted coin being struck, dropped into a bin with other coins, being loaded into a bag of 1,000 coins, then traveling over hundreds of miles by stagecoach. With all that movement and bouncing up and down next to other coins, you're bound to get tiny contact marks from silver metal colliding with other silver metal. The result is contact marks.

Coins that are perfect (or nearly perfect under 10x magnification) such as proofs can be given the highest grade on the grading scale, a PF-70 designation by an independent grading service such as NGC or PCGS. Coins that grade PF-65 or MS-65 or higher are called **Gems** because the strike is sharp, the luster is above average, and there are only few and very minor contact marks or hairlines in the **prime focal area** — Ms. Liberty's cheek, which is relatively easy to see when tilting and twirling the coin under a light source, and the eagle's body and wings as well as the surrounding fields.

An average coin, graded MS-63, will have several contact marks and perhaps marks that appear on Ms. Liberty's cheek or in the fields. Don't forget the reverse. Coins are graded on both sides, even though the obverse side will count more heavily in the final grade determination.

Coins graded MS-60 will have lots of contact marks, and look pretty marked-up, but there will not be an indication of wear, or few slide marks from someone passing the coin back and forth on a hard surface, such as a table.

The toughest coins to grade are those designated Almost Uncirculated (AU-58). These have enough slide marks or slight wear (slightly grayish areas) on the highest surfaces (Ms. Liberty's cheek and hair and the center of the eagle's chest on the reverse) to be considered circulated coins.

Coins graded AU-50 to AU-55 simply have more contact marks and a lesser degree of luster. AU-50s will have thousands of contact marks, such that when you tilt and twirl the obverse radically under a light source, you can see a circular halo in the field between Ms. Liberty's portrait and the stars and letters.

Coins graded Extremely Fine (XF-45) all the way down to Poor-1 have an increasing degree of contact marks and wear due to handling in circulation. It's best to see the grading illustrations given later to determine the degree of wear and, consequently, the coin's grade.

Luster

As the dies, under great pressure, press blank planchets into coins, the metal spreads from the center outward. Metal flows into open spaces on the obverse and reverse dies forming the raised design and letters, and spreads until it reaches the **collar**, whose cavities form the silver dollar's **reeding**. Remember, the obverse and reverse dies are a negative of the coin's design features and metal flows into the dies' recessed areas that form the positive (raised) design of the coin.

A halogen light source can help you see a coin's luster band.

During striking, the metal dies pressing against the planchet create **flow lines** moving out in all directions from the center on the coin's surface. This imparts coin luster. The highest degree of reflectivity is found on **Proof (PF)** coins, struck especially for collectors using very exacting minting processes. Some business strikes have reflectivity similar to that found on proof coins and are described as **Prooflike (PL)** and **Deep Mirror Prooflike (DMPL)**.

PL and DMPL coins were struck for circulation from freshly "basined" dies — highly polished with a fine grit of emery cloth. The flow lines are very tiny for the first few hundred silver dollars struck by these dies. They have the appearance of a deep mirror — you can clearly see your face in DMPL coins, also known as **very early die states**. As the dies continue to wear through use, though, those mirrors become shallower, with the delicate die-flow lines on the coins' surface ultimately degrading, and the surfaces taking on a satiny, highly lustrous, "non-mirror-like" appearance.

The most common way to evaluate reflectivity, and probably the most reliable, is to hold the coin on its edge next to a page of printed matter such as a newspaper where you have marked off inches. You should have a good light source directed toward the coin (but not directly into the coin such that it is reflecting). Then, referring to the DMPL Relativity Scale below, look into the coin's mirrored surface and see how far down your printed scale you can **clearly** read the text.

Cartwheel luster

DMPL Relativity Scale

• Semi-Prooflike (SPL): 1 to 2 inches of reflectivity

• Prooflike (PL): 2 to 4 inches of reflectivity

• Deep Mirror Prooflike (DMPL): More than 4 inches of reflectivity; print must be clearly readable

• Ultra PL: The standard varies; some authorities specify a minimum of 12 inches of reflectivity (assigned by only one grading service, ANACS)

• "Satiny": Refers to no mirror-like reflectivity, but lustrous surfaces that can be average, below average or above average. Mint State 1879s, 1880s 1881s tend to have above average luster.

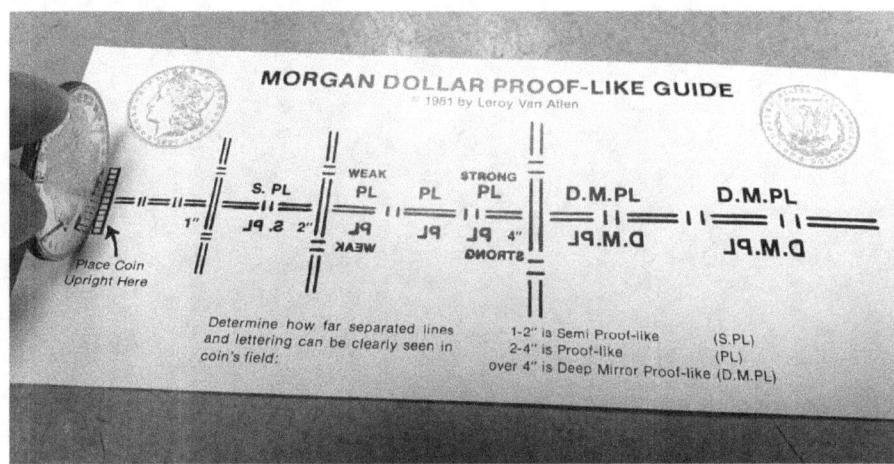

Use the reflectivity scale to determine your coin's proper designation.

It is important to remember that in order to qualify for the luster designations noted above, the entire surface must be mirrored, with no grayish areas or lost reflectivity due to variations in the mirror quality. Normal damage from coins being stored or transported in Mint bags, or **bag marks**, and scuffs are permissible. If only one side of the coin is prooflike, the coin doesn't qualify, unless the grading service offers separate designations for each side of the coin, and even then, usually the obverse must be prooflike in order to count (NGCcoin.com).

Prooflike coins may have been struck after the first few hundred strikes, perhaps into the first thousand or more strikes, until reflectivity is less than 2 inches.

As striking continues, the die deteriorates further, flow lines become more apparent as the dies age, and **middle** and **later die states** can be seen, producing coins that typically have non-reflective luster, growing less lustrous over time. This is the state we see most in coins when dies have made about 10,000 to 100,000 striking impressions.

Coins struck with **very late die states** have dull luster, may have an orange-peel look to the fields, may show die cracks, and may even have rare and desirable **terminal die state** raised bits of metal, called **die breaks** or **cuds** (raised planchet metal at the rim). This is a result of the die starting to break apart from repeated metal-against-metal striking under great pressure.

Toning

Natural toning or as some people call it, tarnish, is acceptable and sometimes highly desirable. It is the result of the coin being in contact with the sulfur in paper, and exposure over time to oxygen and moisture at elevated temperatures, which produce a micro-thin layer of various colors on a coin's surface.

Attractive reverse toning

Morgan dollars stored in brown Wayte Raymond-type albums attain a beautiful **bullet** or **target** type of toning where attractive concentric circles of color can be seen at the coin's periphery. Coins stored in rolls tend to take on toning especially at the ends of the roll. Overlapping colors from the paper folds at the end of the roll may result in an attractive appearance. Coins sitting in Mint bags next to the cloth may take on an attractive texture from the sulfur in the fabric. There may be attractive **crescent** toning at the edges of a coin, with **double or triple crescents** evident, with one-side or wildly attractive two-sided toning.

Toning makes the coin look beautiful, like a piece of art, and can increase the value of a Morgan silver dollar significantly, sometimes doubling or tripling its value, or more. On the other hand, ugly toning can reduce a coin's value. Natural toning may or may not be desirable, but lately more and more collectors demand little, if any, toning. Old-timers and dealers tend to like toning because it reflects a coin's originality.

Overall eye appeal

Earlier, I mentioned that early die strikes produce prooflike or deep mirror prooflike surfaces in a coin's field. Also of note on Ms. Liberty's portrait and other design devices of early die strikes, are frosty surfaces. The contrast between **frosty portraits** and the mirror-like fields gives rise to a **cameo** appearance that is very desirable, like a piece of art. This is produced from fresh, new dies. However, there were times when dies were removed, re-polished and put back into production. Coins struck by these dies may or may not have the striking appearance of beautiful black-and-white contrast cameos.

Among eye-appeal features collectors find desirable are prooflikes, deep mirror prooflikes, cameos and beautifully toned coins. The more attractive the toning, the more desirable it may be. Beautiful two-sided toned coins and spectacular black-and-white frosted cameos tend to bring multiple premiums over their common value. This is where numismatics and art meet.

Because grading is somewhat subjective, independent graders at grading services typically use two graders, then a third grader, the finalizer, to determine grade. Thus, if there is disagreement among the first two graders, the finalizer, the grader with the most experience, swings the vote. The overall appearance is reflected in the final grade.

Grading coins on a numerical scale

As mentioned above, coins are graded from 1 to 70, where 1 is considered Poor and 70 is considered a perfectly struck and preserved coin in the highest possible condition.

An average mint state or proof coin (which includes PL and DMPL coins) is typically graded MS-63 or PF-63. The MS-60 or PF-60 grades are not used very often, but they represent a mint state or proof coin with many contact marks, yet one that has not been in general circulation. MS coins are graded by contact marks, whereas proof coins are graded by the degree of hairlines on the delicate proof surfaces. While both MS and proof coins (also PL and DMPL coins) are graded on overall eye appeal as a final determinant of grade, strength of strike, degree of contact marks and luster are all taken into account when determining an MS or proof grade. PL and DMPL coins are designated on the certification holder by grading services as well.

Though modern proof coins may garner an MS or Proof 70 grade, older coins — those 100 years old or older — are generally not graded higher than MS-68 or PF-68, with MS-65/PF-65 to MS-67/PF-67 and higher being considered Gems.

Perhaps the toughest area of grading is with Almost Uncirculated-58 coins. These are coins that may show a hint of wear from circulation. But in some cases have the look of — and may **"market grade"** anywhere from MS-61 to MS-64. Grading standards have changed over time and many older certified coins in the late 1980s to the late '90s that may have been certified AU-58 may today grade higher upon resubmission to the grading service. It's best to consult a dealer coin-grading specialist on these coins.

Grading circulated coins

Coins that have been in circulation are graded from **Poor 1** (PO-1) to **Almost Uncirculated 58** (AU-58).

Other grades are:
Fair 2 (FR-2)
About Good 3 (AG-3)
Good 4, 6 (G-4, G-6)
Very Good 8, 10 (VG-8, VG-10)
Fine 12, 15 (F-12, F-15)
Very Fine 20, 25, 30 and 35 (VF-20, VF-25, VF-30, VF-35)
Extremely Fine 40, 45 (EF-40, EF-45)
Almost Uncirculated 50, 53, 55 and 58 (AU-50, AU-53, AU-55, AU-58).

Heritage Auctions, the world's largest numismatic auction house (Heritagecoin.com, coins.ha.com/tutorial/coin-grading.s) provides the following grade descriptions for circulated United States coins in general.

Poor (PO-1): Barely recognizable. Large parts of the design will be completely flat. The date may be barely visible or completely missing. Also known as Basal State.

Fair (FR-2): Rims worn well into the design. There should be outlines of some of the images visible on both sides of the coin, but the lettering may be completely gone. Enough of the date should be visible to identify the coin.

About Good (AG-3): Most of the design of the coin will be outlined, but the rims will generally have worn far enough into the design to obliterate parts of the lettering or stars. Sometimes referred to as Almost Good.

Good (G-4, 6): The general design of the coin will be outlined, but there will be very little detail and some parts may be very weak. For the most part, the rim will be intact, but it may wear down to the tops of the letters or stars in some cases. Non-collectors will often refer to their coins as being in "Good" condition; a coin grading Good is actually a very worn coin.

Very Good (VG-8, 10): The coin will have medium to heavy wear, but some details will still be visible. As a rule of thumb, for Seated Liberty coins, Barber coins, Liberty Nickels, and Indian Head Cents, three or more letters of LIBERTY will be visible.

Fine (F-12, 15): The coin will have medium wear, with quite a few details visible and some high spots obviously worn away. As a rule of thumb, for Seated Liberty coins, Barber coins, Liberty Nickels, and Indian Head Cents, all seven letters of LIBERTY will be visible, although some may be very weak.

Very Fine (VF-20, 25, 30, 35): The coin will have medium to light wear overall, and all general details will be visible. As a rule of thumb, for Seated Liberty coins, Barber coins, Liberty Nickels, and Indian Head Cents, all seven letters of LIBERTY will be visible and strong.

Extremely Fine (XF-40, 45): The coin has light wear over the high points only. There may be some traces of mint luster (also commonly abbreviated as EF).

About Uncirculated (AU-50, 53, 55, 58): The coin has wear ranging from extremely light to only a trace of friction on the highest points, along with medium to nearly full luster. AU-58 coins have so little wear that they are often mistaken for Uncirculated coins, hence the nickname "Slider," and in some cases are more attractive than low-end uncirculated coins. It has been said that an AU-58 coin is an MS-63 coin with a trace of wear. AU is sometimes referred to as Almost Uncirculated.

A visual guide

Perhaps the best way for you to determine the approximate grade of your coins is to match them with the following pictures. Note: Not all grades described above are pictured here and are likely not necessary, as chances are you are not planning to become a grading expert. And with most of your coins, except for rare dates, mintmarks and varieties, it really won't matter. Please interpolate to estimate the approximate grades of your coins.

Good-6

Good-6, G-6: The general design of the coin will be outlined, but there will be very little detail and some parts of the design will be very weak. Generally, the full rim will be intact on both the obverse and reverse. Ms. Liberty's hair on the obverse and the eagle on the reverse will be well worn.

Fine-12

Fine-12, F-12: The coin will have medium wear, with quite a few details visible and some high spots obviously worn away. Ms. Liberty's hair will be better defined while the eagle will show some feather detail. The eagle's neck and chest will appear flat, showing considerable wear.

Very Fine-20

Very Fine-20, VF-20, 25, 30, 35: The coin will have medium to light wear overall, and all general details will be visible. The wheat grains on Ms. Liberty's head will be sharp with more hair detail than in lesser grades. There will be more detail to the eagle's neck feathers and some feather detail can bee seen on the eagle's chest.

Extremely Fine-20

Extremely Fine-40, EF or XF-40: The coin has light wear over the high points only. There may be some traces of mint luster. Ms. Liberty's hair is well defined and although there may be a small flat spot on the hair above her ear. There may be small flat spots on the eagle's chest and wing tips.

About Uncirculated-50

Almost (or About) Uncirculated-50, AU-50, 53, 55, 58: The coin has wear ranging from extremely light to only a trace of friction on the highest points, along with medium to nearly full luster. AU-58 coins have so little wear that they are often mistaken for uncirculated coins, hence the nickname "slider," and in some cases are more attractive than low-end uncirculated coins.

Almost Uncirculated coins are best graded under a good light sources so the coin can be radically tilted and twirled. In the areas shown by arrows, AU-50 coins will show a slightly dull grayish (shaded) area in the fields between the letters and design devices. This is due to hundreds of tiny contact marks from circulation. The original luster band swirling around the coin must be present but may be obscured a little by toning. Nevertheless, you should be able to see the luster band through the toning.

AU-53 coins have fewer of these minute contact marks from circulation. AU-55 coins will have even less of this shaded coloring at the coin's periphery. AU-58 coins appear as mint state coins, except several hairlines from circulation will be most noticeable on Ms. Liberty's cheek, the prime focal area of the obverse of the Morgan silver dollar.

Grading mint state coins

Mint state coins, those that have never been in circulation, are graded on a scale from 60 to 70, with an MS-60 being a coin with no wear, but many contact marks. Below are Heritage Auctions' descriptions of uncirculated grading ranges (https://coins.ha.com/tutorial/coin-grading.s), each followed by additional grading tips from me.

Uncirculated

MS-60, MS-61, MS-62: An uncirculated coin with noticeable deficiencies, generally either an overabundance of Mint bag marks, a poor strike, or poor luster. Although most price guides will give a price for coins in MS-60 condition, in many cases this is a very unusual grade, with typical uncirculated pieces often grading somewhere in the MS-62 to MS-64 range depending on the series.

Mint State-60

Grading tips: This represents the ugliest, low end of the uncirculated grade. When the coin is tilted radically and is twirled under a light source, a full mint luster band will be present. There may be many smaller contact marks, a few heavy contact marks, a weak strike, planchet imperfections, or below-average luster.

Select Uncirculated (MS-63)

MS-63: An uncirculated coin with fewer deficiencies than coins in lower uncirculated grades. In general, this will be an uncirculated coin with relatively ordinary eye appeal. Select Uncirculated is sometimes used to refer to a coin grading MS-62.

Grading tips: The silver dollar will exhibit average luster and strike, but may contain a few contact marks, particularly on Ms. Liberty's cheek, a prime focal area.

Mint State-63

Choice Uncirculated

MS-64: An uncirculated coin with moderate distracting marks or deficiencies. These coins generally have average to above-average eye appeal. Choice Uncirculated is sometimes used to refer to a coin grading MS-63.

Grading tips: These are coins which at first glance look above average in strike, luster and eye appeal. They could have been graded MS-65 or higher, but some negative aspect of the coin precludes a higher grade. You might consider these as "Gem minus" grade coins.

Gem Uncirculated

MS-65, MS-66: An uncirculated coin with only minor distracting marks or imperfections. At this point, mint luster is expected to be full, although toning is quite acceptable.

Grading tips: Ms. Liberty's cheek appears clean and smooth, and if marks exist, they are slight and do not distract the viewer. Luster, strike and overall appearance are above average. If your coins look like this, you might consider getting a professional opinion, and you might even want to pay NCG or PCGS to evaluate, grade and authenticate them.

High-end Gem Morgan silver dollars

Again, Heritage Auctions' descriptions, with additional grading tips from me...

Gem-67

Superb Gem Uncirculated

MS-67, MS-68, MS-69: An uncirculated coin with only the slightest distracting marks or imperfections. Toning is still quite acceptable and, in these grades, will usually be pleasing. Many circulating coins even of relatively recent dates are quite rare in such lofty grades, although modern bullion coins and commemoratives are often found in grades as high as MS-69 or even the perfect MS70.

Perfect Uncirculated

MS-70: An utterly flawless coin.

Grading tips, MS-67 to MS-70: Morgan silver dollars in these grades are rarely found. If you believe you have Gem-MS 65 and higher graded coins, you should consider sending them to NGC or PCGS. You can join NGC's Collectors Society or PCGS' Collectors Club and send them off yourself, but you will be better served by working through a local dealer who can often add a dose of wisdom and reality — and the benefit of long experience — to your own grading efforts.

As a professional dealer, I frequently submit coins to NCG and PCGS, and would be happy to help you with this. You can contact me through RCIcoins.com, at Feyms@aol.com or by phone at (201) 859-2337.

Grading PL/DMPL coins, proofs and specialty strikes

Proof coins, prooflike, deep mirror prooflike coins — as well as experimental pattern coins and proofs struck at branch mints rather than Philadelphia — are all graded on the same scale as business strikes, except the criteria are slightly different. (**And note:** Proof (PF), PL, DMPL are not grades, but used as descriptors to reflect the way the coins were manufactured.)

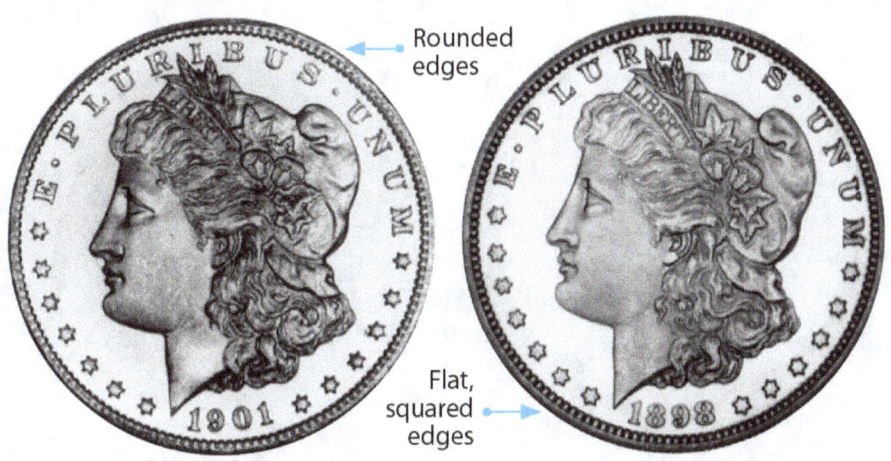

Rounded edges

Flat, squared edges

Rims on **PL and DMPL business strikes** will be rounded instead of flat like proofs. The strike will be weaker than on proofs and the letters will be rounded at the edges. The coin may show contact marks as it was not handled as carefully as proofs.

On **Proofs**, the rims will be squared, sharp, flat and raised. Mirrors will be deep, and the strike sharp and well defined. The coins will exhibit a high degree of preservation with no marks, except perhaps for hairlines on the mirrors' delicate surfaces.

PL and DMPL business strikes are graded mostly by the number and severity of hairlines picked up by the delicate mirrors, perhaps from contact with a tabletop or coin album slide or being even lightly wiped with tissue or a cloth.

Prooflike silver dollars are scarce, and deep mirror prooflike silver dollars are even rarer. They are most prevalent in San Francisco strikes from

1879 to 1882. Although more common PLs and DMPLs command a significant premium over common dollars, better dates and grades should be considered for authentication, grading and certification, especially those whose value exceeds the $300 threshold.

Although proofs and patterns were never intended for circulation, some have found their way into circulation over the years. These can be graded on a scale of PF-1 to PF-58, much the same way business strikes are graded — on the number and severity of hairlines and contact marks picked up on their delicate mirror surfaces.

If you believe your coin is a mishandled proof, it's best to get several opinions from professional numismatists and then a determination from a grading service such as NGC or PCGS.

Though modern proof coins may garner an MS-70 or Proof-70 grade, older coins — those 100 years old or older — are generally not graded higher than MS-68/PF-68, with MS-65-67/PF-65-67 and higher being considered Gems.

STEP 3: Is your coin a proof, specimen or pattern?

The various Mint branches struck proof and specimen coins specifically for the collector market or as presentation pieces. Pattern coins were Mint prototypes. All of them are rare and desirable and command a significant premium.

Proof coins

Proof Morgan dollars, manufactured in relatively small numbers for sale to collectors, were almost always made at the Philadelphia Mint, specially struck to produce deep mirrors and maximum detail. That more rigorous minting process makes it easier to distinguish true proofs from PL/DMPL business strikes that have similar mirrored surfaces:

• Unlike planchets used for business strikes, those for proof coins were carefully selected to be defect-free and were highly polished.

1898 proof Morgan dollar struck at Philadelphia.

• A special press that used heavier pressure and made several impressions on each planchet was used to strike proof coins, which gave them greater detail and a different look than PL/DMPL business strikes. Proofs will have squared, sharp, flat, raised rims and sharp, square edges, and the design elements will be sharp and well-defined.

• Proofs, most of which were never in circulation, will exhibit a high degree of preservation with no contact marks, except perhaps for hairlines on the mirrors' delicate surfaces due to mishandling after minting.

• My advice: When you're not sure whether you have a proof or PL/DMPL business strike, start by consulting several numismatic professionals for their opinion. Then, because of the coin's potential high value, send it to be authenticated, graded and certified by NGC or PCGS.

Specimen coins and branch mint proofs

Specimen strikes are presentation pieces carefully handled by the Mint for special occasions. These may have been made to honor dignitaries or other individuals or commemorate certain events. These and Branch Mint proofs have been graded by third-party services — on RARE occasions only — as something superior to simply a business strike.

It is beyond the scope of this reference to advise on whether you might have a specimen strike or an extremely rare Branch Mint proof, but if your coin has an unusual provenance or pedigree, and is pristine in appearance with deep mirrors, sharp squared rims and is in the highest degree of preservation, you should consider sending it to NGC or PCGS for evaluation.

Pattern Morgan dollars

Rare — and sometimes unique — "pattern" Morgan dollars were prototypes struck to evaluate new designs or specific design features for potential use on business strikes. Patterns are very desirable and worth a significant premium to collectors.

If you think you might have one of these very rare coins, here are some great references:

• You might first visit the Heritage Auctions website (https://coins.ha.com) and register for a free membership. That will give you access to their Auction Archives, where you can search for "Pattern Morgan dollar." You will see large color pictures of Morgan dollar patterns from 1877 and thereafter as well as prices paid for coins at auction in various grades over time.

• 1991. *Comprehensive Catalog and Encyclopedia of Morgan & Peace Dollars* by Leroy C. Van Allen and A. George Mallis, 4th edition, pp. 81-2 (Bob Paul Inc., 648 South St., Philadelphia, PA 19147)

• 1994. *United States Patterns and Related Issues* by Andrew Pollock III, Bowers & Merena Galleries, Inc. (now Stacks Bowers Numismatic Auctions)

• 2003. *United States Pattern Coins, Experimental and Trial Pieces* by J. Hewitt Judd, M.D. (Whitman Publishing)

STEP 4: Spotting valuable VAM die varieties

A die variety is any alteration in a coin's normal design caused by changes made to a die's surfaces both before and during the minting process, often in an attempt to extend the die's working life. Design variations in Morgan silver dollars might have been produced by the individual quirks of new dies, by using damaged, repaired/adjusted or overpolished dies, or using dies with repunched mintmarks or dates. (Don't confuse die varieties with error coins, which are the result of manufacturing mistakes — using the wrong planchet, off-center strikes and so on.)

In 1966, Leroy C. Van Allen and A. George Mallis began cataloging all the known obverse/reverse die pairs used to strike Morgan silver dollars, leading to the publication of their groundbreaking *Comprehensive Catalog and Encyclopedia of Morgan & Peace Dollars* and creating the acronym — VAM — used to describe this collecting specialty. Recognized die varieties are expressed by number, such as VAM-1, VAM-41B, VAM-14.11 and so on. VAMworld.com offers an illustrated reference that includes all varieties from Van Allen and Mallis's book, plus populations and rarity of all known Morgan silver dollar varieties.

Many of the rarest silver dollar varieties, the most desirable and most popularly collected, are shown and priced in the fourth edition of *The Top 100 Morgan Dollar Varieties: The VAM Keys*, which I wrote with Jeff Oxman (2009, Rare Coin Investments/RCI), and which you will find reproduced in the Appendix.

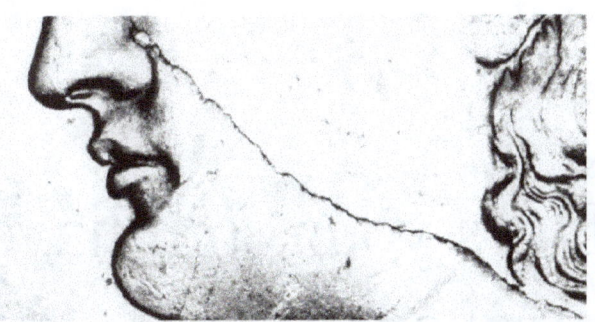

1880-O "Scarface" die break, VAM 1B

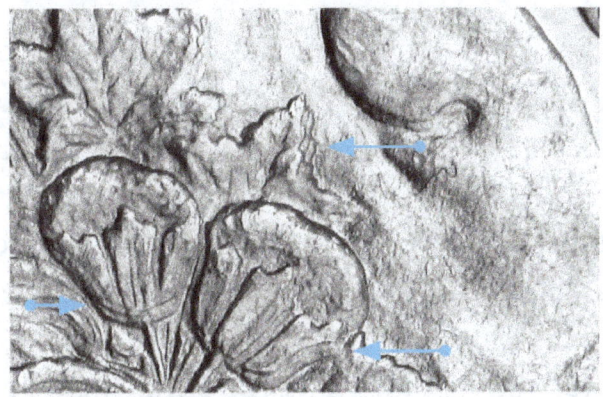

1878-P "7/5"-TF Tripled Blossoms and Leaves "The King," VAMs 44 and 44A

Beyond Van Allen and Mallis: Additional Morgan silver dollar die varieties have been identified and cataloged by Jeff Oxman in his *1878 8-TF Morgan Dollar Attribution Guide, Hot 50 Morgan Dollar Varieties* and *Official Guide to the Morgan Dollar Hit List 40.*

STEP 5: Does your coin have a special provenance?

Silver dollars that have an interesting story, a special provenance, can be worth an additional premium. Coins that were once part of the holdings of famous collectors such as coin dealer John W. Haseltine, Baltimore financier Louis Eliasberg, diplomat R. Henry Norweb and his wife Emery, collector and numismatic writer Farran Zerbe, and world-class collector John Pittman all command additional premiums because they are part of numismatic history.

Perhaps your collection includes a silver dollar that was part of a noted hoard like that left behind in Ted Binion's bunker.

On Sept. 17, 1998, Ted Binion, owner of Las Vegas's Horseshoe Casino, was found dead from a suspected heroin overdose. He had a bunker containing about 110,000 silver dollars that had been used in slot machines from the 1950s forward. The hoard was purchased by a dealer who had them specially certified by NGC as part of the Binion collection, and in 2002, Teletrade auctioned them packaged in NGC special green-labeled holders bearing the "Binion Col." name.

The story of Ted Binion's murder by his girlfriend and her lover, his silver dollar hoard and the court cases that resulted make fascinating reading. I would urge you to do an internet search if you are interested in learning more. I was called in as a consultant to search the hoard for rare die varieties. Further information on Binion's hoard can be found in my *Decade of Top 100 Insights* (2008, Rare Coin Investments/RCI) book.

You may also have a silver dollar from the Redfield Hoard. The wealthy and eccentric LaVere Redfield drove an aged pickup truck and wore overalls, but when he died in 1974, about 400,000 silver dollars were discovered in his basement behind a false wall. Dealers, including Paramount International Coin Company, bought the coins and had them packaged in plastic holders indicating they were from THE REDFIELD COLLECTION. These often bring a premium over the value of similarly graded coins of the same date and mintmark.

Government Services Administration (GSA) hard pack with Uncirculated Carson City Morgan silver dollar, graded by NGC

GSA soft pliobag containing an 1878 8-TF Morgan silver dollar, graded by NGC

The United States government had its own hoard — Morgan silver dollars from 1878 to 1921 that had been left virtually untouched and in mint state in Mint vaults. In the 1970s and '80s, these **Government Services Administration** (GSA) holdings were sold to the public in hard, see-though plastic holders or soft, pliobag plastic holders.

Examples of hard plastic packs include desirable Carson City (CC) mintmarked coins as well as non-CC coins. These always command a numismatic premium. To determine whether you should pay to have your hard-pack GSA coin graded/certified by NGC or PCGS, consider the grade and value (is it worth more than $300?) and the rarity of its date, mintmark and/or die variety.

The soft pliobag example shown here is an ultra rare 1878 8TF (eight tail feather) VAM 14.11 variety, the only one known in a GSA holder and worth a huge numismatic premium. The cost of certification was well worth it. If you have any GSA coins, do not remove them from their holder. Keep the original boxes, papers and envelopes that came with it, as they have numismatic value as well.

If you believe you have a silver dollar that has a special pedigree, check the internet to see if there is a story about it.

STEP 6: Do you have an error coin?

Millions of coins were struck at the U.S. Mints at Philadelphia, San Francisco, Carson City, New Orleans and Denver, and some were bound to be struck in error, perhaps because of a machine breakdown or a machine setting out of place (too little pressure, too much pressure, etc.)

Though each error coin is unique, the general type of error can be used to classify them and provides a basis for valuation. Search online or at ebay.com for coins at a comparable grade with the same type of error to get an idea of what your coin is worth, though certification by an independent authentication and grading service is recommended.

Kinds of minting errors

• **Laminations:** In some cases, the metal in coin blanks was improperly alloyed, causing pieces of metal to flake or peel off a coin's surface. These are called laminations, and areas under them are typically rough. Unless the lamination is large, the coin would not be worth certifying, though it may be worth a small premium to an error collector.

• **Planchet errors:** A flat silver dollar blank was processed through an **upsetting machine** or **upset mill**, where its rim was formed, turning it into a planchet ready for coining. **Type 1 planchet errors** appear as blanks that are the size of a silver dollar but lack a raised rim. **Type 2 errors** are planchets (with a raised rim) that are unstruck. Both are worth a premium as errors and are worth sending to NGC or PCGS for authentication, certification and grading.

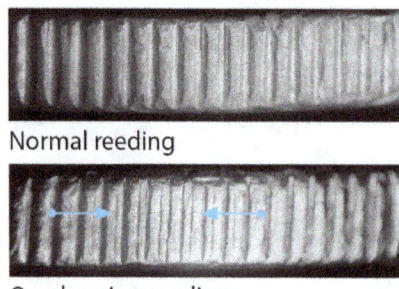

Normal reeding

Overlapping reeding

• **Overlapped reeding:** This is a fairly recent discovery on some New Orleans-minted dollars and 1921 business strikes. At the same time the obverse and reverse dies stamped their designs into a planchet, a separate collar formed the reeding around the edge of a Morgan silver dollar. The Mint equipment that cut reeds into the collars was allowed to cut too long or was repositioned during cutting, resulting in collars that struck coins with overlapping reeding (or "double reeds") on one — or up to four — areas along their edge.

Striking errors

• **Die adjustment pieces:** Planchets were used to make test pieces during setup while striking pressure was adjusted to get coins with the desired detail. If the pressure was set too low, the coins' detail was weak, but more importantly the pressure was too weak to impart the reeding from the collar that held the coin to an exact silver dollar size. These coins lack detail on parts of the obverse and reverse, but also weak reeding, making them rare die adjustment pieces that command a high premium. These should definitely be sent to NGC or PCGS.

• **Misaligned die:** This is another type of adjustment piece, where the obverse and reverse dies are not perfectly aligned top to bottom. If one die is off-center, you might see the design on one side of the coin looking a little off-center. However, it is not so far off-center that the lettering nearest the rim is affected.

• **Rotated dies:** These are easy to spot if you use my method to examine Morgan dollars mentioned earlier. We also discuss coins struck from rotated dies on page 15A in the *Top 100 Morgan Dollar Varieties* book (see Appendix).

• **Strike through:** During the minting process, objects or substances — wire, wood, cloth from a Mint bag, metal scrap, grease, etc. — may have landed between the planchet and dies and gotten "struck into and through" to the planchet. Unless large and very noticeable on mint state coins they do not command a huge premium, but may be worth the cost of certification.

• **Struck through grease:** Die adjustment pieces should not be confused with coins accidentally struck through grease, which have parts of the silver dollar design missing but always have strongly struck reeds at the edge. This more common error does not command a huge premium, but may be worth sending to the grading service if the affected area is large and quite easily noticeable and the coin is in a high grade, perhaps AU or better.

• **Struck through slag:** On some silver dollars, an unappealing black streak can be seen on the coin's surface. That black substance is a metal contaminant, or slag, and almost always detracts from the coin's value.

• **Partial collar:** The edge on a Morgan dollar (the "third side of the coin") is formed by the collar, which imparts the reeding. If the coin is out of position in the collar, it can form what looks like a railroad track, with a smooth "rail" all the way around a portion of the edge and a truncated "track" (reeding) around the rest, either straight or tilted. This is described as a partial collar or a tilted collar. These coins command premiums and should be certified.

• **Mechanical doubling:** This type of doubling, a mistake that occurs during the minting process, is often confused with die doubling, which is caused by a defective die — one that bears a double design image. It does not command any premium. If the dies are not tight in the press, there's a chance the die can move a little in one direction as the coin is struck. This results in a slight doubling of many features in one direction, the direction of the die movement. It can be distinguished from die doubling in that it often appears as a shadow of the original date, mintmark, letters or portrait; it occurs in one direction; there is no split serif seen at the very edges of letters or numbers as you see in die doubling; and the doubling is always lower in the field. Imagine a shearing effect of metal from the tops of a letter struck on a coin to a slightly lower image next to it as the die slips in that direction when striking a coin. Actual die doubling always shows a number or letter doubled at the same height next to it, and often shows a split in the serif. Mechanical doubling does not impart any premium to a coin!

Further information can be obtained from NGC.

• **Die breaks and rim cuds:** Die breaks show up on coins as raised metal that has flowed into a crack or break in the die under the intense pressure of striking. Rim cuds are metal that flowed into a break on the edge of the die, and are seen as raised metal at the rim. These are considered more as **die states** — stages of a die's working life, expressed as **early die state** (when it's new) to **late die state** (when it is worn and may even be cracked or broken). There is a heavy premium for large die breaks and rim cuds on silver dollars. One need only look at the 1887 VAM-1A "Donkey Tail," the 1888-O VAM-1A "Scarface," and the 1891 VAM-2A "Moustache" varieties in the Top 100 book (see Appendix) to see examples of valuable die break silver dollars. The 1921-D VAM-1X "Doubled Rim Cud" in Jeff Oxman's *Hit List 40* book is a good example of a valuable rim cud.

Heavy-premium errors

- **Broad strike:** If the planchet was not contained by the collar during striking, the metal spread out in all directions. These larger-than-normal Morgan silver dollars are desirable errors that command a heavy premium.

Off-center strikes

- **Off-center strike:** This occurs when the coin is struck outside the collar. Naturally, some of the reeding may be missing as well as some of the denticles. Typically, if the off-centering is into the lettering, the coin is considered off-center. The degree to which it's off-center is usually described by percentage — 10% OC, 25% OC, 50% OC, etc. The more off-center, the greater the "WOW" factor and the higher the value. These errors are highly prized among collectors. Certification is highly recommended.

- **Double/multiple strike:** When a coin is not fully ejected after striking, double or even multiple strikes are possible. If the planchet rotates between strikes, this creates multiple images. These errors are highly prized among collectors. Certification is highly recommended.

Double strikes

• **Capped die:** When a coin fails to eject after striking and another planchet feeds in on top of it and is struck, you can get what is called a capped die. The image on that side of the coin is blurred, and partially obliterated. This error is extremely rare.

• **Brockage:** In the case of a capped die, when the design from the second strike is imparted into the first strike, it's called a brockage. This error is also extremely rare and should be certified.

Brockage

STEP 7: Is your silver dollar genuine or a counterfeit?

Morgan dollar counterfeits may have been made in the years when they were originally in circulation, or they may be modern fakes.

And it's not always easy to tell a counterfeit from the real thing. For example, the *Top 100* 1896-O, 1900-O and 1902-O "micro-o" Morgan dollars (see images in the Top 100 book Appendix) and a few others more recently found were discovered to be counterfeits only a few years ago. They are thought to have been counterfeited around the time they were originally in circulation, but after the real silver dollars were minted. Complicating matters, the 1899-O micro o's were found to be genuine. Regardless, these counterfeits are still sought after by variety collectors and are worth a premium.

Chinese counterfeits today have become so good that even knowledgeable numismatists can be fooled, but there are tests that will help you determine whether your coins are real:

• Do you know where your coins came from? If your Morgan silver dollars have been in your family for a long time, say, since before the 1960s, chances are they are genuine.

• If they weigh 26.73 grams for mint state coins and perhaps a little less for circulated dollars, they are likely genuine.

• If they don't stick to a magnet and they make the right "ping" when they are **carefully and gently** pinged on a tabletop, chances are they're real.

• If there are no raised pimples or marks on the coin or spikes coming in from the denticles, and if they have the same look as other silver dollars, chances are they are genuine.

However, if you bought your silver dollars recently and very cheaply, perhaps at a flea market or from another non-numismatic source, and they don't pass these tests, beware — they might be counterfeit. For valuable coins, get an opinion from a local numismatist. Otherwise, you might need to send them to NGC or PCGS for a final determination.

Has it been altered?

If you have a rare date/mintmark combination, you must take special care to ensure your coin has not been altered in some way to deceive you. One of the most commonly encountered fakes is an "S" mintmark added to a genuine 1893 dollar — only 100,000 1893-S Morgan dollars were struck, making it a numismatic rarity that's difficult to find. Other fairly common alterations include a "CC" mintmark added to common 1889 Morgan dollars and changing the final 8 on 1898-S dollars to a 3. Carefully inspect the areas around the mintmark and date. If there is a slight discoloration, or if the flow of metal on the date or mintmark does not look like it was formed during the coin's original strike, it might be altered.

A final word about pricing your Morgan silver dollars

There are several retail coin pricing guides in the marketplace. Perhaps the best known is *The Official Red Book, A Guide Book of United States Coins* by R.S. Yeoman, edited by Kenneth Bressett. Please ensure you are reading the most current yearly edition (Whitman Publishing, LLC). *Coin World* newspaper publishes a *Coin Values Price Guide* monthly (Amos Media) as does *Numismatic News* (Active Interest Media). The *Coin Dealer Newsletter* (CDN Publishing) produces a retail price guide separately, and occasionally for free in the American Numismatic Association's *The Numismatist* monthly magazine. However, most knowledgeable numismatists don't follow these price guides as they represent some of the highest prices that a seller might expect to sell a coin for to a relatively neophyte coin collector.

There are several wholesale coin price guides. These are prices a seller might expect when selling coins to a dealer. These include *The Official Blue Book, A Handbook of United States Coins* by R.S. Yeoman, edited by Ken Bressett (Whitman Publishing, LLC). *The Coin Dealer Newsletter, The CDN Monthly Greysheet*, is often followed by coin dealers as a buying price guide (CDN Publishing). More sophisticated coin dealers use Heritage Auctions' Auction Archives, a site you can sign up for at no cost, and eBay. The former is for higher-value certified coins whereas the latter probably represents the current buy/sell market accurately. But as we mentioned earlier, there's about a 10% seller fee as well as time and effort involved in listing coins for auction on eBay.

The reality is that coin dealers typically buy coins at some percentage (up to 20% is fair) lower than CDN and eBay prices. That percentage often depends on the quality and volume of the coins for sale. As an example, a seller selling 10 lower quality Morgan silver dollars for $1, or about 5%, less than my wholesale price guide of $20 per coin means the dealer stands to make only $10 on the transaction. Now, he is tying up needed money, holding on to coins for which the spot price of silver may go against him, has to pay to ship 10 ounces of coins, and still make money to support his shop or business. Not very enticing is it?

On the other hand, if you sell him 100 uncirculated common silver dollars at $47.50 each, he has room to make $250 or more ($2.50 x 100 at an estimated $50 per coin) on the transaction, which would make it more attractive for him to buy your coins. And, if there are some better dates, grades, varieties and/or errors in the deal, he might be more motivated to pay you closer to what you might expect. Always leave a little room for the dealer to make a profit. Otherwise, why would he buy from you?

This pricing guide will provide you with all the information you need to estimate the approximate value of your Morgan silver dollars. In cases where you have better dates and grades, proofs or patterns, rare die varieties and errors worth in excess of $300, you would be well served to spend money on authentication and grading by NGC or PCGS. In that manner, you should expect to receive a fair value for your coins when it comes time to sell.

Value charts

The values in the charts on the following pages reflect a spot silver price of $17.03.

NOTE: The charts are presented for historical purposes only. You will always find the most recent price guide by keying in...

https://rcicoins.com/value-guide.pdf

Circulated Morgan Silver Dollars

Date/Mintmark	VG-8	F-12	VF-20	XF-40	AU-50	AU-58
1878 8-TF	$50	$55	$60	$70	$90	$105
1878 7-TF Rev '78	30	33	35	38	45	60
1878 7/8-TF	32	35	37	40	50	70
1878 7-TF Rev '79	32	34	36	38	45	60
1878-CC	80	90	100	110	175	225
1878-S	30	35	37	40	45	50
1879	20	23	25	26	30	35
1879-CC	125	150	300	700	2,000	2,750
1879-O	30	34	35	36	40	50
1879-S	20	23	25	26	30	35
1879-S Rev '78	40	45	50	55	65	100
1880	20	23	25	26	30	35
1880-CC Rev '78	115	150	175	200	275	325
1880-CC Rev '79	100	135	150	175	250	300
1880-O	25	27	30	35	40	55
1880-S	20	23	25	26	30	35
1881	20	23	25	26	30	35
1881-CC	275	300	310	325	350	375
1881-O	20	25	27	28	30	35
1881-S	20	23	25	26	30	35
1882	20	23	25	26	30	35
1882-CC	75	80	85	100	120	140
1882-O	20	23	25	26	30	35
1882-O/S	35	40	45	50	65	100
1882-S	20	23	25	26	30	35
1883	20	23	25	26	30	35
1883-CC	75	80	85	100	120	140
1883-O	20	23	25	26	30	35
1883-S	25	26	27	35	75	325
1884	20	23	25	26	30	35
1884-CC	75	80	85	100	120	140
1884-O	20	23	25	26	30	35
1884-S	25	26	27	60	150	1,250

Date/Mintmark	VG-8	F-12	VF-20	XF-40	AU-50	AU-58
1885	$20	$23	$25	$26	$30	$35
1885-CC	425	475	500	525	550	575
1885-O	20	23	25	26	30	35
1885-S	25	26	35	45	75	125
1886	20	23	25	26	30	35
1886-O	25	30	32	35	60	250
1886-S	35	40	55	85	100	150
1887	20	23	25	26	30	35
1887/6	30	35	40	45	115	175
1887-S	23	25	26	27	35	65
1887-O	20	23	25	26	30	40
1887/6-O	35	40	45	50	125	300
1888	20	23	25	26	30	35
1888-O	20	23	25	26	30	35
1888-S	75	85	100	110	120	175
1889	20	23	25	26	30	35
1889-CC	450	625	850	2,250	6,000	16,000
1889-O	20	23	24	25	45	85
1889-S	35	45	50	55	75	125
1890	20	23	25	27	30	35
1890-CC	70	75	80	120	175	275
1890-O	20	23	25	26	35	45
1890-S	20	23	25	26	30	40
1891	20	23	25	26	35	40
1891-CC	70	75	80	100	175	300
1891-O	20	23	25	26	30	85
1891-S	20	23	25	30	35	45
1892	25	27	30	35	60	115
1892-CC	125	150	175	350	550	850
1892-O	20	25	27	30	55	125
1892-S	30	35	85	200	1,100	10,000
1893	100	110	125	175	250	450
1893-CC	225	250	500	1,000	1,850	3,250
1893-O	125	150	225	375	625	1,650
1893-S	2,000	3,500	4,250	6,750	17,500	57,500

Date/Mintmark	VG-8	F-12	VF-20	XF-40	AU-50	AU-58
1894	$600	$650	$700	$750	$850	$1,550
1894-O	30	35	40	65	100	375
1894-S	40	50	75	125	325	475
1895-O	150	175	225	375	800	3,750
1895-S	225	300	475	750	1,100	2,450
1896	20	23	25	26	30	35
1896-O	25	30	32	35	85	275
1896-S	35	40	50	185	650	1,400
1897	20	23	25	26	30	35
1897-O	20	23	25	35	55	250
1897-S	20	23	25	26	30	35
1898	20	23	25	26	30	35
1898-O	20	23	25	26	30	35
1898-S	25	30	35	40	65	110
1899	75	100	125	135	145	150
1899-O	20	23	25	26	30	35
1899-S	25	30	35	45	125	200
1900	20	23	25	26	30	35
1900-O	20	23	25	26	30	35
1900-S	25	30	35	40	55	100
1900-O/CC	40	45	75	100	140	185
1901	30	35	40	70	160	1,000
1901-O	20	23	25	26	30	35
1901-S	25	30	35	45	150	275
1902	25	30	35	37	40	45
1902-O	20	23	25	26	30	35
1902-S	70	75	85	125	150	225
1903	27	30	35	37	40	45
1903-O	225	250	275	300	310	325
1903-S	50	75	150	250	1,250	2,750
1904	25	27	30	33	35	60
1904-O	20	23	25	26	30	35
1904-S	25	30	40	125	450	1,500
1921	18	18	19	19	20	25
1921-D	18	18	20	22	24	30
1921-S	20	22	24	26	28	30

Mint State Morgan Silver Dollars

Date/Mintmark	MS-60	MS-63	MS-64	MS-65	MS-66
1878 8-TF	$155	$200	$350	$875	$4,000
1878 7-TF Rev '78	125	155	300	1,000	7,500
1878 7/8-TF	75	100	170	650	2,750
1878 7-TF Rev '79	100	175	325	1,200	8,000
1878-CC	350	375	425	1,250	4,000
1878-S	55	65	85	200	8,000
1879	55	75	100	425	1,500
1879-CC	3,750	6,350	8,000	20,000	80,000
1879-O	80	200	425	2,000	12,000
1879-S	50	55	65	100	175
1879-S Rev '78	200	550	1,100	4,000	40,000
1880	50	70	100	450	35,000
1880-CC Rev '78	500	575	800	1,250	42,500
1880-CC Rev '79	425	500	525	800	14,500
1880-O	90	300	1,150	12,000	50,000
1880-S	50	55	65	100	175
1881	40	65	115	425	15,500
1881-CC	400	425	450	650	1,050
1881-O	45	60	125	775	6,750
1881-S	50	55	65	100	175
1882	40	65	95	300	950
1882-CC	175	195	215	375	700
1882-O	50	55	65	100	550
1882-O/S	125	450	1,450	42,500	---
1882-S	50	55	65	100	175
1883	50	55	65	100	350
1883-CC	175	195	215	325	700
1883-O	50	55	65	100	250
1883-S	925	1,950	3,750	26,000	120,000
1884	40	65	95	200	650
1884-CC	175	195	215	325	700
1884-O	50	55	65	100	175
1884-S	7950	40,000	115,000	200,000	---

Date/Mintmark	MS-60	MS-63	MS-64	MS-65	MS-66
1885	$40	$65	$95	$115	$175
1885-CC	600	625	650	800	1,600
1885-O	50	55	65	100	175
1885-S	225	275	500	1,450	3,250
1886	50	55	65	100	175
1886-O	775	2,250	7,500	130,000	---
1886-S	300	375	550	1,450	4,000
1887	50	55	65	100	175
1887/6	250	400	500	1,250	6,000
1887-S	110	175	475	1,250	4,250
1887-O	55	100	275	1,250	28,500
1887/6-O	425	1,550	3,000	30,000	---
1888	50	55	65	110	375
1888-O	50	55	65	100	275
1888-S	275	350	625	2,250	42,50
1889	38	45	55	175	625
1889-CC	22,000	35,000	40,000	70,000	250,000
1889-O	225	275	600	2,950	17,000
1889-S	200	275	450	1,250	3,000
1890	40	65	100	725	11,000
1890-CC	475	800	1,000	2,400	29,500
1890-O	65	85	225	1,100	6,000
1890-S	55	85	200	825	1,750
1891	60	145	425	2,750	11,000
1891-CC	425	675	900	3,000	20,000
1891-O	200	325	500	4,000	21,500
1891-S	75	125	300	950	3,000
1892	250	375	850	2,500	42,500
1892-CC	1,000	1,750	2,500	5,000	22,500
1892-O	225	350	600	2,750	35,000
1892-S	35000	60000	---	---	---
1893	750	1,100	1,850	3,250	40,000
1893-CC	4,250	6,500	12,500	65,000	125,000
1893-O	3,000	6,250	14,500	15,000	---
1893-S	150,000	275,000	300,000	750,000	950,000

Date/Mintmark	MS-60	MS-63	MS-64	MS-65	MS-66
1894	$2,750	$4,250	$6,750	$33,000	$75,000
1894-O	1,100	3,750	7,000	50,000	---
1894-S	750	1,050	2,000	5,500	10,500
1895-O	12,500	50,000	80,000	175,000	300,000
1895-S	3,750	5,500	7,000	17,000	75,000
1896	50	55	65	120	300
1896-O	1,400	5,000	30,000	125,000	325,000
1896-S	2,000	3,250	4,650	10,000	65,000
1897	50	55	65	175	550
1897-O	750	3,250	11,500	50,000	80,000
1897-S	65	115	150	425	950
1898	50	55	65	150	375
1898-O	50	55	65	100	175
1898-S	200	425	600	1,250	3,250
1899	200	225	300	700	1,750
1899-O	50	55	65	100	175
1899-S	350	500	700	1,500	2,500
1900	50	55	65	100	400
1900-O	50	55	65	100	275
1900-S	250	375	500	1,150	2,450
1900-O/CC	300	625	800	1,750	3,750
1901	2,800	11,000	50,000	400,000	55,000
1901-O	50	55	65	100	475
1901-S	400	775	1,000	1,850	6,750
1902	75	125	175	275	600
1902-O	50	55	65	110	350
1902-S	325	525	700	1,600	5,500
1903	55	75	95	175	350
1903-O	350	375	400	550	725
1903-S	4,000	6,500	7,500	8,500	12,500
1904	100	200	375	1,650	5,000
1904-O	50	55	65	100	250
1904-S	2,000	4,000	4,500	6,500	17,000
1921	27	32	45	95	400
1921-D	35	50	100	200	600
1921-S	35	50	100	600	2,500

Proof-like strikes   Mirror-like strikes

Date and Mintmark	MS-63 PL	MS-64 PL	MS-65 PL	MS-63 DM	MS-64 DM	MS-65 DM
1878 8-TF	$300	$600	$1,850	$1,000	$3,250	$17,500
1878 7-TF Rev '78	350	750	3,000	1,000	3,500	12,000
1878 7/8-TF	150	400	1450	500	1,250	7,500
1878 7-TF Rev '79	400	800	2,500	1,000	3,500	17,500
1878-CC	500	850	1,725	1,250	2,500	8,250
1878-S	100	175	385	275	1,500	7,000
1879	200	425	1,750	325	1,500	12,500
1879-CC	7,000	8,500	20,000	8,000	15,000	30,000
1879-O	400	875	8,500	1,450	4,000	17,500
1879-S	75	100	185	200	350	1000
1879-S Rev '78	2,250	4,000	8,000	2,500	6,000	14,000
1880	80	325	925	400	1,100	4,000
1880-CC Rev '78	1,150	1,750	5,250	1,750	5,000	14,000
1880-CC Rev '79	525	700	950	750	1,850	5,750
1880-O	1,050	2,450	20,000	1,750	5,750	---
1880-S	75	100	185	200	350	1,000
1881	85	275	1,650	400	975	10,000
1881-CC	500	600	1,200	600	1,050	2,950
1881-O	85	210	2,750	250	800	8,000
1881-S	85	175	185	200	350	1,000
1882	85	225	800	200	995	4,250
1882-CC	225	300	600	375	525	1,650
1882-O	85	225	950	275	925	2,950
1882-O/S	---	---	---	---	---	---
1882-S	75	100	250	325	700	2,000
1883	85	170	425	250	425	1,350
1883-CC	225	250	400	350	500	1,050
1883-O	110	175	175	425	995	
1883-S	5,500	8,500	---	---	---	---
1884	85	110	525	225	775	2,950
1884-CC	225	250	500	350	500	1,050
1884-O	85	110	225	200	350	775
1884-S	38,000	---	---	---	---	---

Date/Mintmark	63-PL	64-PL	65-PL	63-DM	64-DM	65-DM
1885	$85	$110	$185	$185	$375	$900
1885-CC	700	875	1250	800	1,250	2,000
1885-O	85	110	225	175	300	850
1885-S	375	1,650	5,250	1,650	4,250	36,500
1886	85	110	250	175	375	775
1886-O	4,500	---	---	---	---	---
1886-S	550	900	3,150	2,000	7,250	24,000
1887	85	110	225	175	350	850
1887/6	500	950	2,500	2,000	3,250	19,500
1887-S	475	1,850	4,000	2,250	5,750	2,4500
1887-O	200	600	3,850	575	2,000	13,500
1887/6-O	---	---	---	---	---	---
1888	85	110	425	200	400	1,650
1888-O	85	110	500	200	500	3,250
1888-S	425	850	3250	800	2,150	13,000
1889	85	110	675	250	775	3,000
1889-CC	50,000	75,000	220,000	55,000	85,000	---
1889-O	750	1,500	6,000	1,500	5,850	24,500
1889-S	600	1,150	3,750	1,500	3,750	27,000
1890	160	350	1,625	425	1,350	12,500
1890-CC	950	1,450	6,500	1,250	2,750	10,000
1890-O	120	350	1,550	300	1,250	8,250
1890-S	135	325	1,625	450	2,550	7,750
1891	700	1,650	---	1,600	4,000	20,000
1891-CC	800	1,250	4,250	1,750	3,650	24,500
1891-O	1600	3,500	---	2,500	5,000	30,000
1891-S	200	350	2,000	625	2,750	16,000
1892	750	1,650	5,000	1,500	2,750	16,000
1892-CC	2,300	2,500	12,000	4,000	8,250	31,500
1892-O	4,250	6,500	---	9,000	20,000	40,000
1892-S	85,000	---	---	---	---	---
1893	---	---	---	---	---	---
1893-CC	9,000	21,500	85,000	20,000	40,000	80,000
1893-O	8,500	---	---	19,000	65,000	---
1893-S	---	---	---	---	---	---

Date/Mintmark	63-PL	64-PL	65-PL	63-DM	64-DM	65-DM
1894	---	---	---	$25,000	$50,000	---
1894-O	22,000	---	---	---	---	---
1894-S	1,400	2,750	8,500	5,000	15,500	---
1895-O	55000	95000	---	---	---	---
1895-S	7,000	9,000	27,000	9,000	15,000	35,000
1896	85	120	325	185	375	825
1896-O	---	---	---	23,000	35,000	---
1896-S	8,500	---	---	17,000	---	---
1897	85	150	350	200	400	2,000
1897-O	8,500	---	---	22,000	30,000	---
1897-S	115	200	700	250	950	2,000
1898	85	110	400	200	400	950
1898-O	85	110	175	185	450	1,000
1898-S	450	850	3250	850	2,650	12,500
1899	375	475	1,100	500	1,000	2,200
1899-O	85	140	325	225	450	1,150
1899-S	450	900	1,950	900	3,500	17,000
1900	85	250	2,750	2,500	8,000	---
1900-O	85	100	300	425	750	4000
1900-S	350	800	2,200	5,500	12,000	25,000
1900-O/CC	---	---	---	---	---	---
1901	20,000	---	---	---	---	---
1901-O	85	145	450	400	1,050	7,750
1901-S	1,100	2,750	6,500	8,000	16,000	20,000
1902	1,000	1,750	2,600	5,750	7,250	15,000
1902-O	85	110	400	400	2,000	11,500
1902-S	1850	3000	8500	---	---	---
1903	450	785	1,250	1,900	4,250	19,000
1903-O	450	875	2,000	550	1,650	5,500
1903-S	10000	12500	16000	---	---	---
1904	1,250	2,950	20,000	20,000	35,000	60,000
1904-O	85	110	175	200	350	1000
1904-S	4,750	6,500	10,000	12,000	14,000	---
1921	200	450	1,550	2,000	3,500	10,000
1921-D	1,000	2,500	4,250	2,500	5,500	8,000
1921-S	2,000	4,750	13000	---	---	---

I hope you have enjoyed this comprehensive guide to understanding and pricing your Morgan silver dollars. The same kind of analysis can be applied to Peace dollars and all other United States coins as well as foreign coins, medals, paper money, and other related numismatic items. If you have a large collection and need help from a professional, please feel free to contact me at:

Michael S. Fey
Rare Coin Investments
P.O. Box C
Ironia, NJ 07845
RCIcoins.com
(201) 859-2337 or FAX (973) 252-0481
feyms@aol.com

APPENDIX: Top 100 Morgan Silver Dollars, The VAM keys

TOP 100
Morgan Dollar Varieties

THE VAM KEYS

By Michael S. Fey, Ph.D.
and Jeff Oxman

FOURTH EDITION
4th

Top 100
Morgan Dollar Varieties

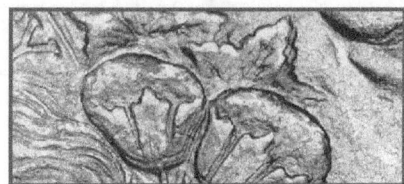

The VAM Keys

By Michael S. Fey, Ph.D.
and Jeff Oxman

Fourth Edition / 2009
Ironia, New Jersey

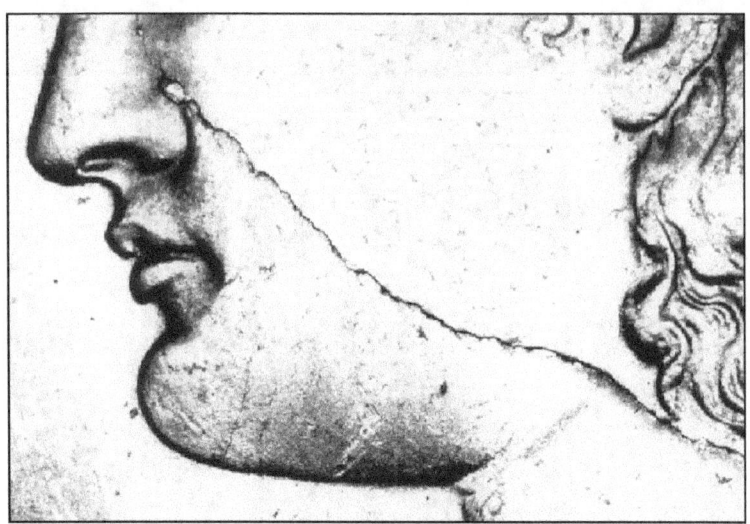

1888-O "Scarface" variety, VAM 1B Late Die State

Top 100 Morgan Dollar Varieties: The VAM Keys

By Michael S. Fey, Ph.D., and Jeff Oxman

Copyright © 2009 Rare Coin Investments
P.O. Box C, Ironia, New Jersey 07845

ISBN: 978-0-9653645-5-3
Library of Congress Control Number: 2008943284

Cover photos of 1878 7/3-TF VAM 44 Morgan dollar: Tom Mulvaney

Editing and design: Mary Jo Meade

TABLE OF CONTENTS

Welcome to the Revolution i
Acknowledgments...vi
VAM Collecting: A Primer xiv
The *Top 100* Challenge..xix
How to Use This Book..xxiii

The Top 100 Morgan Dollar Varieties: The VAM Keys

1878

8-TF Doubled "RIB" / **VAM 5** 2
8-TF First Morgan Dollar / **VAMs 9, 9A**...............3
8-TF Wild Eye Spikes / **VAM 14.11*** 4
8-TF Doubled "LIBERTY" / **VAM 15**....................5
8-TF Doubled Lips & Profile / **VAM 23** 6

7/3-TF / **VAM 32** 7
7/7-TF / **VAMs 41, 41B**....................................8
7/5-TF Tripled Blossoms & Leaves / **VAMs 44, 44A**..........9
7/0-TF Doubled Talons / **VAM 45**......................10

7-TF Rev. '78 Doubled "RIB" / **VAM 70** 11
7-TF Rev. '78 Type I Obverse / **VAMs 100-1, 100-2**........12
7-TF Rev. '78 Tripled Blossoms / **VAMs 115, 198****........13
7-TF Rev. '78 Tripled Star / **VAMs 117, 141, 141A** 14
7-TF Rev. '78 Tripled "R" / **VAM 171** 15
7-TF Rev. '78 Short Wheat Leaf / **VAMs 203, 203A** 16
7-TF Rev. '78 Tripled "R" / **VAM 220** 17
7-TF Rev. '78 Washed-Out "L" / **VAM 223**.......................18

CC Doubled Leaves / **VAM 6** 19
CC Lines in Eagle's Wing / **VAM 11** 20
CC Doubled Leaves / **VAM 18** 21
CC Doubled Leaves / **VAMs 24, 24A**...............22

*Replaces VAM 11, which was never confirmed.   **Formerly VAM 199.1

1878

S Long Center Arrow Shaft / **VAMs 26, 27, 56, 57,
58, 59, 60, 62, 72** 23

1879

O/Horizontal O / **VAMs 4, 28** 24

S Rev. '78 / **VAMs 4, 6, 9, 23, 25, 34, 34A, 34B, 35,
39, 42, 43, 46, 50, 51, 52, 56 (56A), 66, 67** 25

CC "Capped Die" Mintmark / **VAM 3** 26

1880

Knobbed "8" / **VAM 1A** 27
8/7 "Spikes" Overdate / **VAM 6** 28
8/7 "Crossbar" Overdate / **VAM 7** 29
8/7 "Ears" Overdate / **VAM 8** 30
8/7 "Stem" Overdate / **VAM 9** 31
80/79 Overdate / **VAM 23** 32

CC 80/79 Rev. '78 / **VAM 4** 33
CC 8/7 High & Low Overdates / **VAMs 5, 6** 34

O 80/79 "Crossbar" Overdates / **VAMs 4, 5** 35
O 8/7 "Ear" Overdates / **VAMs 6, 6A, 6C** 36
O Doubled Ear / **VAM 43** 37
O "Hangnail" Variety / **VAM 48*** 38
O 8/7 "Ear/Hangnail" Overdate / **VAM 49**** 39

S 80/79 Diagonal Overdates / **VAMs 8, 9** 40
S 8/7 "Crossbar" Overdate / **VAM 10** 41

1882

O/S Flush / **VAMs 3, 3A, 3 Early Die State** 42
O/S Recessed / **VAMs 4, 4 Early Die State** 43
O/S Broken / **VAMs 5, 5 Early Die State** 44
O/O Mintmark / **VAM 7** 45

* Formerly VAM 1A   ** Formerly VAM 6B

1883

Sextupled Stars / **VAM 10** 46

O/O Mintmark / **VAM 4** 47

1884

"Dot" Varieties / **VAMs 3, 4** 48

O/O Mintmark / **VAM 6** 49

1885

S/S Mintmark / **VAMs 6, 9** 50

1886

Line in "6" & Line thru "M" / **VAMs 1A, 1A1, 21*** 51
Doubled Arrows / **VAM 17** 52

O "E" on Reverse / **VAM 1A** 53

S/S Mintmark / **VAM 2** 54

1887

Donkey Tail / **VAM 1A** 55
7/6 Overdate / **VAM 2** 56
Doubled Date / **VAM 5** 57
"Alligator Eye" / **VAMs 12, 12A** 58

O Doubled Date / **VAM 2** 59
O 7/6 Overdate / **VAM 3** 60
O Doubled Stars / **VAM 5** 61
O Pitted Reverse / **VAMs 22A**, 22B** 62

S/S Mintmark / **VAM 2** 63

1888

Doubled Ear / **VAMs 11, 11A** 64

*Formerly VAM 1B   **Formerly VAM 22

1888

O "E" on Reverse / **VAM 1A**...................................... 65
O "Scarface" / **VAM 1B**... 66
O "Hot Lips" / **VAM 4**.. 67
O Doubled Arrows / **VAM 9**.. 68
O Oval "O" Mintmark / **VAMs 2, 5, 6, 17, 18, 21, 24, 34**...... 69

1889

"Barwing" / **VAMs 19A*, 19B, 22**................................ 70

O "E" on Reverse / **VAMs 1A1, 1A2**............................... 71
O Oval "O" Mintmark / **VAMs 2, 2A**............................... 72
O Doubled Date / **VAM 6**... 73

1890

CC "Tailbar" / **VAM 4**... 74

1891

Doubled Ear/"Moustache" / **VAMs 2, 2A, 2B** 75

CC "Spitting Eagle" / **VAM 3**.................................... 76

O "E" on Reverse / **VAMs 1A1, 1A2, 1A3**......................... 77

S Doubled Stars / **VAM 3**.. 78

1892

O Doubled Ear / **VAM 5**.. 79

S Doubled Date / **VAM 2**... 80

1893

Doubled Stars / **VAM 4** 81

1895

S "S/Horizontal S" / **VAM 4**..................................... 82
*Formerly VAM 5A

1896

Doubled Stars / **VAM 4**.. 83
"8" in Denticles / **VAM 19**.. 84
O Micro "o" Mintmark / **VAM 4** 85

1897

Pitted Reverse / **VAM 6A**... 86

1899

O Micro "o" Mintmark / **VAMs 4, 5, 6, 31, 32** 87
S Doubled Date / **VAM 7** 88

1900

Doubled Reverse / **VAMs 11, 24** 89
O Micro "o" Mintmark / **VAM 5** 90
O Doubled Stars / **VAMs 15, 15A** 91
O Die Break thru Date / **VAM 29A**...................................... 92
O/CC Mintmark / **VAM 9**... 93
O/CC Mintmark / **VAMs 7, 7A, 8, 8A, 8B,
        10, 10A, 11, 12**... 94

1901

"Shifted Eagle" / **VAM 3** 95

1902

Doubled Ear / **VAM 4**.. 96
O Micro "o" Mintmark / **VAM 3** 97

1903

S Small "s" Mintmark / **VAM 2** 98

WELCOME TO THE REVOLUTION

By Jeff Oxman

There were some great moments in the 20th century. Charles Lindbergh flew solo across the Atlantic in 1927. Amelia Earhart soared across the Pacific Ocean in 1935. Neil Armstrong stepped onto the moon in 1969. And variety collecting, building a base in the 1970s and '80s, literally took off into the stratosphere in the late 1990s. Whoa, wait a minute, you say! Variety collecting can't compare in importance with these other events! And of course, you're right. But in numismatics, collecting by "die variety" has become a virtual revolution – one that the authors believe has changed the way U.S. rare coins are collected today.

In 1893, A.G. Heaton published a small 54-page volume entitled *A Treatise on the Coinage of the United States Branch Mints*, which transformed the landscape of American numismatics. Prior to this time, most hobbyists were only incidentally concerned with coinage struck at U.S. branch mints, and coin cabinet space was most often given to the best possible specimen of each date, not each date and mintmark. To this way of thinking, a nice 1884 silver dollar struck at the New Orleans Mint would be as desirable as any from the Philadelphia, San Francisco or Carson City mints.

Fast forward to the present and look at the direction numismatics has taken. In this day and age, every collector is aware that the "right" mintmark can make a huge difference in terms of value, but some might be surprised by the order of magnitude. An 1884-O Morgan dollar in Gem BU condition has a current *Greysheet* value of $158. But think about this – its San Francisco Mint counterpart, the 1884-S, in the same grade is listed in the *Greysheet* at $190,000!

Of course, it's not just the date and mintmark that are important. The value of any particular coin is based on a laundry list of factors, including wear, contact marks, strike, luster, and eye appeal. Looking back, it was our contention when the first *Top 100* book was released in 1997 that the "die variety" of every silver dollar would become an increasingly important determinant of value. Thirteen years later, this is indeed the case, as date, grade and variety now form a metric that ultimately establishes the coin's value. Without question, the revolution is here!

A look in the rear-view mirror

If collecting by mintmarks was a quantum leap for the 19th century mind, imagine what their reaction would be to collecting by "die variety." Along with 200mph sports cars, bullet trains, and a one-world financial system, numismatics has also changed radically. In the 21st century, it's the die varieties in most 20th-century coin series that represent the "keys." If you haven't thought about it, look no further than the venerable Lincoln cent. When I was piecing together my first set of "pennies" in the 1950s, pressing coin after coin into a blue pennyboard, the 1909-S VDB with its ultra-low mintage of 484,000 was the undisputed "king" of the series. Indeed, owning one was the stuff of which dreams were made.

But the 1909-S VDB is no longer king. Now, the most exciting Lincoln cent is not the 1909-S VDB, but varieties such as the 1969-S Doubled Die or the 1922 Plain (No-D) varieties. Before you smirk, a Mint State 64 red 1969-S Doubled Die sold in 2008 for $126,500, and the 1922 Plain is listed in the *Greysheet* at $130,000 in MS65. By comparison, a 1909-S VDB in the same grade is readily obtainable for about $6,000. Oh, how the mighty have fallen!

Turn the page to the Buffalo nickel series. The two "keys" in the current market are the 1916/1916 Doubled Die and the 1918/7-D Overdate, both of which are die varieties. In the Mercury dime series, two of the most prized coins are the 1942/1-P and the 1942/1-D varieties. The most expensive

Standing Liberty quarter is the 1918/7-S Overdate, and so on. The story is much the same across the board in U.S. numismatics, as more and more varieties become the big premium coins, even to non-variety collectors!

"Knowledge is King"

Okay, but what about silver dollars? Collecting Morgan and Peace dollars by die variety really got its start in the 1960s with the independent efforts of Leroy Van Allen and A. George Mallis. Yes, a number of collectors and dealers were aware of various varieties before this, but the mid-1960s represented a time of intense growth, not only in terms of knowledge, but also in collector demand for U.S. silver dollars. The fact that the U.S. Treasury was at that time disbursing millions of Uncirculated dollars at face value certainly didn't hurt, either. The public immediately recognized the incredible potential, and in what seemed like the wave of a magic wand, these cartwheels went from being the ugly stepsister of American numismatics to the queen of the ball!

By 1971 a collaboration of Van Allen and Mallis resulted in the first VAM Book (VAM is the acronym for **V**an **A**llen and **M**allis), which served to establish VAM collecting as a viable segment of the hobby. These were exciting times. Research into how the first Morgan dollars were developed flowed from the pens of researchers. The minting process came under detailed study, so that errors and varieties could be better explained. And most importantly, there appeared to be a boundless energy on the part of collectors to uncover new Morgan dollar die varieties. What was the result of all this unbridled enthusiasm? Over the next two decades, the number of known VAM varieties exploded to almost 2,000, and then almost doubled again in the years since.

But today there is a problem. Of the thousands of varieties known, only a fraction of that number spark the interest of hobbyists. For instance, of the 87 known 1881-S die varieties, none currently produces a premium in the marketplace. What's wrong? Actually, there's nothing wrong – it's just that VAM collecting requires a clearer focus. And that is the purpose of this book – to supply the reader with specific information about the *Top 100* varieties in the Morgan dollar series in order to highlight those varieties which are collected, bought and sold on a premium basis.

And there are some Morgan dollar varieties that produce tremendous premiums. Need an example or two? In 2007, a West Coast VAM collector purchased an 1882-O for less than $500, and because it was the *ultra-rare* 1882-O/S Early Die State VAM 4, he sold it for something in the vicinity of $30,000. Recently, another VAM enthusiast purchased an 8-TF VAM 14.12 for $95 and sold the same coin in a VAMquest Auction for more than $9,500. The point is this: A collector might encounter just such coins as these at a dealer's table, and armed with the right information (that's where this book comes in!), he or she would have the necessary knowledge to purchase a major rarity without paying a penny more than the cost of the common non-variety. An impossible scenario? No, it happens time and again for those collectors who know and understand variety collecting!

The wave of the future

Today, there is a growing trend in numismatics toward more and more specific knowledge about the coins we collect. At the same time, the experts are bemoaning the fact that local coin clubs (which once were the backbone of the hobby) are disappearing at an alarming rate. The few clubs that are surviving are the so-called specialty clubs. What do they specialize in? From the Fly-In Club, which focuses on Indian cents, to the Society of Silver Dollar Collectors, which specializes in Morgan and Peace dollar varieties, most successful clubs specialize in one particular coin series and the important die varieties in that series. Indeed, variety collecting is riding the crest of the wave, and collecting Morgan dollar varieties by VAM number is spearheading this trend.

So, enjoy this fascinating specialty, and you'll find yourself on a numismatic adventure. The days are far behind us when a handful of pocket change can produce treasures for your coin collection. But we are still living in a time when cherry-picking rare Morgan dollar varieties from a dealer's stock, or even identifying those in your own collection, will produce that same pounding of the heart and racing pulse that collectors over the centuries have enjoyed.

The authors welcome this opportunity to share some of the excitement that has made VAM collecting one of the true frontiers of modern numismatics. All we can say is that for those who seek the thrill of the hunt, this specialty is for you!

Jeff Oxman (left) and Michael Fey

THANKS!
Acknowledging the VAMers

By Michael Fey

Silver dollars! You gotta love 'em. Those big, beautiful cartwheels of yesteryear conjure thoughts of the Wild West, the Comstock Lode and westward expansion – a time of trade among men (and women) in real silver, when money was real money and not just fiat currency pretending to be real money. In the current recessionary economic climate, these beautiful silver dollar cartwheels are worth saving as they now contain about $10 to $15 of silver that continues to increase in value over time. Try getting the same value appreciation from our current coinage!

Silver dollar collectors often evolve from novice to advanced as they learn more about their hobby or investment. The first collection is typically one of dates and mintmarks that may be a mix of Circulated-to-Mint State grades, depending on rarity and cost. After careful thought, observation and an initial study of the literature about the series, collecting pursuits gradually give way to the rarer, but perhaps not proportionately as expensive, Proof-like (PL) or Deep Mirror Proof-like (DMPL) specimens. Often, collectors will notice extensive die cracks and breaks on Morgan dollar PL/DMPLs, suggesting that the dies didn't last very long before they broke apart. The more they read, learn and experience, the more they come to realize that these dollars are likely to be rarer than others of the same date. As the collector continues to acquire reference books and learn more, he/she will ultimately start collecting rare silver dollar varieties as a way to acquire greater rarity. The specimens are much more interesting examples as well, and may be acquired for nearly the same amount of money than could be spent for the relatively more common specimens. Naturally, it represents a better investment of both time and money – and it's far more fun!

Initially, collectors seeking more information may have turned to *The Comprehensive Catalog and Encyclopedia of Morgan & Peace Dollars* by Leroy Van Allen and A. George Mallis. We are indebted to these authors as the Founding Fathers of VAM collecting – indeed, the "VAM" name is an acronym made up of their initials. Numismatists such as Francis Klaes, Neil Shafer, Walter Breen, Bill Fivaz and Randy Campbell were all early pioneers of VAM collecting and deserve due credit for making significant contributions to VAM discovery, publication and promotion.

I especially want to acknowledge Jeff Oxman as my mentor and co-author of the *Top 100 Morgan Dollar Varieties: The VAM Keys*. VAM collecting rested mostly on Jeff's shoulders from the latter part of the 1980s to the late '90s. It could not have been in better hands when Jeff founded the Society of Silver Dollar Collectors (SSDC) in the winter of 1988. Along with his most excellent publication, the *SSDC Journal*, Jeff nurtured VAM collecting from its infancy until such time as the spark began to ignite into the brightly burning blaze it is today. Thanks also go to the American Numismatic Association (ANA) for inviting me and Jeff to give Summer Seminar classes and present Numismatic Theatres about silver dollar variety collecting throughout the years.

Jeff went on to produce some excellent references on silver dollar varieties – *The 1878 Morgan Dollar 8-TF Attribution Guide* and *The 1878 Morgan Dollar 7/8-TF Attribution Guide* (both with co-author Les Hartnett), the *Official Guide to the Hot 50 Morgan Dollar Varieties*, the *Official Guide to the Top 50 Peace Dollar Varieties* (with co-author David Close, M.D.), and now the *Hit List 40*. These classic references, and a growing number of Internet resources such as VAMlink.com and VAMquest.com, have generated increased interest and contributed to the rapid growth of silver dollar variety collecting.

I would be remiss if I didn't mention the world-class photographic efforts of Tom Mulvaney, whose unsurpassed images of silver dollars, as well as other numismatic types, have inspired our generation. Bill Fivaz, through Jeff Oxman's series of books, also did a superb job of photographing close-up desirable features on Morgan and Peace dollar varieties. John Baumgart's photographic and programming efforts were essential in developing a series of computer CD wizards for silver dollar varieties. It's these very images that excite many of us today.

Thanks to Randy Campbell, Michael Faraone and John Roberts, author of the "About VAMs" column in *Coin World*, new Morgan and Peace varieties and particularly *Top 100s* were recognized by the ANACS grading service from 1997 forward, a significant step toward establishing credibility and a trading market.

Thanks to the forward thinking of NGC President Mark Salzberg and NGC's Research Director, David Lange, *Top 100* and other Morgan and Peace dollar varieties were, starting in 1998, recognized by the NGC grading service. Shortly thereafter, James Taylor, Keith Love, J.P. Martin and others at the ICG grading service followed suit (Taylor and Martin are now employees of ANACS). Larry Briggs, founder of the SEGS grading service and longtime VAM aficionado and expert, also attributed *Top 100* and other VAMs on the holder's label. Larry continues to be a world-class expert on Morgan and Peace dollar varieties, and is one of the most knowledgeable experts when it comes to 1878-S varieties.

David Wang, Ph.D., is to be congratulated for his 2001 publication, *A Guide to the 1879-S Reverse of 1878 Morgan Silver Dollars*. Working with Leroy Van Allen, Calvin Cherry, William Eubanks and me via e-mail, Dave was the first to bring a sense of order to this niche of variety collecting. To our knowledge he was the first in numismatics to use the Internet as a medium for rapid communication to finally define this series that was confusing to everyone.

We wish to acknowledge and thank Mark Kimpton,

M.D., who brought a passion for collecting and a keen sense of observation to silver dollar variety collecting. Mark went on to discover hundreds of new clashed Morgan and Peace dollar varieties, including many *Top 100s*, and published a book titled *Elite Clashed Morgan Dollars* in 2005, all of which earned him the title "Founding Father of Clashed Morgan Dollars."

We would also like to acknowledge veteran collector Rob Joyce for his 2003 book, *Fun with 1921 – Denver Morgan Dollars with Die Breaks, Die Gouges and Filled Dies*. He and Jim Hart became the experts in this fascinating area of variety collecting. Unfortunately, Jim passed away in 2003, just as friend and fellow variety collector extraordinaire Terry Armstrong passed in 2001.

Thanks go to Marcy Gibbel, Managing Editor of *COINage Magazine*, and Mike Gumpel, who in the Fall of 2003 began publishing *Top 100* values in their monthly. Soon thereafter, Mark Ferguson of *Coin World* began publishing pricing for select silver dollar varieties. We would like to recognize Harry Miller and *Numismatic News* for their efforts to continue to follow pricing in this burgeoning area of collecting. And Shane Downing and Keith Zanner of CDN, Inc., are to be recognized for providing a sense of wholesale *Greysheet* values for common silver dollar varieties.

At the First Annual SSDC VAM Thing in 2003, John Baumgart stepped up as the SSDC's Internet maven. John is to be recognized for his tireless efforts in assembling and delivering the weekly electronic version of SSDC news to members through VAM-E.

The "California Contingent," consisting of Dennis Halladay, Logan McKechnie and Tim Cannard, began publication of the *VAMView* quarterly in 2005, and the following year expanded its distribution to all SSDC members electronically. Its impact has been widespread, and in 2006 *VAMview* broadened its focus to include a retail pricing guide.

PCGS began attributing silver dollar varieties in 2005 and

brought in Michael Faraone, formerly of ANACS, as their primary variety attributor. Silver dollar variety collecting has not been the same since. PCGS added new credibility as well as new dealer and collector clientele to the market. Prices soared.

With all that was happening throughout the years, Leroy Van Allen stayed the course, attributing hundreds of potential discoveries, some significant, some not. Leroy published yearly VAM Book supplements, provided photographs for Dr. Kimpton's book, and published nearly a dozen monographs on various areas of Morgan and Peace dollar varieties. His tireless efforts and dedication to this area of collecting earned him a Lifetime Achievement Award in 2007 from the American Numismatic Association, an award well deserved. Leroy, on behalf of the VAM collecting community, we all salute you!

But acknowledging silver dollar variety collectors is only part of the story. Thanks also go to the dealers who sacrificed their time and hard-earned money to provide liquidity to the market and to promote VAM collecting to their customers. Dealers such as Larry Briggs, Gene Henry, Paul Marino, Jonathan Parrella, Bob Campbell, Gene Gress, Pete Goydas, Sal Germano, John Guilde, Jack Beymer, Grant Campbell, Tim Carroll, Michael Cotta, Tom DeLorey, Orv Detrick, Bill Grider, Robert Harlow, Val Homes, Al Johnbrier, Eric Justice, Allan Kreuzer, Wayne Miller, Warren Mills, Bob Minichino, Alex Nocerino, Richard Nachbar, Robert Paul, Tom Payne, Ken Potter, Robert Reithe, Jason Pasciuti, Allen Rowe, Dr. Arnold Saslow, Randy Schultz, John Schuck, Ralph Solomon, Richard Stelfox, Dan Walker, Bob Walter, and many more.

Thanks to Jim Halperin, Brian Koller and David Lisot of Heritage Auction Galleries for their efforts to accurately attribute and promote silver dollar varieties in their market-leading auction venue, a venue which is now setting many new price records. Thanks to Q. David Bowers, Scott Mitchell and Vicken Yegparian of Stacks/ANR for their efforts to attribute VAMs in their auctions. Likewise, thanks to Bowers & Merena Auctions, Superior Galleries, and Ira and Larry Goldberg Auctioneers. Thanks to Mary Counts and Dennis Tucker of Whitman Publishing, LLC, and author Q. David Bowers, who in 2004 published *The Official Red Book of Morgan Silver Dollars: A Complete History and Price Guide*. Through this book, most of the *Top 100* Morgan dollar varieties went public via retail book distributors throughout the nation.

A special thanks to world-class numismatists Leroy Van Allen, Bill Fivaz, Larry Briggs, John Roberts, Mark Kimpton, David Wang, and Rob Joyce for their informative contributions to the *Top 100*. In this era of silver dollar variety collecting, these numismatists are a Who's Who of VAMs.

THE LIST

This is an abbreviated list of silver dollar variety collectors who continue to hunger for knowledge and yearn for the thrill of the hunt, and who continue to contribute to the history, growth and popularity of silver dollar variety collecting. When compared with large cent and bust half collectors, we are still in our infancy. Your names will hereinafter be inscribed as part of silver dollar variety collecting history.

Del **Alder**
William **Allen**
Frank **Aratari**
Terry **Armstrong***
Michael **Ash**
Bob **Barkey**
Frank **Barton**
John **Baumgart**
Cindy **Bedwell**

James **Bedwell**
Stephanie A. **Begonja**
Martin **Bell**
Frank **Belmont**
Jim **Berrier**
Jack **Beymer**
Charles **Bishop**
Rick **Bonazza**
George **Booze**

David **Borofski**
Q. David **Bowers**
Floyd **Bradford**, Jr.
John **Bradley**
Dan **Brady**
James **Brake**
Kenneth **Bressett**

Steven **Brewer**
Larry **Briggs**
Will **Camp**
Bob **Campbell**
Grant **Campbell**
Randy **Campbell**
Richard **Carlson**
Scott **Carlson**
Jim **Carr**
Tim **Carroll**

Claudio Cepeda, M.D.
Calvin Cherry
Clayton Christiansen
Robert Clark
Hartley Cole
Ralph Cole
Earl Collison
Lawrence Coole
Michael Cotta
J.W. Courter
John Coxe
Haver (Dan) Danner
Mark Davis
Lee Day
Richard DeKrauze
Tom DeLorey
Rick DeSanctis
Orv Detrick
Johann Diaz
Blair Diffenderfer
Ron Dintermann
Mike Dlugosz
Lance Dohe
David Druzisky
Bryan Eckenrode
Sherwood Elkind
David Emery
Michael Emswiler
Casmier Fadze
Brian Fanton
Mike Faraone
John Feigenbaum
Carl Feldman
Gabor Ferencz

Mark Ferguson
Martin Field*
Bill Fivaz
Brent Fogelberg
Coleman Foster
Kevin Frank, Sr.
Daniel Frazon
William Friend
Sal Fusco
Lloyd Gabbert
Larry Galbraith
Jeff Garrett
Paul Geiersbach
Sam Gelberd
Ray Gelewski
Sal Germano
Roland Girardet
Rusty Goe
Pete Goydas
Brian Greer
Bill Grider
John Gulde
Mike Gumpel
Henry Habenicht
Dennis Halladay
Clarence Hale
Don Hansen
Greg Hanson
Robert Harlow
Tim Harris
C. Ash Harrison
Richard Harrison
James Hart*
Tim Henrichs
Gene Henry
Brandon Hicks
Steve Hodges
Bob Hoebake
Dorell Hoffner
Val Homes
Fred Howe
Jim Huffman
John Hunter

Ralph Huntzinger
Steve Hyatt
Henry James
Keith James
J. Robert Jankosky
David Janus
Al Johnbrier
Brad Johnson
Darryl Johnson
Don Johnson
Ronald Johnson
Terry Jones
Robert Joyce
Eric Justice
Donald Kagin
Thomas Kern
Robert Kevorkian
Mark Kimpton, M.D.
Mark Kleiman
Paul Kobierecki
Michael Koch
Brian Koller
Alan Kreuzer
Mike Krowczyk
Jim Lafferty
Richard Lang
Dave Lange
Mel Larson
William K. Latour
Wendell Leavitt
Max Lebow, M.D.
Jack Lee
Donald Lenke
Joe Lewis
Craig Lickenbrock
David Lisot
James Lottes

Maximilian Lucas
Michael Lucyk
Ed McCafferty
Logan McKechnie
Mal McKittrick
Ken McLean
Ron Madonia
Michael Maggi
Yvonne Malinowski
Charles Mamiye
Charles Marino
Paul Marino
Tom Martin
Tom Matterness
Ricardo Medina
Alan Meghrig
Jonathan Meyer
Harry Miller
John Miller
Wayne Miller
Warren Mills
Bob Minichino
Scott Mitchell
Charles Moore
Ryan Moretti
Lenny Mormino
H. "Crae" Morton
Wali Motorwalla
Alfred Moy
Larry Muehl
John Murray
Richard Myers
Richard Nachbar
Robert Namiat
Ronald Nelson, M.D.
Michael Nevin
Alex Nocerino
Ellis Nordyke
Bob Orlando
Nathan Owens

Jeff **Oxman**
Tim **Page**
Steven **Palmisano**
Russ **Panchelli**
Jonathan **Parrella**
Jason **Pasciuti**
John **Pasciuti**
Tony **Patchin**
Robert **Paul**
Richard **Pawley**
Tom **Payne**
Theodore **Peiffer**
David **Percy**
Philip **Perdue**
Paul **Pierce**
Ken **Potter**
George **Powell**, Jr.
Richard **Prouty**
Paul **Puckett**
Edward **Rautmann**
Robert **Reithe**
Jeffrey **Rex**
Dan **Rhame**
Richard **Ripkowski**
John **Roberts**
Charles **Robinson**
James **Roland**
Joe **Rouillard**
Allen **Rowe**
D. Lavar **Rush**
John **Rusinko**
Steve **Sabella**
Jim **Sabrowski**
Sam **Salvo**
Steve **Saris**
Arnold **Saslow**
Jeffrey **Scalici**

John **Schuck**
Lawrence **Schuffman**
E.R. (Randy) **Schultz**
Marc **Serafine**
Frank **Setteducato**
Jason J. **Sharon**
Jay **Shattuck**
Joseph **Shirley**
Al **Simmons**
Victor **Skidmore**
Clark **Smith**
Darrell **Smith**
James **Smith**
Orville **Smith**
Chris **Smolinski**
Ralph **Solomon**
Sal **Stagnitta**
Fred **Stanley**
Tony **Stanley**
J.T. **Stanton**
Robert **Steinegger**
Richard **Stelfox**
Gary **Stewart**
Bob **Stone**
Barry **Stuppler**
Thomas **Sutton**
Anthony **Swiatek**
Steve **Szcerbiak**
James **Taylor**
Tom **Testagrose**, Jr.
Richard **Thomas**
Michael **Torgrimson**
Scott A. **Travers**
Lee **Tucker**, Jr.
Jack **Turner**
James **Turner**
Jim **Turner**

Leroy **Van Allen**
John **Vignola**
Dan **Walker**
Terry **Wallace**
Bob **Walter**
Robert **Ward**
W. Hoyt **Warren**
Jonathan **Wengel**
Ray **Williams**
Fred **Wilson**
John **Wilson**
Richard **Wismar**
Albert **Wood**
Myron **Xenos**
Bob **Yauger**
James **Young**
Richard **Zink**

---

* Deceased

VAM Collecting: A Primer

The VAM attribution system is a series of identifying numbers assigned to individual die varieties for each date and mintmark. This nomenclature makes it possible to refer to any particular silver dollar variety in the series simply by using its "VAM Number." For example, in 1888 a specific die pair from the New Orleans Mint struck what is affectionately known as the "Hot Lips" variety. To distinguish this obverse and reverse die combination from all others dated 1888-O, Van Allen and Mallis assigned the "Hot Lips" variety its own VAM Number, in this case, VAM 4. Hence, only a coin struck by this pair of dies is a VAM 4 for this date.

Each date in the Morgan and Peace dollar series has its own set of reference numbers, beginning with VAM 1 and proceeding as high as necessary to accommodate all of the known die varieties for that date and mintmark. For 1880-S, the VAM numbers go from 1 to 85 (as of February 2009, refer to the current VAM Supplements published periodically by Leroy Van Allen (see pages 26B-27B). For 1880-CC the VAM numbers run only to VAM 10.

Many collectors have written us and said, "There's so much to know in VAM collecting!" This is true, but with a little dedication and patience, the terminology is within reach of every collector.

VAM terminology

VAM – An acronym for **V**an **A**llen and **M**allis. The term "VAM" has now become synonymous with the system of cataloging Morgan and Peace dollar die varieties. Each die variety is now called a VAM. Leroy Van Allen and A. George Mallis first joined forces in the late 1960s to produce their original volume on U.S. silver dollar varieties, entitled the

Guide to Morgan and Peace Dollars. This seminal work was first privately published in 1971, and Leroy Van Allen still catalogs silver dollars and publishes periodic supplements to the book.

VAM Book – Five years later, in 1976, the authors expanded "The Guide" to create their magnum opus, the *Comprehensive Catalogue and Encyclopedia of U.S. Morgan & Peace Silver Dollars.* This was expanded again in 1991 to a Third Edition and again in 1997 in a fourth, which has now received universal acceptance as the "VAM Book." The first quarter of the book deals with the background and development of the Morgan dollar. The next two quarters of the book present a sequential listing of Morgan dollar varieties by date. Each variety has been assigned a VAM Number, is described as to its distinctive attributes and is pictured so that a collector can readily identify it. The final quarter of the book features a similar presentation of Peace dollar varieties.

The VAM Book is highly recommended as a necessary reference for all Morgan dollar collectors. If you need a copy of this important resource, please check with your local coin dealer or numismatic weekly newspapers such as *Coin World* or *Numismatic News*, or visit our websites, **www.rcicoins.com** and **www.vamlink.com.**

VAM Numbers – In the VAM Book, each die variety is assigned a unique identifying number called a VAM Number. As new varieties are discovered, they are given the next available number. For example, VAM 85 is the most recently discovered 1880-S die variety, but should a new variety come to Leroy Van Allen's attention, it would be designated VAM 86.

Die Pair – Every Morgan and Peace dollar has been struck by two dies. This occurs within the confines of a collar die which imparts the reeding and also serves to prevent the planchet from expanding beyond its specified diameter.

Together, the obverse and reverse are considered a die pair. Every coin produced by this pair of dies has the same VAM Number. If one die breaks, which was a continual problem at the various Mints, the remaining die may be paired with a new die. Coins struck by the new die pair would have one obverse or reverse in common with the old die pair, but for purposes of attribution, this new pair would be assigned a new VAM Number. The upshot is that each die pair is unique.

VAM Number with a capital letter and/or number following it – Each VAM Number denotes a particular die pair, and a letter after the VAM Number, as in VAM 1B, indicates

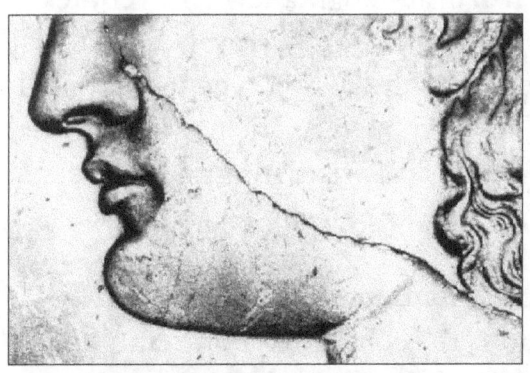

The classic 1888-O "Scarface"

the presence of some feature on the obverse or reverse that Van Allen and Mallis felt was worthy of special note.

For instance, the 1888-O VAM 1 is the "normal" die pair for this date. 1888-O VAM 1B refers to the same die pair, but a much later die state. 1888-O VAM 1B is called the "Scarface" variety and is the terminal die state of the obverse die with a major die break across Liberty's cheek.

If the 1888-O VAM 1B is an earlier die state of the "Scarface" variety, it may have a number following it, as with VAM 1B1. And if it is a Very Late Die State (there being several die stages known with the "Scarface" designation), the coin may be listed as a VAM 1B5. Since variety collectors and investors are likely to want the most dramatic variety feature of the "Scarface," they would seek an example of the 1888-O VAM 1B5. However, some VAM collectors might want to collect a rare die progression set of all the "Scarface" listings, from Early Die State 1B1 to 1B5.

Types I-IV – Designations for identifying obverse design types. Types I and II were used only in 1878. Type III obverses were used after Types I and II in 1878 and then were used exclusively through 1904. Type IV was a newly engraved design used only in 1921. Images differentiating these obverse design types are given in the most recent VAM book.

Reverse Types A-D – Designations for identifying reverse design types. Type A reverses, known as 8-Tailfeather reverses, were employed only for a short period of time in the spring of 1878. Type B followed and is now referred to as the 7-Tailfeather, Parallel Arrow Feathers, flat breast, "Reverse of '78." These are mostly found in 1878, although a few leftover dies were used for 1879-S and 1880-CC. Type C reverses were first used in 1878 and continued to be the design type found on all Morgan dollars through 1904. Type D was the newly engraved design used only in 1921. Images differentiating these reverse design types are provided in the most recent VAM Book.

Die Designations – For attribution purposes, the VAM Book assigns die designations to each VAM. For example, a $III^11 \cdot C^2b$ designation for a variety would simply mean that the obverse for this Morgan was the third design (III), first working hub design (^{1}), and the first reported obverse working die (1). The reverse would be the "C" design, second working hub design (^{2}), and the "b" indicates the second reported reverse working die. The obverse and reverse die designations are separated in VAM by a dot.

Please keep in mind, that it is not of key importance to remember or even understand the assignment of VAM numbers or die designations to make a *Top 100* find. Just match up your dollar exactly to the photo and key identification features and you've got it!

For more information about the assignment of VAM Numbers, refer to the VAM Book.

THE SSDC
TOP 100 CHALLENGE

Whether you are a collector, investor or a little bit of both, the thrill of the hunt and the satisfaction of completing a set can make VAM collecting both fun and rewarding.

In our past challenge, the Society of Silver Dollar Collectors (SSDC) offered a $1,000 award to the first new SSDC member who completed a set of the First Edition *Top 100* in any grade by the year 2000. The only stipulation was that the set be submitted to the SSDC so that the attributions could be corroborated. Michael Andrew was the winner of that $1,000 award. This set did not include every variety, or the current new discoveries, but did include examples from every *Top 100* variety class.

To the best of our knowledge, no one has been successful in assembling a complete collection of the First Edition *Top 100* Morgan varieties in Mint State, or with all coins listed in each of the *Top 100* classes, although several SSDC collectors (including the authors) are getting close. Such a collection would be an amazing numismatic accomplishment.

The authors are prepared to offer another award of $5,000 to any SSDC collector who completes a collection of the Fourth Edition *Top 100* in Mint State – certified by a major grading service – by January 1, 2010. We would also publicize the winner's achievement in the numismatic media. Only SSDC members are eligible, and the winner must agree to be the subject of a press release. See page 24A for an SSDC membership application.

OTHER TOP 100 CHALLENGES

Fortunately, there are many other collecting challenges that involve *Top 100* Morgans and other Morgan varieties listed in the Fourth Edition of the VAM Book, the *Comprehensive Catalog and Encyclopedia of Morgan & Peace Dollars* by Leroy C. Van Allen and A. George Mallis. Some are quite formidable undertakings, while others are less difficult to achieve...

1.) Completing a set of **1878 Morgan 8-Tailfeather** dollars, including the first Morgan dollar variety struck, the VAM 9. This includes VAMs 1 through 23 and 14.1 through 14.20 and comprises a 41-coin set. The set may be expanded to include all known reed counts, as different collars were used to strike some varieties. The authors rate this as an **ULTIMATE** challenge (Rarity 7+), since to the best of our knowledge, only two collectors have ever assembled a complete 8-Tailfeather set. Numerous collectors and dealers are currently building one.

2.) Completing a set of the so-called **1878 7/8-Tailfeather** dollars. This includes VAMs 30-45 and is considered by the authors to be **VERY DIFFICULT** (Rarity 6+). Several dozen examples of the VAM 44 are currently known in all grades, and VAMs 32, 34, and 45 are also quite difficult to find. Some collectors have successfully completed this set in Circulated grades, and very few have completed it in Mint State. If you want a greater challenge (Rarity 8), try putting together this set in BU or with Proof-like or Deep Mirror Proof-like surfaces, with the various known non-clashed and clashed dies. The VAM 34A with clashed obverse is a Rarity 8 coin! There may only be one complete set like this!

3.) Completing a set of **Morgan Micro "o" mintmarks**. This collection includes an example of the 1880-O Micro "o";

1896 Micro "o"; 1899 Micro "o" VAMs 4, 5, 6, 31 and 32; the 1900-O Micro "o"; and the 1902-O Micro "o", along with contrasting examples of the normal "o" mintmark for each year. The 1903 Small "s" and the 1921-D (with the normal Micro "D" mintmark) would make interesting additions to this collection. Since most of the later-date Micro "o" Morgans are quite rare, the authors would rate this collection as **VERY DIFFICULT** (Rarity 6+) in Circulated grades, and perhaps unachievable (Rarity 8) in BU. To our knowledge, several collectors have completed a Micro "o" collection in low Circulated grades, but no complete sets have ever entered the marketplace. This would likely be a raw set, since the grading services no longer certify the 1896, 1900 and 1902 Micro "o" Morgans as Mint products because they believe these coins were struck outside the Mint and are contemporary counterfeits.

4.) Completing a **full set of VAM die varieties for a particular date and mintmark** of your choice. Take your pick. Chances are good that you will become an expert in that date and mintmark and will discover one or more new and perhaps rare die varieties. You too can leave your mark in numismatic history by contributing knowledge to a particular series. Sound far-fetched? In just the past 13 years, since publication of the First Edition of the *Top 100* book, dealers and collectors have discovered several hundred new varieties, some of which are in this Fourth Edition.

More collecting options

You may wish to start your collection by targeting a set of the 1878-S B1 (long center arrow shaft) reverses – an **EXTREMELY DIFFICULT** and challenging nine-coin set (Rarity 8) in Circulated grades, and perhaps unachievable in BU. To our knowledge, there are perhaps only two completed sets in Circulated grades. Or how about a collection of the

19 known 1879-S "Reverse of 1878" Morgan varieties in Circulated grades or BU condition? There may only be one Circulated set. The 10 known 1900 "O/CC" over-mintmarks with clashed varieties present an interesting challenge in Circulated grades because of the difficulty in finding VAMs 7, 7A and 9 (Rarity 7). This set becomes almost unachievable in BU (Rarity 8).

You may also wish to start with something less challenging, such as a three-coin set of the 1882 "O/S" overdates, VAMs 3, 4, and 5 (Rarity 4). Later, you may want to include Early Die States of these coins, which would increase your challenge to Rarity 7+ because of the difficulty in finding the VAM 4 EDS. Or you may wish to assemble a collection of the *Top 100* doubled dies, a collection of *Top 100* overdates, *Top 100* repunched dates or mintmarks, rare die breaks, "E" reverses, or pitted reverses. Or, you might just collect your favorite rare *Top 100* VAMs.

Whichever VAMs you decide to collect, be assured you are doing something worthwhile. A collection of rare Morgan dollar varieties will be a source of enjoyment far into the future. And if the past decade is any indication, the potential is there for significant price appreciation as well.

Begin by defining your objective. Then, we recommend that you read as much as you can about the subject – subscribe to *Top 100 Insights and Value Guide* and become a member of the SSDC to keep up with the latest information. Then, join in the thrill of the hunt for the *Top 100* VAM Keys and venture into the 8-TFs, *Hot 50, Hit List 40* or any of the other series of Morgan and/or Peace dollars that may strike your fancy.

Happy Hunting!

HOW TO USE THIS BOOK
A Key to the Fourth Edition

The concept for the *Top 100 Morgan Dollar Varieties: The VAM Keys* was simply this: to create a pocket-sized field guide with an easy-to-understand, easy-to-use format that enables you to first identify the *Top 100* varieties, then quickly and efficiently attribute them. This book was written in response to the need for on-the-spot attribution at coin shows and shops, auctions or anywhere else.

We've expanded the Fourth Edition to include the latest new discoveries, pricing information and condition census data, and added references that allow you to further explore any particular interests. The VAM value charts in this new edition include two more grade categories than those in earlier editions, and we've added population data for each variety, including counts for PL and DMPL specimens.

We have also added supplementary information about such topics as rotated-die and wide-reeding varieties, Micro "o" VAMs, and the rank order of *Top 100* PL and DMPL VAMs in two appendices.

Although we have provided what we feel are the most important images of *Top 100* Morgans – the photos you will need for accurate attribution – we have not included images of every single variety in a series. If we had, this wouldn't be a quick and handy little pocket-sized book anymore.

In This Section

The Format xxiv
Coin Grading Scale and Rarity Scale xxvi
About Values xxvii
Abbreviations used throughout the book xxviii
References and Reference Codes xxx

A

1878-P 8-TF Doubled "RIB"

B ■ **VAM:** 5 / 8-Tailfeather Reverse / **PF:** 8

C ■ **Ref:** F, FS (1-1878-005), O1, OCD, R, V

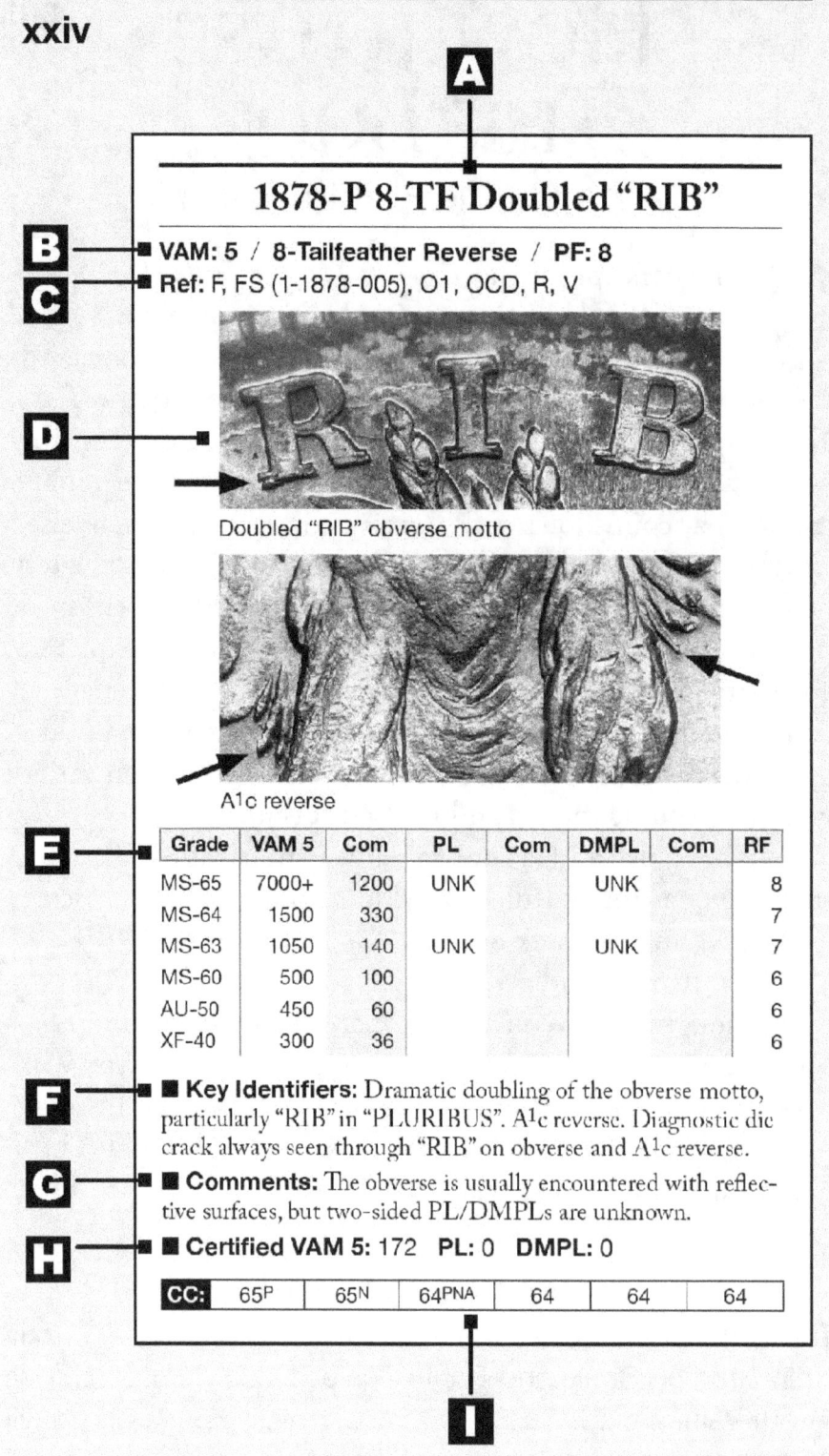

Doubled "RIB" obverse motto

A1c reverse

E

Grade	VAM 5	Com	PL	Com	DMPL	Com	RF
MS-65	7000+	1200	UNK		UNK		8
MS-64	1500	330					7
MS-63	1050	140	UNK		UNK		7
MS-60	500	100					6
AU-50	450	60					6
XF-40	300	36					6

F ■ **Key Identifiers:** Dramatic doubling of the obverse motto, particularly "RIB" in "PLURIBUS". A1c reverse. Diagnostic die crack always seen through "RIB" on obverse and A1c reverse.

G ■ **Comments:** The obverse is usually encountered with reflective surfaces, but two-sided PL/DMPLs are unknown.

H ■ **Certified VAM 5:** 172 **PL:** 0 **DMPL:** 0

CC:	65P	65N	64PNA	64	64	64

I

A / Title – Date, mintmark, and popular variety description.

B / Identification – VAM Number as listed in the Fourth Edition of the VAM Book, a more complete variety-type description, and the Popularity Factor (PF, a scale – from a low of 1 up to 10 – that measures demand for a particular variety).

C / References – Where to look for deeper information on a particular variety. Author reference codes (see page xxx) and Fivaz/Stanton Numbers are included where applicable.

D / Photos – Arrows indicate key pick-up points.

E / Value Estimates –

Column 1: Six grade levels
Column 2: Value of VAM through grades (see page xxvi)
Column 3: Value of a non-variety or common coin
Column 4: Value of VAM with PL surfaces
Column 5: Value of non-variety or common PL coin
Column 6: Value of VAM with DMPL surfaces
Column 7: Value of non-variety or common DMPL coin
Column 8: Rarity Factor estimate based on number of certified specimens known to exist (see page xxvi)

F / Key Identifiers – Important pick-up points on the coin for identification purposes. **Note:** Minor differences in die varieties have been omitted.

G / Comments – Information about a particular variety. **Note:** New *Top 100* die marriages have been discovered. Several varieties may exist in a variety class, so we have provided extended listings beginning on page 2A.

H / Number Certified – Combined populations of PCGS, NGC, ANACS and SEGS coins, with PL and DMPL totals.

I / Condition Census – The Finest Known and the five next-best specimens, and grading services, if certified.

GRADING SCALE

Grades are given on a 70-point grading scale:

G	Good	4 or 6
VG	Very Good	8 or 10
F	Fine	12 or 15
VF	Very Fine	20, 25, 30, 35
XF	Extra Fine	40 or 45
AU	About Uncirculated	50, 53, 55 or 58
MS	Mint State	60 through 70
UNC	Uncirculated	
BU	Brilliant Uncirculated	

RARITY SCALE

R-8	Unique or Nearly Unique	Several
R-7	Extremely Rare	Few tens
R-6	Very Rare	Several hundred
R-5	Rare	Several thousands
R-4	Very Scarce	Tens of thousands
R-3	Scarce	Hundreds of thousands
R-2	Not So Common	Several million
R-1	Common	Tens of millions

Note: The higher-end rarity scale of a particular *Top 100* variety may change (typically, decrease) over time as more specimens are found. The lower end of the rarity scale should not change significantly. Assigning rarity values is not an exact science. After all, how can anyone know how many examples exist at any given time? The rarity values given in this book are based on the authors' knowledge and experience, historical data and periodic mathematical compilations.

Data in Column 2 of the value chart on each variety's page represent the authors' estimate of the retail value of each variety in a particular grade, based on auction results and private treaty transactions. **Note:** Some very rare Morgan dollar varieties, including those among the Finest Known, may never have been sold, or may sell only rarely. A plus sign (+) next to the value indicates that this coin may be bought or sold for significantly more than the price given.

Data in Column 3 are the corresponding non-variety values, based on commonly accepted wholesale values, as found in the *Coin Dealer Newsletter Bluesheet* and/or *Greysheet*, (Division of CDN, Inc). These values may fluctuate from day to day, with changes in the rare coin or bullion markets.

    Readers are cautioned to obtain current price listings and up-to-date *Top 100* prices when determining the value of their coins. RCI publishes a quarterly newsletter called the *Top 100 Value Guide* with the most current pricing of varieties listed in this book. Readers are urged to obtain current pricing information, as pricing in this book will quickly become out-of-date.

Data in Columns 4 and 5 offer estimates of the variety and non-variety values for the same VAM with Proof-like (PL) surfaces. If a variety is not known to have PL surfaces, this area will likely be blank.

Data in Columns 6 and 7 offer estimates of the variety and non-variety values for the same VAM with Deep Mirror Proof-like (DMPL) surfaces. If a variety is not known to have DMPL surfaces, this area will likely be blank.

Data in Column 8 are estimates of the rarity of a particular VAM in a particular grade, based on the scale given in the Fourth Edition of the VAM Book (see previous page).

ABBREVIATIONS

0/9	Overdate/Underdate numerals in the date
7/6	Overdate/Underdate numerals in the date
7/8-TF	The so-called "7 over 8-Tailfeather Reverse"
7/X	7/8-TF with X number of tips showing
8/7	Overdate/Underdate numerals in the date
80/79	Overdate/Underdate numerals in the date
A	ANACS (Condition Census section)
ANACS	ANACS grading service
AU	About Uncirculated (grading terminology)
BU	Brilliant Uncirculated
-CC	Carson City mintmark
CDN	Coin Dealer Newsletter
DDO	Doubled die obverse
DDR	Doubled die reverse
DM	Deep Mirror Proof-like (Condition Census section)
DMPL	Deep Mirror Proof-like
EDS	Early Die State
F	Fine (grading terminology)
FS	Fivaz-Stanton (in reference listings on VAM pages)
I	PCI grading service
LDS	Late Die State
M	Morgan's initial as designer
Mult.	Multiples (Condition Census section)
N	NGC grading service (Condition Census section)
NGC	Numismatic Guaranty Corporation of America
NTH	Has **N**ot **T**raded **H**ands
-O	New Orleans mintmark
Obv.	Obverse
O/CC	"O" mintmark repunched over "CC" mintmark

O/O	Repunched New Orleans mintmark
O/S	"O" mintmark repunched over "S" mintmark
OPL	Proof-like surface on obverse only
ODMPL	Deep Mirror Proof-like surface on obverse only
P	PCGS grading service (Condition Census section)
-P	Struck at Philadelphia (no mintmark)
PAF	Parallel Arrow Feathers on the B reverse
PCGS	Professional Certification Grading Service
PCI	Photo Certification Institute
PF	Popularity Factor
PL	Proof-like
R	Raw, not certified (Condition Census section)
Rev.	Reverse
RF	Rarity Factor
RPD	Repunched date
RPL	Proof-like surface on reverse only
RDMPL	Deep Mirror Proof-like surface on reverse only
RPM	Repunched mintmark
-S	San Francisco mintmark
S	SEGS grading service (Condition Census section)
SAF	Slanted Arrow Feathers on the C reverse
SPL	Semi-Proof-like
S/S	Repunched San Francisco mintmark
TF	Tailfeathers
TDO	Tripled die obverse
TDR	Tripled die reverse
UNK	Unknown
VAM	Van Allen/Mallis
VAR	Various
VF	Very Fine (grading terminology)
VLDS	Very Late Die State
XF	Extremely Fine (grading terminology)

REFERENCES

Note: Letter and letter-number codes in **BOLD** represent their corresponding titles in the references line on VAM pages.

B Breen, Walter. *Walter Breen's Complete Encyclopedia of U.S. and Colonial Coins*. New York: Doubleday, 1998.

D Fey, Michael S. *A Decade of Top 100 Insights, For the Advanced Morgan Dollar Collector*. Ironia, NJ: RCI, 2008.

F Fivaz, Bill, and J.T. Stanton. *The Cherrypickers' Guide to Rare Die Varieties*. Third Edition. Wolfeboro, NH: Bowers & Merena Galleries, Inc., 1994.

FS Fivaz, Bill, and J.T. Stanton. *Cherrypickers' Guide to Rare Die Varieties*. Fourth Edition, Volume II. Atlanta, GA: Whitman Publishing, LLC, 2006. **Note:** The FS numbering system changed between editions, so references for some VAMs include two FS numbers – one from 1994 and one from 2006.

J Roberts, John. *Long Nock: A Guide to the 1878-S B1 Reverse Varieties*. VAMview and VAMS and More, 2008.

K Kimpton, Mark. *Elite Clashed Morgan Dollars*. Ironia, NJ: RCI, 2005.

O1 Oxman, Jeff, and Les Hartnett. *1878 Morgan Dollar 8-TF Attribution Guide*. Third Edition. North Hills, CA: VAMstar.com/VAMstar Publishing, 2008.

O2 Oxman, Jeff, and Les Hartnett. *1878 Morgan Dollar 7/8-TF Attribution Guide*. Third Edition. North Hills, CA: VAMstar.com/VAMstar Publishing, 2004.

Oxman, Jeff. *Official Guide to the Hot 50 Morgan Dollar Varieties*. Second printing. North Hills, CA: VAMstar.com/ VAMstar Publishing, 2008.

Oxman, Jeff. *Official Guide to the Morgan Dollar Hit List 40*. North Hills, CA: VAMstar Publishing, 2009.

OCD Oxman, Jeff, and John Baumgart. *Attribution Wizards on CD (2000-2008):* 8-TFs, 7-TFs (including 7/8-TFs), *Hot 50* Morgan Dollar Varieties, 1879-S Reverse of '78s, *Hit List 40* Morgan Dollar Varieties, and *Top 50* Peace Dollars. Contact John Baumgart, P.O. Box 3882, Barrington, IL 60011; John.Baumgart@comcast.net.

R Yeoman, R.S., edited by Kenneth Bressett. *The Official Red Book: A Guide Book of United States Coins.* Atlanta, GA: Whitman Publishing, LLC, 2004.

Q Bowers, Q. David. *A Guide Book of Morgan Silver Dollars: The Official Red Book.* Atlanta, GA: Whitman Publishing, LLC, 2004.

V Van Allen, Leroy C., and A. George Mallis. 1991/2004. *Comprehensive Catalog and Encyclopedia of Morgan & Peace Dollars.* Fourth Edition. Philadelphia, PA: Bob Paul, Inc., 1999.

Van Allen, Leroy C. VAM Book Supplements 1992-current. Revised 2008. Leroy Van Allen, P.O. Box 196, Sidney, OH 45365.

Van Allen, Leroy C. *Morgan Dollar 8 & 7 Over 8 Tail Feather Story.* Revised 2006.

V2 Van Allen, Leroy C. *Micro O Mint Mark on Morgan Dollars.* Revised April 2005.

V3 Van Allen, Leroy C. *1921-P Infrequently Reeded or Wide Reeding Morgan Dollar Attribution Guide.* Revised 2004.

W Wang, David T. *A Guide to the 1879-S Reverse of 1878 Morgan Silver Dollars.* David T. Wang, 2001.

We dedicate this book to those
adventurers who love the
thrill of the hunt.

May your quest for the elusive
Top 100 VAM Keys
be successful!

Knowledge is King!

TOP 100
Morgan Dollar Varieties

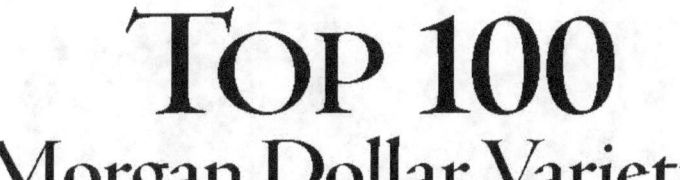

THE VAM KEYS

VAM: 5 / **8-Tailfeather Reverse** / **PF: 8**
Ref: F, FS (1-1878-005), O1, OCD, Q, R, V

Doubled "RIB" obverse motto

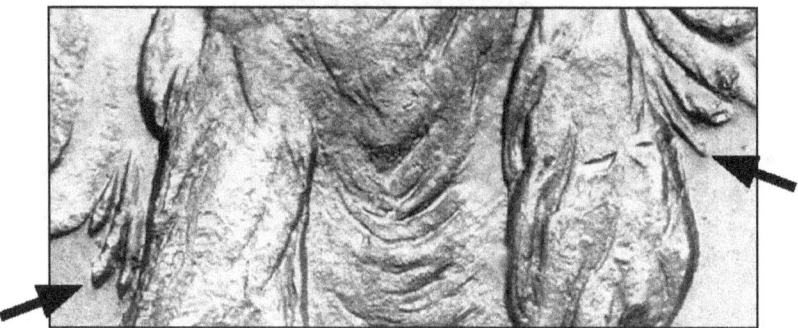

A¹c reverse

Grade	VAM 5	Com	PL	Com	DMPL	Com	RF
MS-65	7000+	1200	UNK		UNK		8
MS-64	1500	330					7
MS-63	1050	140	UNK		UNK		7
MS-60	500	100					6
AU-50	450	60					6
XF-40	300	36					6

■ **Key Identifiers:** Dramatic doubling of the obverse motto, particularly "RIB" in PLURIBUS. A¹c reverse. Diagnostic die crack always seen through "RIB" on obverse and A¹c reverse.

■ **Comments:** The obverse is usually encountered with reflective surfaces, but two-sided PL/DMPLs are unknown.

■ **Certified VAM 5:** 172   **PL:** 0   **DMPL:** 0

CC:	65ᴾ	65ᴺ	64ᴾᴺᴬ	Mult.		

VAMs: 9, 9A / **8-Tailfeather Reverse** / **PF:** 10
Ref: F, FS (1-1878-009), O1, OCD, Q, V

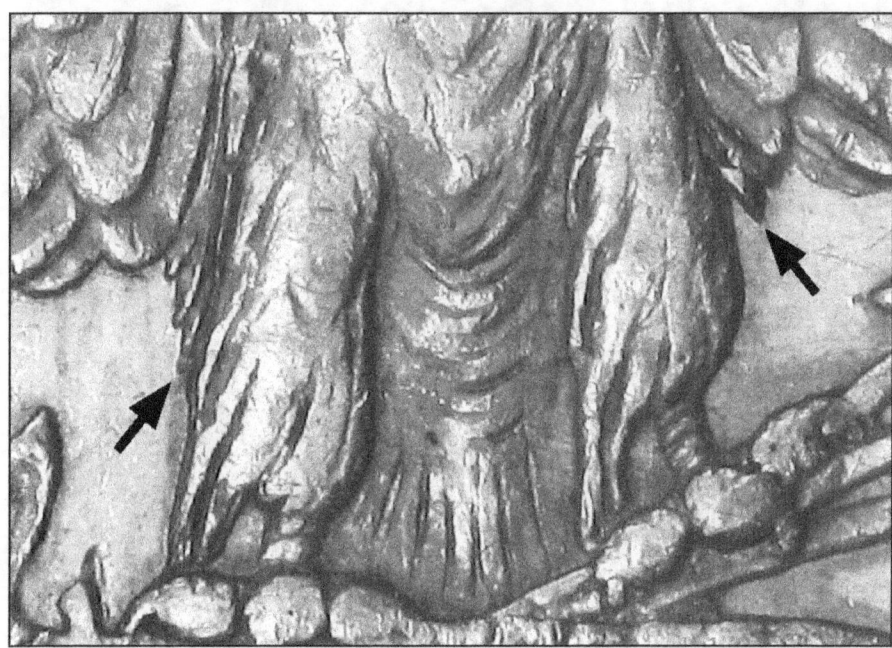

A^{1}h reverse

Grade	VAM 9	Com	PL	Com	DMPL	Com	RF
MS-64	20K	330	20K+	450	20K+	4100	8
MS-63	11.5K	140	11.5K+	350	11.5K+	750	8
MS-60	6000	100	6000+	150	6000 +	300	7
AU-50	1000	60					6+
XF-40	700	36					6
VF-30	400	31					6

■ **Key Identifiers:** Unique engraved feather, resembling a comma, is visible between the eagle's wing and body on the right side. A^{1}h reverse.

■ **Comments:** *Ultra rare* and highly desirable in MS. Known specimens are typically Proof-like because of the reverse die's short production life. Later die state VAM 9A shows clash marks.

■ **Certified VAMs 9, 9A:** 293   **PL:** 2   **DMPL:** 7

CC:	64PL[N]	64[N]	64[N]	63DM[A]	63[P]	63[N]

VAM: 14.11 (formerly 11) / **8-Tailfeather Reverse** / **PF:** 10
Ref: F, FS (1-1878-014), O1, OCD, V

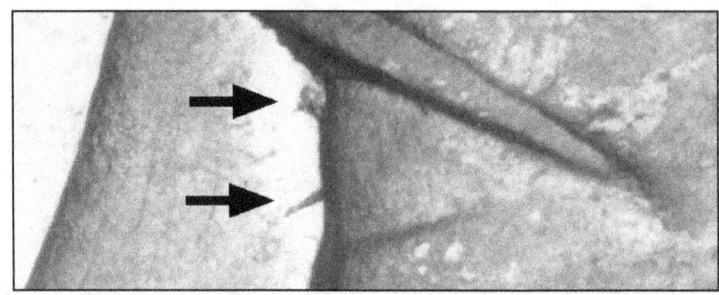

Two "wild" eye spikes extend from the eyeball.

A1c reverse

Grade	VAM 14.11	Com	PL	Com	DMPL	Com	RF
MS-65	NTH	1200	UNK		UNK		8
MS-64	NTH	330					8
MS-63	>20K	140	UNK		UNK		7+
MS-60	18K	100					7+
AU-50	10K	60					7+
XF-40	7500	36					7+

■ **Key Identifiers:** *Ultra rare* die marriage with unique eye spikes on the obverse and A1c reverse (same as VAM 5). Always seen with a Proof-like obverse.

■ **Comments:** This variety replaces the VAM 11 of earlier editions, as VAM 11 is not believed to exist. A key variety for *Top 100* and 8-TF sets. Discovered by Les Hartnett in 1995.

■ **Certified VAM 14.11:** 14 **PL:** 0 **DMPL:** 0

CC:	67P	65N	65N	64N	63N	63A

VAM: 15 / **8-Tailfeather Reverse** / **PF:** 8
Ref: F, FS (1-1878-015), O1, OCD, Q, V

Doubled LIBERTY obverse

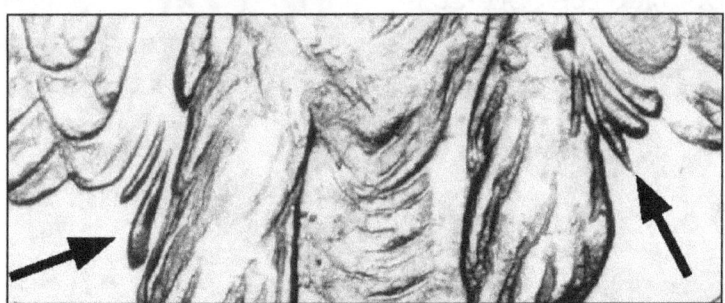

A^{1}e reverse

Grade	VAM 15	Com	PL	Com	DMPL	Com	RF
MS-65	NTH	1200	NTH	1750	NTH	17K	8
MS-64	NTH	330	NTH	450	NTH	4100	7
MS-63	1675	140	1675+	350	2150+	750	7
MS-60	1150	100	1250+	150	1500+	300	6
AU-50	600	60					6
XF-40	325	36					6

■ **Key Identifiers:** Strong doubling of LIBERTY on obverse. The reverse is an A^{1}e, which is shared with VAM 10. Normally seen with reflective surfaces.

■ **Comments:** This often-overlooked obverse/reverse combination, a very scarce die pair, is usually found Proof-like. Even rarer than the 8-TF VAM 5. Very rarely seen in Circulated grades.

■ **Certified VAM 15:** 99   **PL:** 44   **DMPL:** 23

CC:	65DM^P	65DM^N	64DM^P	64DM^A	64DM^A	64PL^{PNA}

VAM: 23 / **8-Tailfeather Reverse** / **PF:** 7
Ref: F, O1, OCD, V

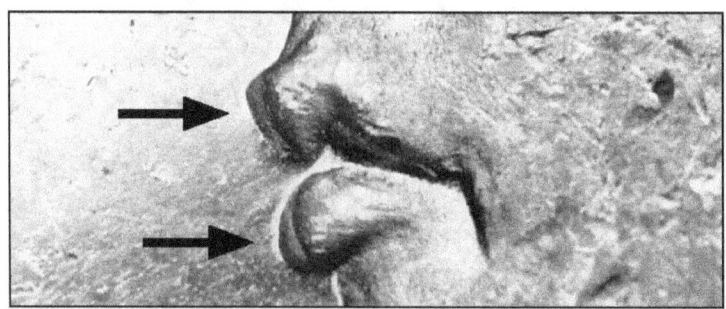

Doubled lips obverse

A^2/A^{1}b reverse

Grade	VAM 23	Com	PL	Com	DMPL	Com	RF
MS-65	UNK	1200	UNK	1750	UNK	17K	8
MS-64	1000	330	1250+	450	NTH	4100	7+
MS-63	550	140	600+	350	1200+	750	7
MS-60	275	100	300	150	600	300	6
AU-50	100	60					6
XF-40	50	36					6

■ **Key Identifiers:** Strong doubling of Liberty's nose, lips and chin on the obverse. A^2/A^{1}b reverse. Van Allen currently believes this reverse to be struck from multiple hubbings.

■ **Comments:** Scarce in all grades. Seen in Mint State Prooflike grades with nice cameo contrast.

■ **Certified VAM 23:** 337 **PL:** 111 **DMPL:** 78

CC:	64DMP	64DMP	64PLN	64PLA	64PLA	64PLA

VAM: 32 / "7/8"-Tailfeather Reverse / **PF:** 8
Ref: B (5504), FS (1-1878-032), O2, OCD, V

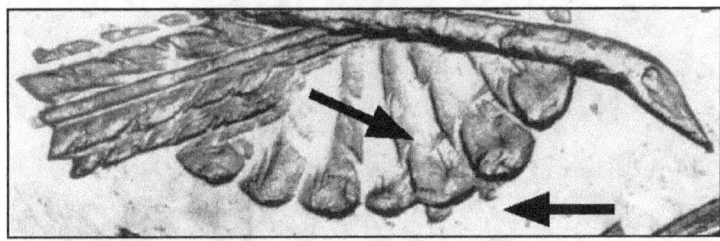

VAM 32 reverse *(Top 100)*

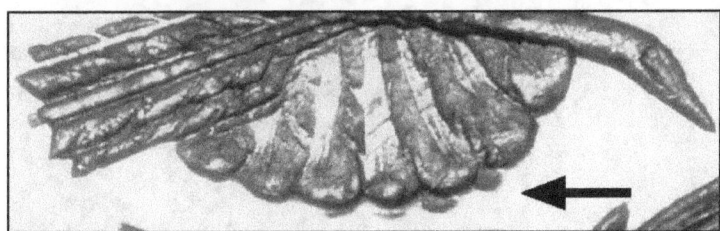

VAM 34 reverse *(Hot 50)* for comparison

Grade	VAM 32	Com	PL	Com	DMPL	Com	RF
MS-64	2500	330	3500+	400	7500+	4800	8
MS-63	1550	235	1750	325	2500+	1000	7
MS-62	1250	115	1500	200	2000	350	7
MS-60	1000	95	1250	130	1500	125	7
AU-50	350	60					6
XF-40	275	36					6

■ **Key Identifiers:** Three distinctive tailfeather tips protrude from under the eagle's normal set of seven. A diagonal die-polishing line is visible in an over-polished area above the feathers (photo). VAM 32 should not be confused with the *Hot 50* VAM 34, which is also quite scarce – even *ultra rare* – with an obverse clash mark at the neck. VAM 32 can be found unattributed among slabs with "weak 7/8" designations.

■ **Comments:** Because of its short production run, the VAM 32 is often found with Proof-like surfaces.

■ **Certified VAM 32:** 124 **PL:** 29 **DMPL:** 29

CC:	64DM^PNA	Mult.				

VAMs: 41, 41B / **"7/8"-Tailfeather Reverse** / **PF:** 7
Ref: B (5505), K, O2, OCD, Q, V

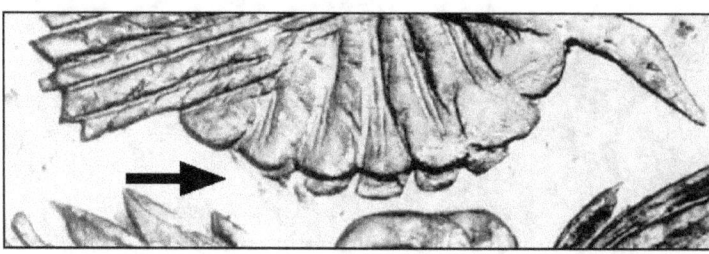

VAM 41 reverse

VAM 41B showing die clash by neck

Grade	VAM 41	Com	PL	Com	DMPL	Com	RF
MS-64	500	330	NTH	400	NTH	4800	7+
MS-63	400	235	300	200	NTH	1000	7
MS-62	300	115	200	150	1750+	350	6
MS-61	150	95	150	125	400+	200	6
MS-60	75	60					6-
AU-50	50	36					5+

■ **Key Identifier:** Extensive and unmistakable tailfeather doubling.

■ **Comments:** This VAM shows the strongest, most complete doubling of the eagle's tailfeathers of any so-called "7/8"-TF variety. Sometimes seen with deeply reflective DMPL surfaces. VAM 41B shows a clashed "n" from "In God we trust" in the obverse field below Ms. Liberty's neck (refer to Kimpton, 2005).

■ **Certified VAMs 41, 41B:** 404   **PL:** 24   **DMPL:** 30

CC: 64DM^{PNA}	Mult.				

VAMs: 44, 44A / **"7/8"-Tailfeather Reverse** / **PF:** 10
Ref: B (5506), F, FS ($1-001) ($1-1878-044/001), K,
       O2, OCD, Q, V

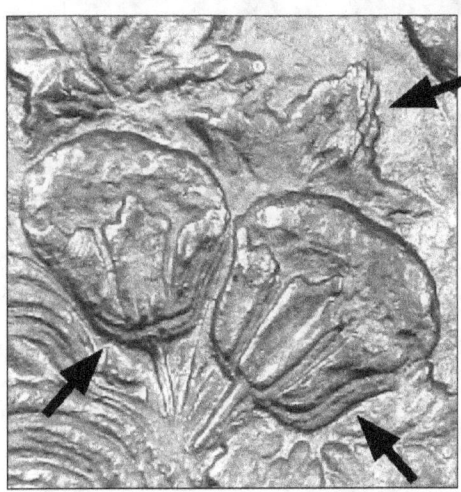

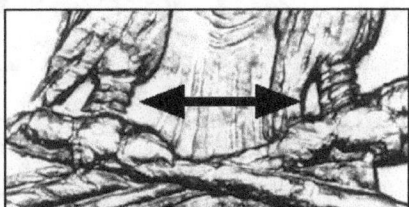

Strongly doubled legs

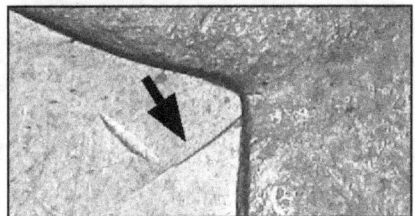

Tripled blossoms and leaves   Die clash on VAM 44A

Grade	VAM 44/44A	Com	PL	Com	DMPL	Com	RF
MS-63	UNK	235	UNK	1750	UNK	1000	8
MS-62	20.7K+	115	22K+	1500	25K+	350	7+
MS-60	12K+	95	12.5K+	1250	15K+	200	7+
AU-50	7500	60					7
XF-40	6000	36					6+
VF-30	2500	25					6+

■ **Key Identifiers:** The bottom edges of the blossoms and leaves in Liberty's headdress are tripled. The reverse is the same as VAM 33, with doubled legs and an extra five small tailfeathers.

■ **Comments:** Considered by most specialists to be the No. 1 Morgan dollar variety. Usually seen with Proof-like surfaces. VAM 44A shows evidence of clashed dies, even on Proof-like specimens. A radial die crack at 10 o'clock suggests a short-lived obverse die.

■ **Certified VAMs 44, 44A:** 102   **PL:** 12   **DMPL:** 3

CC:	62PL[P]	62PL[A]	62[A]	61DM[A]	60PL[R]	55[A]

VAM: 45 / **"7/8"-Tailfeather Reverse** / **PF:** 8
Ref: B (5507), O2, OCD, V

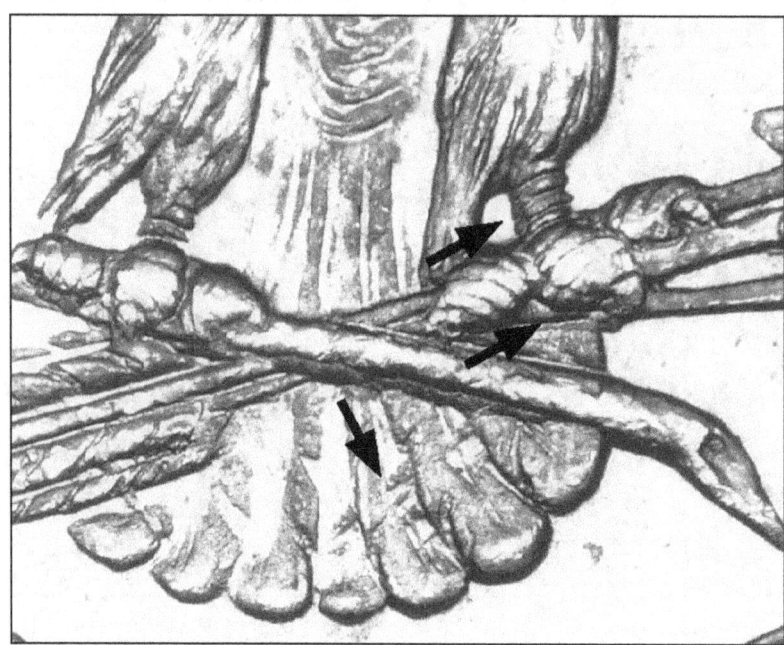

Doubled talons on reverse

Grade	VAM 45	Com	PL	Com	DMPL	Com	RF
MS-65	2500+	1850	3500+	2500	UNK	17K	8
MS-64	1000+	330	1250+	400	6000+	4800	7
MS-63	400	235	500	200	1500+	1000	7
MS-62	350	115	400	150	600	350	6+
MS-60	200	95	250	125	400	200	6+
AU-50	100	60					6

■ **Key Identifiers:** Eagle's legs and talons are doubled toward the left. Heavy diagonal die-polishing line in heavily polished-out tailfeathers.

■ **Comments:** Often seen with Proof-like surfaces.

■ **Certified VAM 45:** 189   **PL:** 17   **DMPL:** 2

CC:	65PL[A]	65[A]	64PL[PNA]	Mult.		

VAM: 70 / **7-Tailfeather "Reverse of '78"** / **PF:** 7
Ref: B (5509), O2, OCD, V

Doubled "RIB" obverse

The "A" of AMERICA touches the eagle's wing.

▶ 7-TF parallel arrow feathers with the B1 long nock reverse

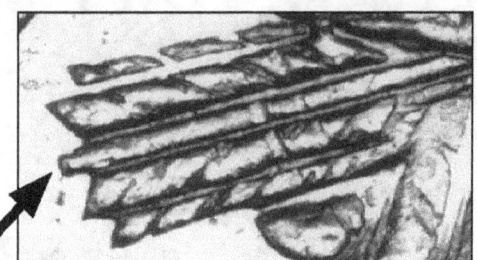

Grade	VAM 70	Com	PL	Com	DMPL	Com	RF
MS-65	2365+	950	UNK	2000	UNK	9000	8
MS-64	450	200	600+	300	2500+	1700	7+
MS-63	350	80	450	110	650+	450	7
MS-62	250	65	350	100	400	150	6+
MS-60	150	55					6+
AU-50	115	33					6

■ **Key Identifiers:** Dramatic doubling of the obverse motto, particularly the lower serifs of "RIB" in PLURIBUS. The bundle of arrows on the reverse has a long center arrow shaft (B1) and Parallel Arrow Feathers (PAF).

■ **Comments:** The doubling is almost identical to that found on the 8-TF VAM 5 obverse. This is the scarcest 1878 7-TF B1 reverse.

■ **Certified VAM 70:** 246 **PL:** 69 **DMPL:** 19

CC:	65P	64DMA	64PLA	64PLA	64N	Mult.

VAMs: 100-1, 100-2
7-Tailfeather "Reverse of '78" / **PF:** 6
Ref: B (5511), F, O2, OCD, V

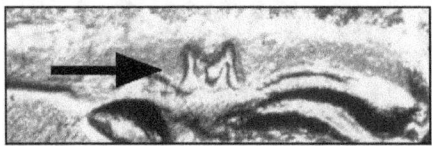 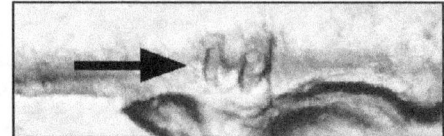

Scarce obv. Type I incuse "M"   Common Type II raised "M"

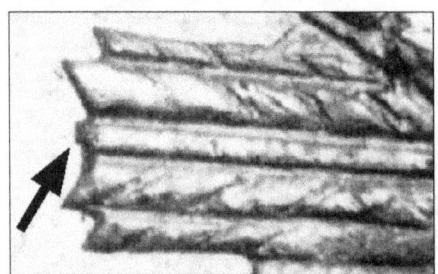 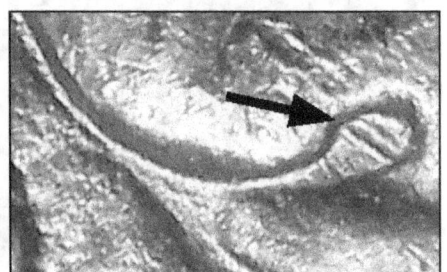

B² rev. with short arrow shaft   Doubled lines in Liberty's cap

Grade	VAM 100-1 100-2	Com	PL	Com	DMPL	Com	RF
MS-65	1250	950	UNK	2000	UNK	9000	7+
MS-64	350	200	500	300	NTH	1700	6+
MS-63	150	80	200	110	NTH	450	6
MS-62	120	64	150	100	200	150	6
MS-60	80	55					6-
AU-50	60	33					5

■ **Key Identifiers:** Type I obverse with evenly divided ear and incuse designer's initial. Reverse with short center arrow shaft (B²). Relatively straight die crack on "D" of DOLLAR for 100-1, whereas 100-2 shows a slight blip and is not straight.

■ **Comments:** The only known early 8-TF Type I obverse die (incuse "M") used with a B reverse die. All others were used with 8-TF dies. 100-2 is thought to be much rarer than 100-1. 100-1 has a small die scratch through the "A" of DOLLAR on the reverse.

■ **Certified VAMs 100-1, 100-2:** 333   **PL:** 12   **DMPL:** 6

| **CC:** VAMs100-1/100-2 | 65ᴺ | 65ᴺ | 65ᴬ | 65ᴬ | 64DMᴾᴬ | Mult. |

VAMs: 115, 198 (formerly 199.1)
7-Tailfeather "Reverse of '78" / PF: 8
Ref: D, FS (1-1878-115), O2, OCD

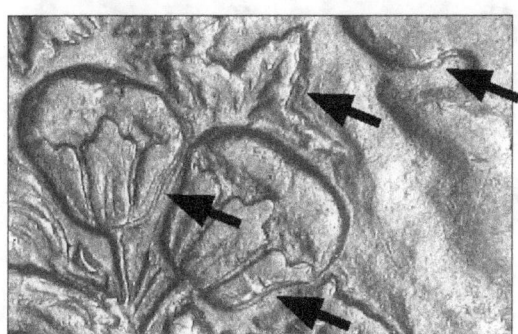

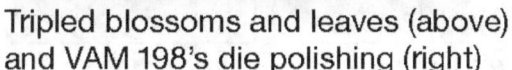

Tripled blossoms and leaves (above)
and VAM 198's die polishing (right)

Grade	VAM 115 or 198	Com	PL	Com	DMPL	Com	RF
MS-63	2500	80	UNK	110	UNK	450	8
MS-60	625	65					7+
AU-58	565	55					7
AU-50	250	33					6
XF-40	75	20					5
VF-30	50	10					5

■ **Key Identifiers:** On VAMs 115 and 198, the blossoms and leaves in Liberty's headdress have moderately tripled right edges. Both reverses have short arrow shafts (B[2] type).

■ **Comments:** Both varieties are rare in Mint State. VAM 115 is rarer overall. Prior to its discovery, it is likely that many early ANACS-certified VAM 115 dollars were actually VAM 198. VAM 198 shows more extensive die polishing in the eagle's left wing and at the right junction between the wing and leg.

■ **Certified VAM 115:** 250   **PL:** 1   **DMPL:** 0
■ **Certified VAM 198:** 229   **PL:** 1   **DMPL:** 0

CC: VAM 115	64[N]	64[N]	63[A]	62[PNA]	Mult.	
VAM 198	62PL[A]	62[PNA]	Mult.			

VAMs: 117, 141, 141A
7-Tailfeather "Reverse of '78" / **PF:** 7
Ref: O2, OCD, V

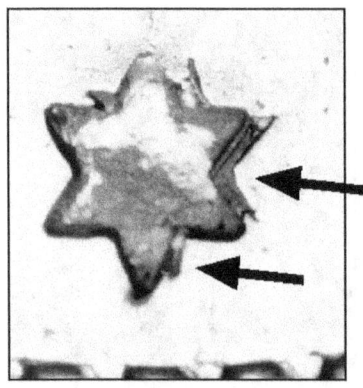
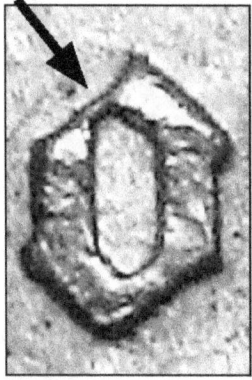
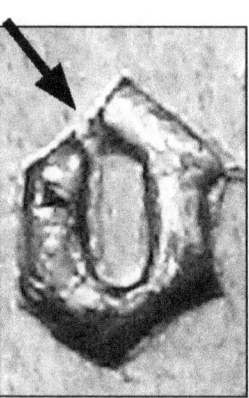

Tripled-star obverse   VAM 117   VAM 141

Grade	VAM 117/141	Com	PL	Com	DMPL	Com	RF
MS-65	NTH	950	NTH	2000	UNK	9000	8/7
MS-64	400/300	200	NTH/400	300	NTH	1700	7+/7
MS-63	300/150	80	NTH	110	NTH	450	7/6
MS-62	160/85	65	300/150	100	400/200	150	6/6-
MS-60	125/75	55					6/5
AU-50	100/55	33					5/5

■ **Key Identifiers:** The second star from the right of the date is spectacularly tripled. VAM 141 can be distinguished from VAM 117 by the broken top of the "o" in "God" on the reverse motto (B^{2}b reverse). The "o" on VAM 117 is not broken (B^{2}a reverse). A recently discovered VAM 141A shows a shallow diagonal die gouge on the upper side of the eagle's left wing tip.

■ **Comments:** VAM 117 is much scarcer than VAM 141 and now commands higher prices.

■ **Certified VAM 117:** 200   **PL:** 3   **DMPL:** 1
■ **Certified VAMs 141, 141A:** 357   **PL:** 28   **DMPL:** 7

CC: VAM 117	64PL^A	64^{PNA}	Mult.			
VAMs 141/141A	66^N	65PL^P	65PL^N	65^P	65^N	64DM^A

VAM: 171 / **7-Tailfeather "Reverse of '78"** / **PF:** 8
Ref: O2, OCD, V

Tripled "R" obverse

Parallel Arrow Feathers (PAF) reverse

Grade	VAM 171	Com	PL	Com	DMPL	Com	RF
MS-64	850+	200	UNK	300	UNK	1700	8
MS-63	750+	80	750+	110	UNK	450	7
MS-62	700	65	UNK	100	UNK	150	6
MS-60	250	55					6
AU-50	150	33					5
XF-40	125	20					5

■ **Key Identifiers:** The bottom left serif of "R" in PLURIBUS is tripled, showing two clear notches on the left in a stairstep fashion. Cotton blossoms are strongly tripled to the south, offering a nice "Wow" factor.

■ **Comments:** The same obverse die was later used with a C reverse (see VAM 220). Both are rare and desirable.

■ **Certified VAM 171:** 180   **PL:** 1   **DMPL:** 0

CC:	65N	63PNA	Mult.			

VAMs: 203, 203A / **7-Tailfeather "Reverse of '79"**
PF: 8
Ref: K, O2, OCD, V

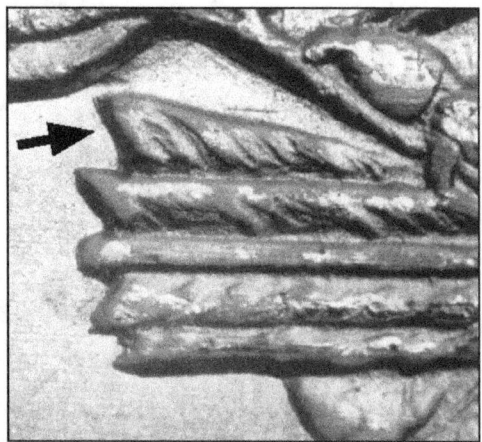

Short wheat leaf on obv.   Slanted arrow feather, C reverse

Grade	VAM 203/203A	Com	PL	Com	DMPL	Com	RF
MS-65	2500+	2000	UNK		UNK		7+
MS-64	575	420					6+
MS-63	200	130	UNK		UNK		6
MS-62	150	75					6
MS-60	100	60					6
AU-50	70	34					5

■ **Key Identifiers:** The leftmost wheat leaf in Liberty's head-dress is shorter than normal because of over-polishing. Slanted Arrow Feather (SAF) C reverse. VAM 203A was struck from strongly clashed dies and has a strong incuse "n" on Ms. Liberty's neck from "In God we trust" on the reverse.

■ **Comments:** This VAM has long been recognized as a rarity and is among the Big Three C reverse varieties. The VAM 203A currently commands a higher price than the VAM 203.

■ **Certified VAMs 203, 203A:** 237   **PL:** 0   **DMPL:** 0

CC:	65PN	Mult.				

VAM: 220 / **7-Tailfeather "Reverse of '79"** / **PF:** 9
Ref: B (5515), O2, OCD, V

 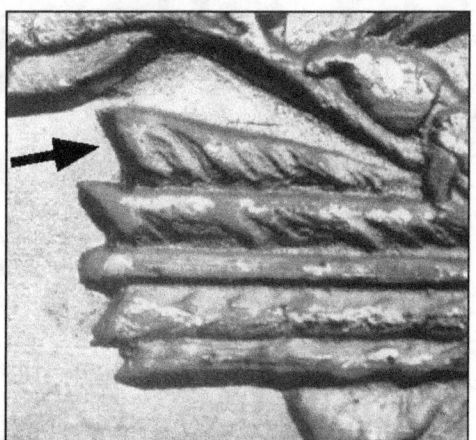

Tripled serif on the "R" in PLURIBUS

Slanted top arrow feather with a C reverse

Grade	VAM 220	Com	PL	Com	DMPL	Com	RF
MS-64	NTH	420	UNK		UNK		8
MS-63	UNK	130					8
MS-62	NTH	75	UNK		UNK		7+
MS-60	1000	60					7+
AU-50	400	34					7
XF-40	150	21					6+

■ **Key Identifiers:** The bottom left serif of "R" in PLURIBUS on the obverse is tripled, showing two clear notches. Slanted Arrow Feather (SAF) C reverse.

■ **Comments:** In terms of rarity, this highly sought after variety is the No. 1 1878-P "Reverse of '79" business strike VAM variety. VAM 220 is very rare in Mint State.

■ **Certified VAM 220:** 187 **PL:** 1 **DMPL:** 0

CC:	64ᴾ	62ᴾ	61ᴾᴺᴬ	Mult.		

VAM: 223 / **7-Tailfeather "Reverse of '79"** / **PF:** 7
Ref: B (5514), O2, OCD, V

Weak "L" in LIBERTY

Slanted top arrow feather with a C reverse

Grade	VAM 223	Com	PL	Com	DMPL	Com	RF
MS-64	1325+	420					8
MS-63	360	130	UNK		UNK		7+
MS-62	275	75					7
MS-60	250	45					6
AU-50	100	34					6
XF-40	50	21					6

■ **Key Identifiers:** The top of the "L" in LIBERTY is over-polished, as are the leading strands of hair just under it. Slanted Arrow Feather C reverse.

■ **Comments:** Infrequently encountered in Mint State.

■ **Certified VAM 223:** 235   **PL:** 1   **DMPL:** 0

CC:	64P	64A	63PNA	Mult.		

VAM: 6 / **Doubled Die Obverse** / **PF:** 8
Ref: B (5522), FS (1-1878cc-006), Q, V

Obverse doubled blossoms and leaves

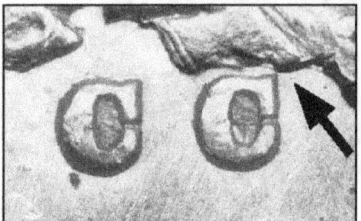

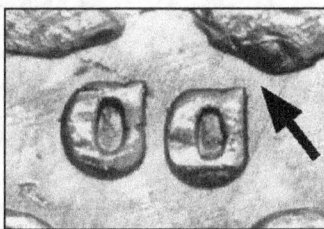

VAM 6's mintmark almost touches the wreath.

VAM 18's mintmark sits away from the wreath.

Grade	VAM 6	Com	PL	Com	DMPL	Com	RF
MS-65	NTH	1300	UNK	2400	UNK	8200	8
MS-64	NTH	500	NTH	600	UNK	2300	7+
MS-63	650+	300	NTH	450	UNK	1300	7
MS-60	450	175					6+
AU-50	150	125					6
XF-40	125	100					5

■ **Key Identifiers:** The leaves in Liberty's headdress, her ear, the date and the stars are all strongly doubled.

■ **Comments:** VAM 6 and VAM 18 have the same strongly doubled blossoms-and-leaves obverse. The "CC" on VAM 6 almost touches the wreath, the only such instance in the Morgan dollar series. VAM 6 seems undervalued in grades of MS-63 and better.

■ **Certified VAM 6:** 284 **PL:** 6 **DMPL:** 0

CC:	65S	64PLN	64PN	Mult.		

VAM: 11 / **Die Polishing Lines on the Reverse** / **PF:** 7
Ref: B (5523), Q, V

▶ Polishing
lines in
the eagle's
wing

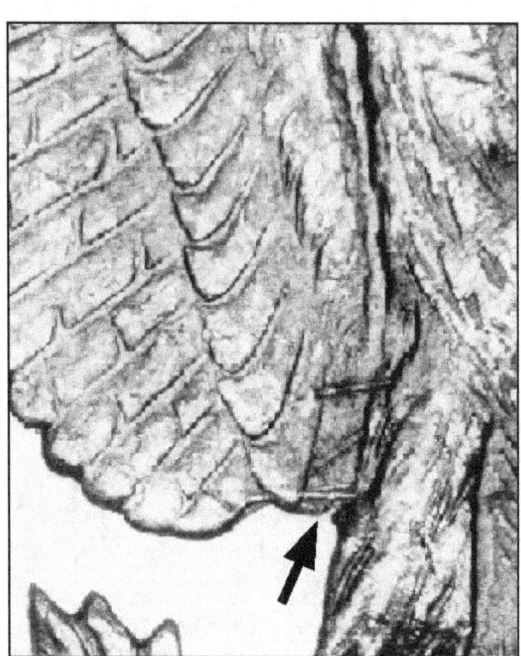

Grade	VAM 11	Com	PL	Com	DMPL	Com	RF
MS-66	NTH	4500	UNK		UNK		8
MS-65	1700+	1300	NTH	2400	NTH	8200	7+
MS-64	625	500	750	600	2500+	2300	6+
MS-63	450	300	600	450	1500	1300	6
MS-62	300	175	400	325	450	350	6-
MS-60	200	125	125				5+

■ **Key Identifier:** Heavy die-polishing lines at the base of the eagle's right wing.

■ **Comments:** This variety is obtainable in all grades up through MS-65 and is often seen with reflective surfaces. Its popularity exceeds its rarity. Some specimens found in GSA holders.

■ **Certified VAM 11:** 616   **PL:** 68   **DMPL:** 50

CC:	66P	66P	66N	66N	65DMA	65DMA

VAM: 18 / **Doubled Die Obverse** / **PF:** 9
Ref: B (5522) FS (1-1878cc-018), Q, V

 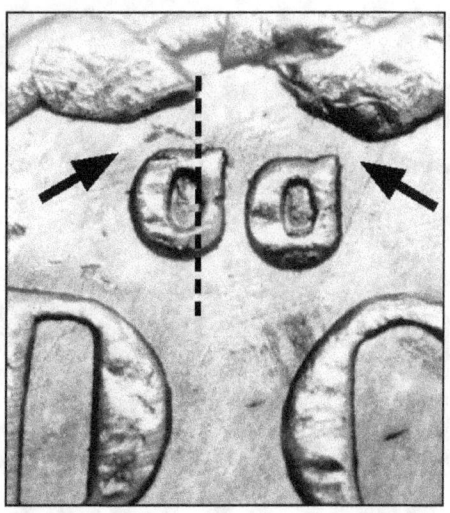

Obverse doubled blossoms and leaves

"CC" sits away from the wreath. Note alignment with bow.

Grade	VAM 18	Com	PL	Com	DMPL	Com	RF
MS-64	3000+	500	3500+	600	UNK	2300	8
MS-63	1500+	300	2000+	450	UNK	1300	7+
MS-62	1250+	250	1500+	325	UNK	350	7+
MS-60	1000+	175					7+
AU-50	800	145					7+
XF-40	250	100					7

■ **Key Identifiers:** The leaves in Liberty's headdress, her ear, the date and the stars are all strongly doubled. Note the downward slope and alignment of the mintmark with the bow.

■ **Comments:** VAMs 6 and 18 have the same doubled-blossoms-and-leaves obverse. The VAM 18 "CC" mintmark displays die chips, slopes downward and does not touch the wreath. VAM 18 is much rarer and more desirable than VAM 6. It is often seen with Proof-like surfaces and has been found in GSA holders.

■ **Certified VAM 18:** 56 **PL:** 17 **DMPL:** 0

CC:	64PL[P]	63PL[A]	63PL[A]	62PL[P]	62PL[N]	61PL[A]

VAMs: 24, 24A / **Doubled Die Obverse / PF:** 9
Ref: B (5523), Q, V

Doubled leaves and blossoms
on the obverse

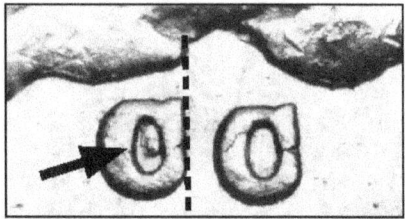

Wide "CC"
with dot;
note align-
ment with
bow.

▶ Denticle
lump above
the "U" on
VAM 24A

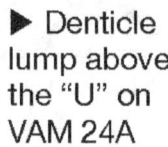

Grade	VAM 24	Com	PL	Com	DMPL	Com	RF
MS-61	NTH	185	NTH	225	UNK		8
MS-60	NTH	175					7+
AU-58	NTH	150					7+
AU-50	700	145					7+
XF-40	285	100					7
VF-30	100	85					6+

■ **Key Identifiers:** The leaves in Liberty's headdress are doubled, but NOT her ear, the date or the stars.

■ **Comments:** Rarer than VAM 6, VAM 24 has almost identical doubling on the leaves, but the mintmark has a dot of metal inside the left "C". Note alignment of left "C" to bow. Very rare in Mint State. John Roberts' discovery of the VAM 24A, a later and more common stage of VAM 24, displays a lump from the denticles above the second "U" in PLURIBUS (photo by John Roberts).

■ **Certified VAM 24:** 131 **PL:** 5 **DMPL:** 0

CC:	61PL[N]	61[N]	61[A]	60[N]	60[P]	58[PNA]

VAMs: 26, 27, 56, 57, 58, 59, 60, 62, 72
B^1 Reverse / **PF:** 10
Ref: B (5517), D, J, Q, V

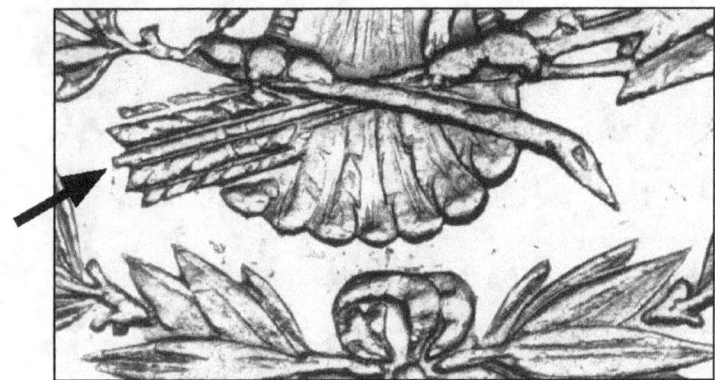

Long center arrow shaft with B^1 reverse

Grade	B^1 Rev VAMs	Com	PL	Com	DMPL	Com	RF
MS-63	5500+	57	UNK		UNK		8
MS-60	1500+	50					7+
AU-58	1200+	35					7
AU-50	975+	29					7
XF-40	500	21					6+
VF-30	400	19					6+

■ **Key Identifier:** On the B^1 reverse, the notch at the back end of the center arrow shaft (the nock) is much longer than on the more common B^2 reverse.

■ **Comments:** There is a well-documented history of striking problems with 1878-S B^1 reverse varieties minted in San Francisco. Nine die pairs are known. All are rare, but VAMs 60, 62 and 72 are *ultra rare*. Only a few BUs have been discovered for ALL of the 1878-S B^1 reverse varieties. Only two complete Circulated sets are known! See page 2A, and refer to John Roberts, 2008.

■ **Certified VAMs:** 653   **PL:** 0   **DMPL:** 1

*CC:	64N	63N	63N	62DMA	61A	58PNA

*Includes all die pairs.

VAMs: 4, 28 / **Repunched Mintmark** / **PF:** 8 and 9
Ref: B (5528), D, FS ($1-002) ($1-1879-O-004 &
      $1-1879o-028), Q

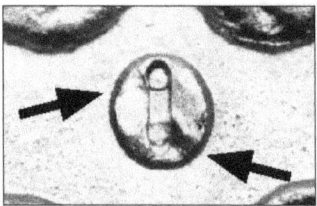

◀ Two curved lines are visible inside the repunched New Orleans mintmark.

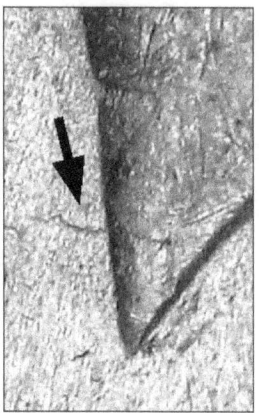

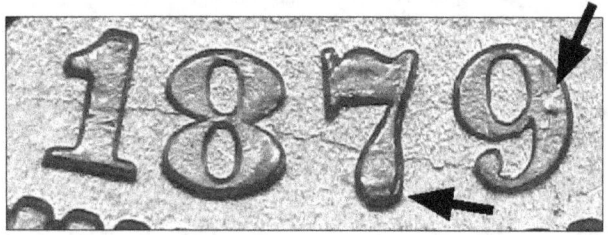

VAM 28 with die crack through the date has doubling on the "7" and a dot on the "9".

VAM 4 with die crack at the "Vee" of Liberty's neck

Grade	VAM 4/28	Com	PL	Com	DMPL	Com	RF
MS-64	1500+/NTH	450					8/8
MS-63	1100+/NTH	160					7/7+
MS-62	750/NTH	80					7/7+
MS-60	500/2400	60					7/7+
AU-58	300/1000	35					6/7+
AU-50	125/600	24					5/7+

■ **Key Identifiers:** VAMs 4 and 28 share the same reverse. Curved lines are clearly visible at the top and bottom interior of the mintmark.

■ **Comments:** VAM 28 is much rarer than VAM 4. These scarce VAMs are the only known "O/Horizontal O" varieties in the Morgan dollar series.

■ **Certified VAM 4:** 390 **PL:** 3 **DMPL:** 1
■ **Certified VAM 28:** 31 **PL:** 0 **DMPL:** 0

CC: VAM 4	64[A]	63[PA]	Mult.			
VAM 28	63[N]	63[A]	62[P]	62[A]	61[N]	58[PNA]

VAMs: 4, 6, 9, 23, 25, 34, 34A, 34B, 35, 39, 42, 43, 46, 50, 51, 52, 56 (56A)*, 66, 67 / **B Reverse** / **PF**: 10

Ref: B (5531), D, FS ($1-1879s-901), Q, R, V, W

Scarce PAF "Reverse of '78" (B reverse)

Common SAF "Reverse of '79" (C reverse)

Grade	Com '79-S Rev '78 VAMs	Com	PL	Com	DMPL	Com	RF
MS-66	36K	325					8
MS-65	6325	150	8250	175	17K	1000	7
MS-64	1150	55	1250	65	5500	300	6
MS-63	545	40	650	50	2700	75	5
MS-60	200	32					5
AU-50	100	20					4

■ **Key Identifiers:** This reverse has the flat breast and Parallel Arrow Feathers (PAF) characteristic of the B reverse.

■ **Comments:** VAMs 34B, 56, 66 and 67 are recent discoveries and considered *ultra rare*. VAMs 6, 23, 34A and 51 are rare, and especially so in Mint State. Rarer VAMs are likely found with one- or two-sided Proof-like surfaces. Prices given are for common varieties, but can vary significantly depending on variety, grade and rarity. No complete sets are known in any grade! Refer to page 4A, and David Wang's comprehensive 2001 guide.

■ **Certified VAMs:** 3,620 **PL:** 188 **DMPL:** 15

CC: Com '79-S Rev '78 VAMs	66PL[N]	66[P]	66[P]	65DM[N]	66PL[N]	65PL[N]

*Larry Briggs recently found a VAM 56 LDS; he anticipates that Leroy Van Allen will designate it VAM 56A.

VAM: 3 / **Medium Over Small Mintmark** / **PF:** 7
Ref: B (5533), Q, R, V

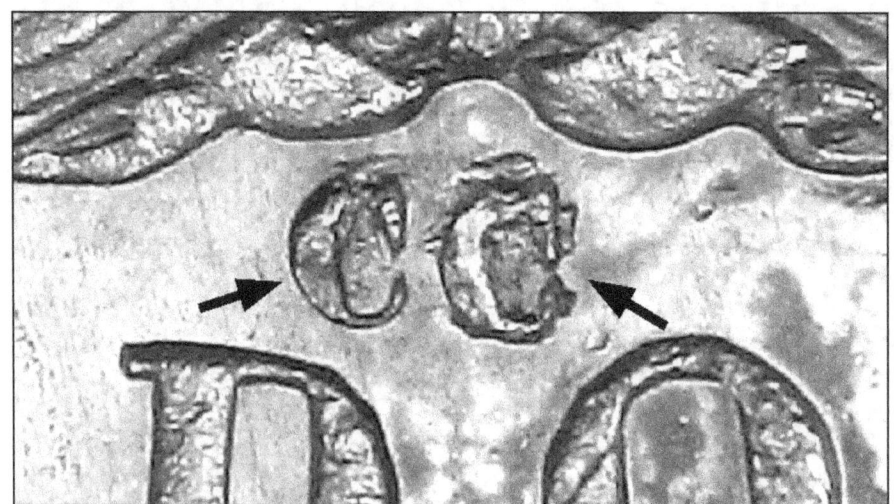

Repunched medium mintmark over remains of small mintmark

Grade	VAM 3	Com	PL	Com	DMPL	Com	RF
MS-66	NTH	40K					8
MS-65	40K+	25K	30K+	25K	52K+	40K	7+
MS-64	10K	8000	21K	9000	30K	25K	7
MS-63	5500	5500	6000	5500	NTH	11.5K	6
MS-60	3200	3200					5
AU-50	1500	1500					4

■ **Key Identifier:** A medium "CC" mintmark with evidence of an underlying small "CC" mintmark.

■ **Comments:** Now becoming more popular than the so-called "perfect mintmark" variety, the VAM 3 is scarcer – and more interesting – particularly in high grades. Long considered a semi-key date. Compare the population, rarity and pricing of this variety with data for other *Top 100* VAMs to gain perspective on the overall rarity of other *Top 100* coins. Because of its relatively high price, the market has yet to fully appreciate its rarity.

■ **Certified VAM 3:** 4,114   **PL:** 107   **DMPL:** 51

CC:	68N	65DMP	65DMN	65PNA	Mult.	

VAM: 1A / **Die Break thru Date** / **PF:** 8
Ref: Q, R, V

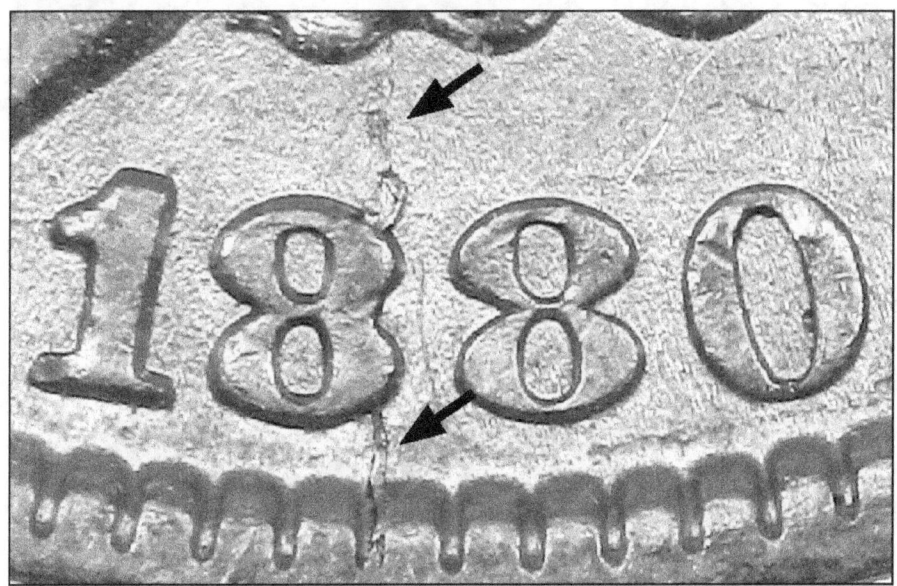

Large die break through the date

Grade	VAM A1	Com	PL	Com	DMPL	Com	RF
MS-61	NTH	32	UNK		UNK		8
MS-60	NTH	30					8
AU-58	650+	28					7
AU-50	550	22					7
XF-40	350	19					7
VF-30	125	18					6

■ **Key Identifier:** Large die break from the rim up through the right side of the "8" in the date.

■ **Comments:** Rare in all grades and *ultra rare* in BU. The VAM 1A is still undervalued, but there is growing appreciation for its true rarity. Early die states without the full die break command a lesser premium.

■ **Certified VAM 1A:** 191 **PL:** 0 **DMPL:** 0

CC:	61ᴺ	60ᴬ	*58ᴺ	58ᴾᴺᴬ	Mult.	

*Binion Hoard

VAM: 6 / **"8/7" Overdate** / **PF:** 10
Ref: B (5535), FS ($1-003) ($1-1880-006), R, V

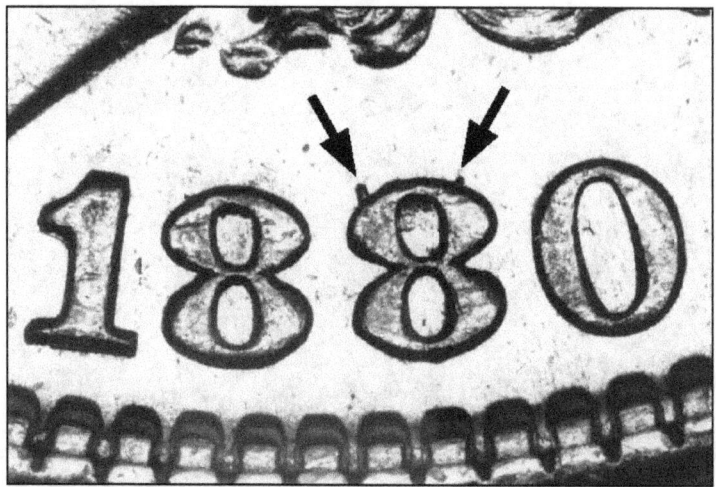

"8/7" overdate feature

Grade	VAM 6	Com	PL	Com	DMPL	Com	RF
MS-64	12650+	115	UNK		UNK		8
MS-63	800+	40					7
MS-62	650+	35					7
MS-60	575+	30					7
AU-58	425+	28					6
AU-50	200+	22					5

■ **Key Identifiers:** Dramatic remains of an underlying "7" inside the top loop of the second "8" in the date, and spikes atop the "8".

■ **Comments:** Relatively few BU specimens are known. This is a heavy-premium variety. The Van Allen specimen, a PCGS MS-64, sold in Spring 2008 for a record $12,650.

■ **Certified VAM 6:** 519   **PL:** 0   **DMPL:** 0

CC:	64P	64A	64A	63A	62PNA	Mult.

VAM: 7 / **"8/7" Overdate** / **PF:** 9
Ref: B (5535), FS ($1-004) ($1-1880-007), V

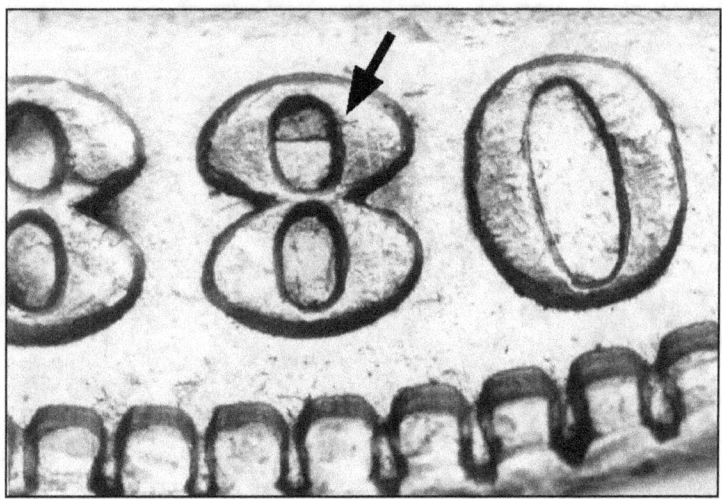

"8/7" overdate feature

Grade	VAM 7	Com	PL	Com	DMPL	Com	RF
AU-58	1500+	28					7+
AU-55	1350+	24					7+
AU-50	1250	22					7
XF-40	450	19					6+
VF-30	350	18					6+
VF-20	250	17					6

■ **Key Identifier:** Recessed "crossbar" easily seen inside the top loop of the second "8" in the date.

■ **Comments:** Rare in all grades and still no Mint State specimens known! A heavy-premium variety.

■ **Certified VAM 7:** 161 **PL:** 0 **DMPL:** 0

CC:	58^PNA	Mult.				

VAM: 8 / **"8/7" Overdate** / **PF:** 10
Ref: B (5535), FS ($1-005) ($1-1880-007), V

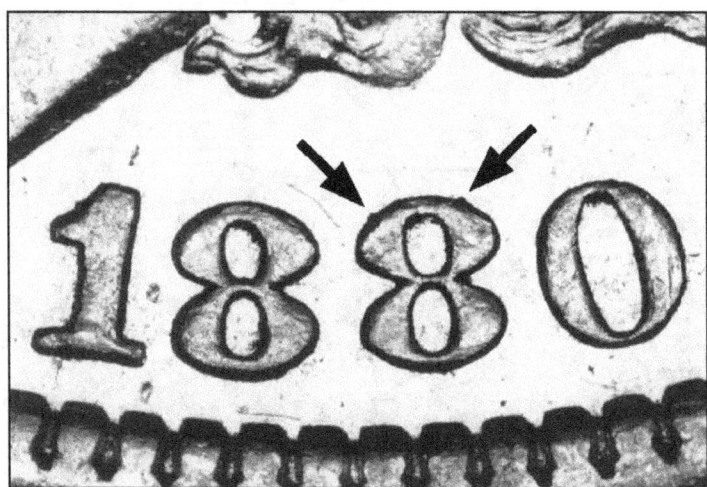

"8/7" overdate feature

Grade	VAM 8	Com	PL	Com	DMPL	Com	RF
MS-62	NTH	32	UNK		UNK		8
MS-60	NTH	30					8
AU-58	NTH	28					7+
AU-50	1380	22					7
XF-40	875	19					7
VF-30	500	18					7

■ **Key Identifier:** Two small "ears" are visible atop the second "8" in the date.

■ **Comments:** Even rarer than VAMs 6 and 7, but less easily attributed, especially in grades below AU. VAM 8 is in high demand from VAM collectors. *Ultra rare* in Mint State. Worth a heavy premium in all grades.

■ **Certified VAM 8:** 56   **PL:** 0   **DMPL:** 0

CC:	62A	61S	58PNA	Mult.		

VAM: 9 / **"8/7" Overdate** / **PF:** 8
Ref: FS, V

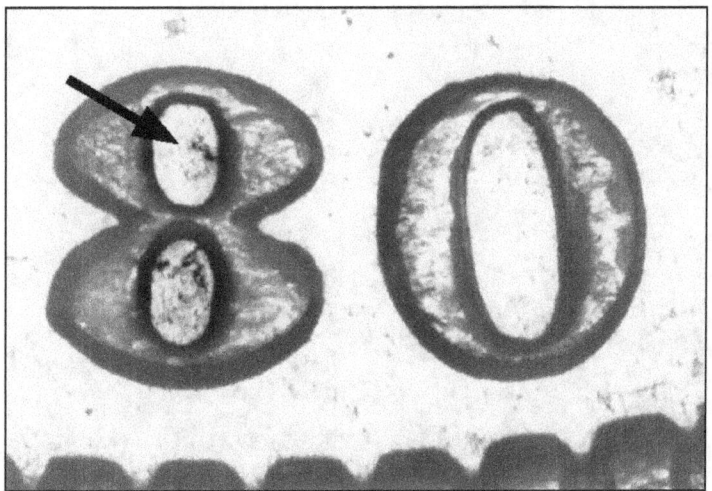

"8/7" overdate feature

Grade	VAM 9	Com	PL	Com	DMPL	Com	RF
MS-65	2370+	600	UNK	2000	NTH	4700	7+
MS-64	950	110					7
MS-63	600	40					6+
MS-62	300	35					6
MS-60	250	30					6
AU-50	100	19					4

■ **Key Identifiers:** Diagonal markings inside the top and bottom loops of the second "8" in the date.

■ **Comments:** While not nearly as rare as VAMs 7 and 8, the VAM 9 is desirable as part of the core 1880-P overdate set and still commands huge premiums.

■ **Certified VAM 9:** 209 **PL:** 0 **DMPL:** 2

CC:	66P	66P	65DMN	65PNA	Mult.	

VAM: 23 / **"80/79" Overdate** / **PF:** 9
Ref: B (5534), FS ($1-1880-023), V

"80/79" overdate feature

Grade	VAM 23	Com	PL	Com	DMPL	Com	RF
MS-62	2100+	32	UNK		UNK		8
MS-60	1500+	30					7+
AU-58	750	28					7+
AU-50	600	22					7
XF-40	525	19					6
VF-30	150	18					6

■ **Key Identifiers:** "Ear" atop right side of second "8", and the remains of an underlying "9" on the surface of the "0".

■ **Comments:** *Ultra rare* in Mint State. The VAM 23 is the most dramatic variety in the Morgan dollar series, with the remnants of the first date appearing on the surface of the digits of the date.

■ **Certified VAM 23:** 159 **PL:** 0 **DMPL:** 0

CC:	62P	62N	62A	61PNA	Mult.	

VAM: 4 / **"80/79" Overdate with B Reverse** / **PF:** 8
Ref: B (5551), FS ($1-1880CC-004), Q, R, V

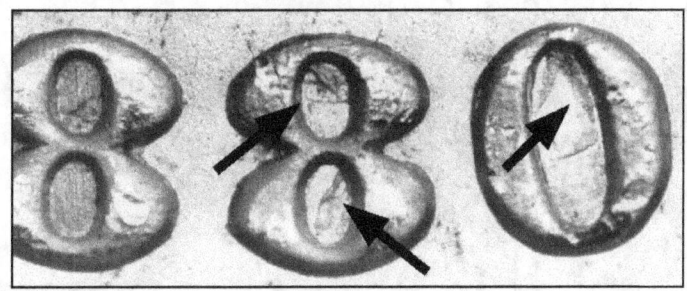

"80/79" overdate feature

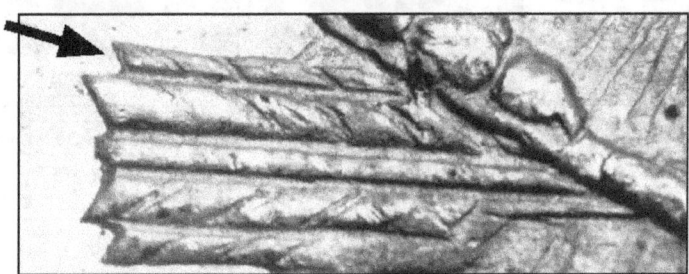

Parallel Arrow Feather (PAF) B reverse

Grade	VAM 4	Com	PL	Com	DMPL	Com	RF
MS-66	4300	2500		UNK		UNK	7+
MS-65	2300	1200	4400	1500	11500	7800	7
MS-64	975	550	2100	700	6000	2300	6+
MS-63	575	475	1300	425	1550	800	6
MS-62	500	465					6
MS-60	475	450					5

■ **Key Identifier:** Remains of an underlying "79" are clearly visible in the last "8" and the upper half of the "0" in the date.

■ **Comments:** VAM 4, along with VAM 7, both with the Parallel Arrow feather (PAF) B reverse are worth a premium over their Slanted Arrow Feather (SAF) C reverse counterparts.

■ **Certified VAM 4:** 1,058   **PL:** 41   **DMPL:** 31

CC:	66PNA	Mult.				

VAMs: 5, 6 / **"8/7" Overdates with C Reverse** / **PF:** 7
Ref: B (5553, 5554), FS-($1-005.2) ($1-1880cc-005 &
$1-1880cc-006), Q, R, V

 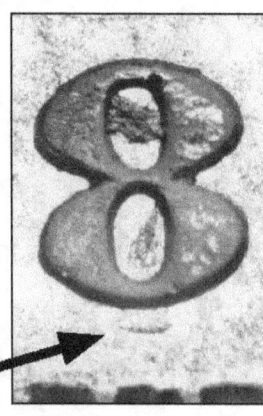 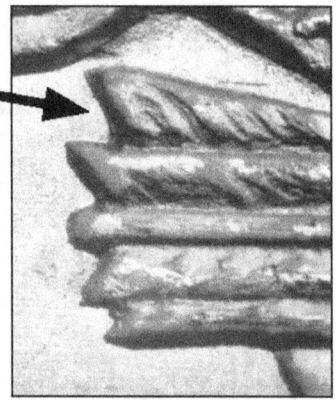

VAM 5 "8/7"   VAM 6 "8/7"   Slanted Arrow Feather
high overdate   low overdate   (SAF) reverse

Grade	VAM 5/6	Com	PL	Com	DMPL	Com	RF
MS-66	2550	2500		UNK		UNK	7
MS-65	1250	1200	1600	1500	8050	7800	6+
MS-64	600	550	750	700	2400	2300	6
MS-63	525	475	570	425	850	800	5
MS-62	475	465					4
MS-60	450	450					4

■ **Key Identifiers:** The dates of both VAMs show dramatic remains of an underlying "7", set high on VAM 5, low on VAM 6.

■ **Comments:** Although not rare, these VAMs are extremely popular because they represent two of the clearest overdates in the Morgan dollar series. VAM 5 is scarcer than VAM 6. Found in GSA holders.

■ **Certified VAM 5:** 517   **PL:** 98   **DMPL:** 42
■ **Certified VAM 6:** 405   **PL:** 51   **DMPL:** 42

CC: VAM 5	67[A]	66[PNA]	Mult.			
VAM 6	66PL[N]	66PL[N]	66PL[A]	66PL[A]	66[PN]	Mult.

VAMs: 4, 5 / **"80/79" and "8/7" Overdates** / **PF:** 7
Ref: B (5540), FS ($1-1880o-004 & $1-1880o-005), Q, R, V

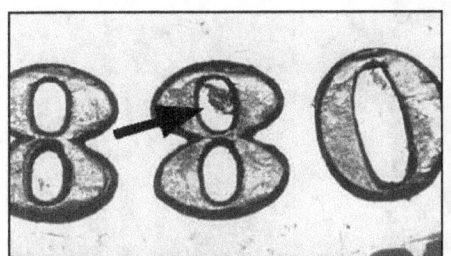

VAM 4 obverse overdate

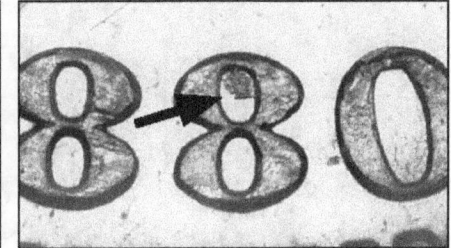

VAM 5 obverse overdate

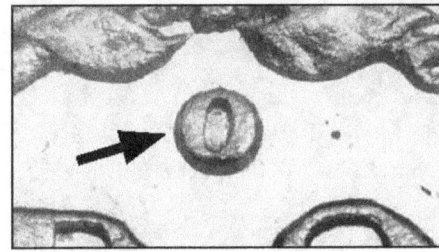

VAM 4 reverse Micro "o"

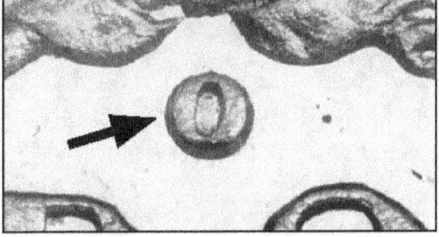

VAM 5 medium Oval "O"

Grade	VAM 4/5	Com	PL	Com	DMPL	Com	RF 4/5
MS-65	NTH	23K	UNK	25K	UNK	56K	8
MS-64	2100+	1500	NTH	1600	UNK	7K	7+
MS-63	1400	300	1500	350	2200	1200	7
MS-60	250	50					6/6+
AU-58	200	45					6/6+
AU-50	75	40					5/6

■ **Key Identifier:** The remains of a "7" in the top loop of the "8" of the date, in the form of a "crossbar."

■ **Comments:** The VAM 5 with an Oval "O" mintmark is about three times more scarce than the VAM 4 with a Micro "o". VAM 4 is often found with Proof-like surfaces.

■ **Certified VAM 4:** 499   **PL:** 38   **DMPL:** 50
■ **Certified VAM 5:** 177   **PL:** 19   **DMPL:** 3

CC: VAM 4	65P	64PNA	Mult.			
VAM 5	64PLN	64PLA	64PLA	64PLA	64PN	Mult.

VAMs: 6, 6A, 6C / **"8/7" Overdates** / **PF:** 7
Ref: B (5539), FS, K, Q, V

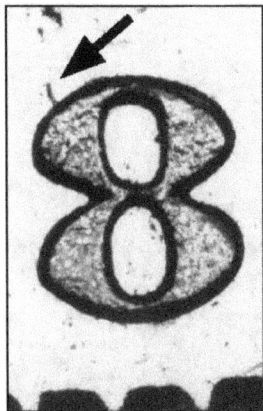
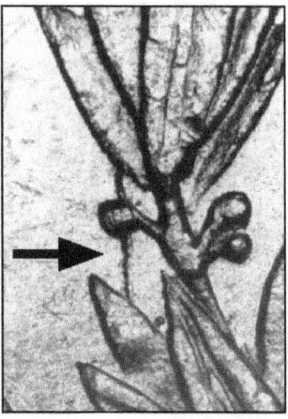

Ear overdate
on second "8"

VAM 6A reverse, die
gouge in left wreath

VAM 6C die clash
with letter transfer

Grade	VAM 6/6A & 6C	Com	PL	Com	DMPL	Com	RF 6/6A & 6C
MS-64	2.6K/1.7K	1500	NTH	1600	NTH	7K	8/7
MS-63	1K/550	300	NTH	350	NTH	1200	7/6
MS-62	750/350	110					7/6
MS-60	500/175	45					7/5
AU-58	425/150	40					6/5
AU-50	150/75	21					5/4

■ **Key Identifiers:** A small arc curves upward from the left top of the second "8" in the date. VAM 6A has a reverse die gouge on the outer side of the upper right wreath (viewer's left). VAM 6C shows a strong multiple-letter die clash on the obverse from the reverse (refer to Kimpton, 2005).

■ **Comments:** All three have the same obverse. VAM 6, without the reverse die gouge, is much scarcer than VAMs 6A and 6C.

■ **Certified VAM 6:** 123 **PL:** 1 **DMPL:** 0
■ **Certified VAMs 6A, 6C:** 721 **PL:** 12 **DMPL:** 5

CC: VAM 6	63P	63A	63A	62P	62P	61PLA
VAMs 6A/6C	65P	65N	64DMA	64DMPNA	Mult.	

VAM: 43 / **Doubled Die Obverse** / **PF:** 8
Ref: Q, V

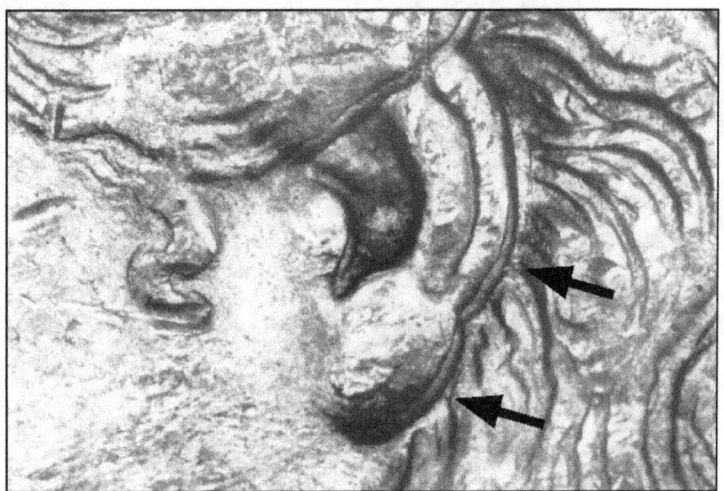

Obverse doubled ear

Grade	VAM 43	Com	PL	Com	DMPL	Com	RF
MS-63	600+	300	UNK		UNK		7+
MS-62	525	110					7
MS-61	435	45					6
MS-60	400	40					6
AU-50	150	21					6
XF-40	100	18					5

■ **Key Identifiers:** Liberty's ear is doubled along the outside back and bottom edges. The eyelid is also doubled.

■ **Comments:** Its true rarity has not yet been appreciated by most variety specialists, as evidenced by its low population.

■ **Certified VAM 43:** 200 **PL:** 1 **DMPL:** 0

CC:	64P	64N	63PA	Mult.		

VAM: 48 (formerly 1A) / **Die Gouge on Reverse** / **PF:** 6
Ref: FS ($1-005.1), Q, V

Die gouge through far left tailfeather

Grade	VAM 48	Com	PL	Com	DMPL	Com	RF
MS-64	1700+	1500	NTH	1600			7+
MS-63	500	300	NTH	350			7
MS-62	450	110					7
MS-60	155	45					7
AU-58	125	40					6
AU-50	90	21					5

■ **Key Identifiers:** A die gouge, whimsically called the "Hangnail," is evident beneath the eagle's tailfeathers on the left side.

■ **Comments:** Because of its obvious variety feature, VAM 48 is popular with variety and non-variety collectors alike.

■ **Certified VAM 48:** 547   **PL:** 4   **DMPL:** 0

CC:	64PNA	Mult.				

VAM: 49 (formerly 6B) / **"8/7" Overdate** / PF: 9
Ref: B (5539), FS ($1-1880o-048), K, Q, V

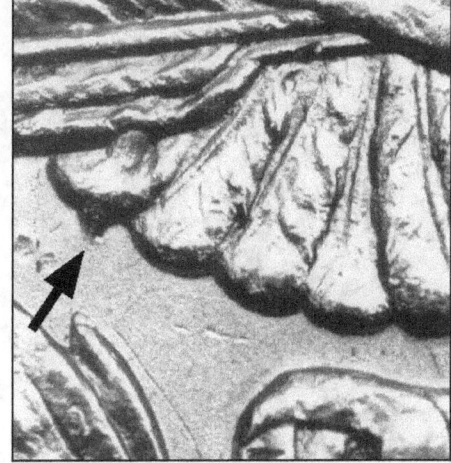

"8/7" overdate feature   Reverse die gouge ("Hangnail")

Grade	VAM 49	Com	PL	Com	DMPL	Com	RF
MS-63	1800+	300	UNK		UNK		8
MS-62	1500+	110					7+
MS-60	1250	45					7+
AU-58	1100	40					7+
AU-50	900	21					7
XF-40	350	18					6+

■ **Key Identifiers:** A small arc curving upward from the left top of the second "8" in the date. VAM 49 is also paired with the "Hangnail" reverse.

■ **Comments:** VAM 49 is still considered to be the key 1880-O overdate. Few BU specimens are known. The market has yet to fully appreciate the rarity and value of this interesting die marriage.

■ **Certified VAM 49:** 115   **PL:** 0   **DMPL:** 0

CC:	63P	63A	63A	63A	62P	62A

VAMs: 8, 9 / **"80/79" Overdates** / **PF:** 7
Ref: B (5545), Q, R, V

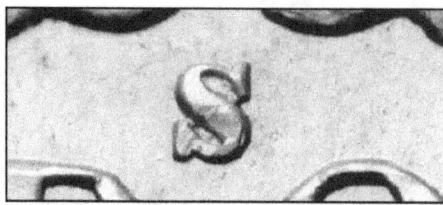

Medium "S" VAM 8 reverse

"80/79" overdate feature on VAMs 8 and 9

Large "S" VAM 9 reverse

Grade	VAM 8/9	Com	PL	Com	DMPL	Com	RF
MS-67	1450	750	UNK		UNK		8
MS-66	450	325	NTH		NTH		7+
MS-65	375	150	350	175	875	580	7
MS-64	180	55	200	75	700	250	6
MS-63	160	40	140	50	300	68	5
MS-60	75	30					4

■ **Key Identifier:** Prominent die fill in top loop of the second "8" in the date with diagonal markings.

■ **Comments:** Although both VAMs have the same obverse, VAM 8 has a medium "S" mintmark and VAM 9 has a large "S". VAM 9 is scarcer than VAM 8, and they both trade for about the same premium.

■ **Certified VAM 8:** 710   **PL:** 76   **DMPL:** 86
■ **Certified VAM 9:** 440   **PL:** 78   **DMPL:** 55

CC: VAM 8	68[P]	67[PNA]	Mult.			
VAM 9	68[N]	67[PNA]	Mult.			

VAM: 10 / **"8/7" Overdate** / **PF:** 8
Ref: B (5547), Q, V

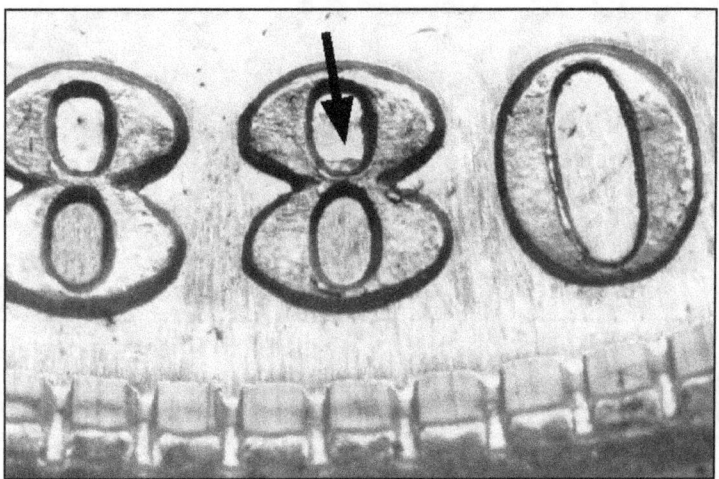

"8/7" overdate feature

Grade	VAM 10	Com	PL	Com	DMPL	Com	RF
MS-66	775	325	UNK		UNK		8
MS-65	460	150	NTH	175	1150	580	7+
MS-64	375	55	450	75	NTH	250	7
MS-63	275	40	350	50	NTH	68	6+
MS-62	155	35					6
MS-60	100	30					5

■ **Key Identifier:** Horizontal markings at the bottom inside of the upper loop of the second "8" in the date.

■ **Comments:** The VAM 10 is the "stopper" of the 1880-S overdate set and is quite desirable.

■ **Certified VAM 10:** 261   **PL:** 1   **DMPL:** 3

CC:	66PNA	Mult.				

VAMs: 3, 3A, 3EDS / **"O/S" Over-mintmark** / **PF:** 10
Ref: B (5567), FS ($1-005.25) ($1-1882o-003), Q, R, V

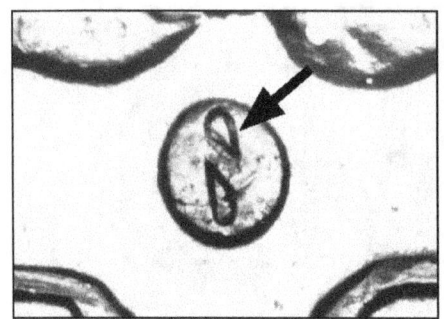
"O/S" feature

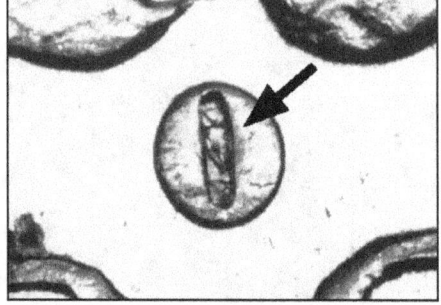
Rare EDS of the same variety

Grade	VAM 3/EDS	Com	PL	Com	DMPL	Com	RF
MS-65	45K	1100	UNK		UNK		7
MS-64	2700	80					6
MS-63	950/NTH	45					5
MS-62	475/NTH	37					4
MS-60	200/400	35					4/7 EDS
AU-50	75/200	24					4/6+ EDS

■ **Key Identifiers:** Strong diagonal crossbar inside the "O" and flush with the mintmark, with tiny raised dots of metal from a rusted die on much of the reverse.

■ **Comments:** Three die states are known. An EDS shows less of the diagonal crossbar, but is worth significantly more than later die states and is highly underappreciated in all grades. A recently discovered LDS VAM 3A shows a partial clash of "us" from "trust" on the reverse.

■ **Certified VAMs 3, 3A*:** 7,517   **PL:** 0   **DMPL:** 0
■ **Certified VAM 3EDS:** 209   **PL:** 0   **DMPL:** 0

CC: VAMs 3/3A	**64PNA	Mult.				
VAM 3EDS	63P	63N	63A	63A	63A	62PA

*Combined VAMs 3, 4, and 5. **Higher grades may be found among non-attributed 1882 O/S certified coins.

VAM: 4, 4EDS / **"O/S" Over-mintmark** / **PF:** 10
Ref: B (5567), FS ($1-005.25) ($1-1882o-004), Q, R, V

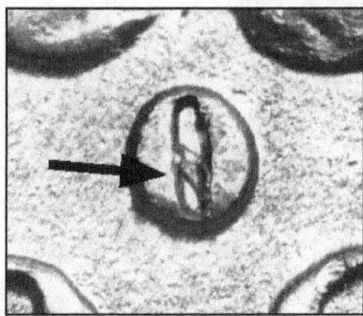
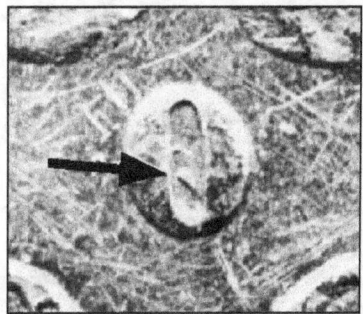

"O/S" feature   Rare EDS of same variety

Grade	VAM 4/ EDS	Com	PL	Com	DMPL	Com	RF
MS-65	45K	1100	UNK		UNK		7
MS-64	2700	80					6
MS-63	950/NTH	45	UNK		33K*	2.7K	5/8 EDS
MS-62	475/NTH	37					4/8 EDS
MS-60	200/NTH	35					4/7+ EDS
AU-50	75/1800	24					4/7+ EDS

■ **Key Identifiers:** Strongly recessed diagonal crossbar in the "O" mintmark, with tiny raised dots of metal from a rusted die on much of the reverse.

■ **Comments:** Two die states are known. An *ultra rare* Early Die State shows less of the diagonal crossbar. It is highly desirable and worth a huge premium. The EDS is likely to show reflective surfaces.

■ **Certified VAM 4*:** 7,517 **PL:** 0 **DMPL:** 0
■ **Certified VAM 4EDS:** 23 **PL:** 0 **DMPL:** 1

CC: VAM 4	**64PNA	Mult.				
VAM 4 EDS	63DMP	63PN	62DMP	58A	55PNA	Mult.

*Combined VAMs 3, 4, and 5. **Higher grades may be found among non-attributed 1882 "O/S" certified coins.

VAM: 5, 5EDS / **"O/S" Over-mintmark** / **PF:** 10
Ref: B (5567), FS ($1-1882o-005), Q, R, V

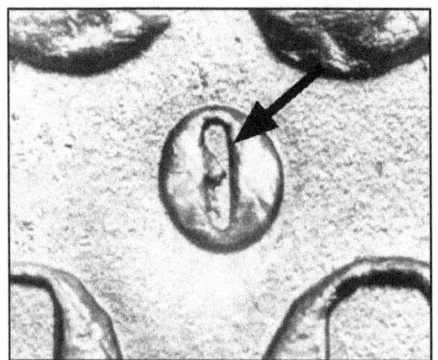

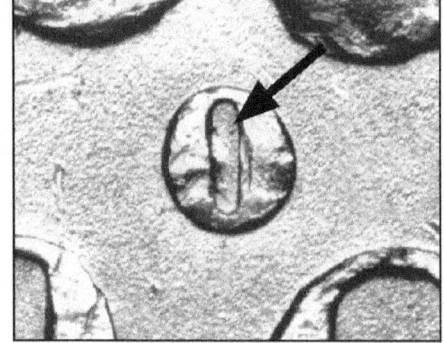

"O/S" feature   Rare EDS of the same variety

Grade	VAM 5/ EDS	Com	PL	Com	DMPL	Com	RF
MS-65	45K	1100					7
MS-64	2700	80					6
MS-63	950/NTH	45	UNK		UNK		5/8 EDS
MS-62	475/NTH	37			10K	75	4/8 EDS
MS-60	200/NTH	35			4K	50	4/7+ EDS
AU-50	75/200	24					4/7 EDS

■ **Key Identifiers:** Broken diagonal crossbar in the "O" mint-mark, with tiny raised dots of metal from a rusted die on much of the reverse.

■ **Comments:** Two die states are known. A rare Early Die State shows less of the broken diagonal and is worth significantly more. The EDS, which is still underappreciated, is likely to show reflective surfaces.

■ **Certified VAM 5*:** 7,517 **PL:** 0 **DMPL:** 0
■ **Certified VAM 5EDS:** 113 **PL:** 4 **DMPL:** 4

CC: VAM 5	**65[N]	64[N]	64[PNA]	Mult.		
VAM 5EDS	63[N]	62DM[N]	62DM[A]	62[PA]	Mult.	

*Combined VAMs 3, 4, and 5. **Higher grades may be found among non-attributed 1882 "O/S" certified coins.

VAM: 7 / **Repunched Mintmark** / **PF:** 7
Ref: Q, V

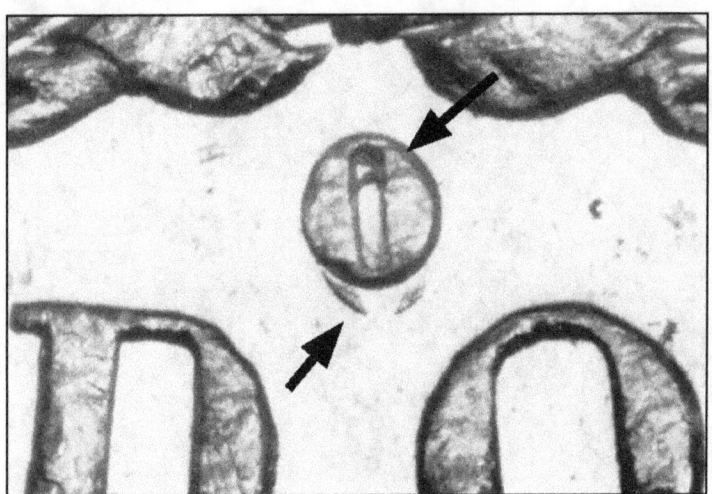

"O/O" mintmark

Grade	VAM 7	Com	PL	Com	DMPL	Com	RF
MS-66	NTH	8K					8
MS-65	NTH	1100	NTH	1250	NTH		7
MS-64	300	80	400	125			6
MS-63	225	45	250	50			5
MS-62	150	37	200	45			4
MS-60	70	35	50				4

■ **Key Identifier:** Strong remains of a second "O" mintmark inside the "O" as well as below it.

■ **Comments:** One of the most dramatic "O/O" varieties in the Morgan dollar series. VAM 7 is usually offered for a premium in all grades.

■ **Certified VAM 7:** 1,283 **PL:** 8 **DMPL:** 3

CC:	66P	65PNA	Mult.			

VAM: 10 / **Doubled Die Obverse** / **PF:** 10
Ref: V

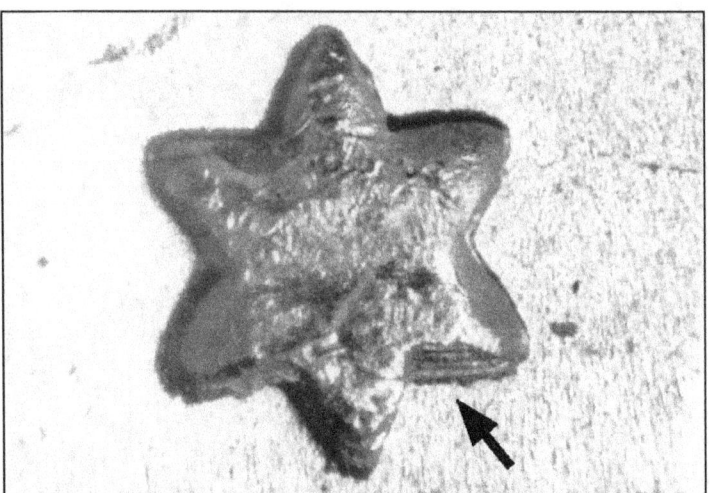

The first star to the right of the date

Grade	VAM 10	Com	PL	Com	DMPL	Com	RF
MS-64	NTH	65	UNK		UNK		8
MS-63	2200+	45					8
MS-62	825+	40					7
MS-60	500+	35					7
AU-50	250	20					7
XF-40	200	18					6+

■ **Key Identifier:** Stars to the right of the date show six doublings on the bottom edges.

■ **Comments:** Seldom encountered, the VAM 10 is still underappreciated for its rarity. Take care not to confuse this Morgan with VAM 9, another rare doubled-star variety, but different from the one pictured here. Demand for VAM 10 has increased over the past decade with a greater appreciation for its unique features and rarity.

■ **Certified VAM 10:** 105   **PL:** 0   **DMPL:** 0

CC:	64P	64P	64A	63PN	Mult.	

VAM: 4 / **Repunched Mintmark** / **PF:** 7
Ref: Q, V

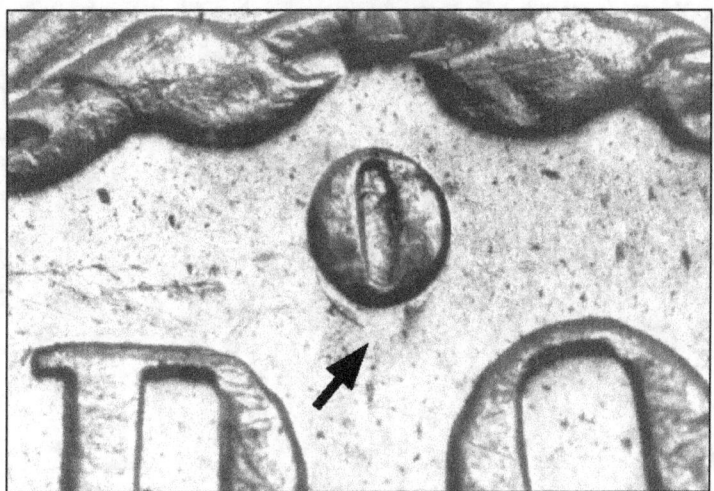

"O/O" repunched mintmark

Grade	VAM 4	Com	PL	Com	DMPL	Com	RF
MS-66	NTH	500					8
MS-65	NTH	250	NTH	450	NTH	1150	7
MS-64	200	60	250	100	600+	340	6
MS-63	175	45	200	50	250	90	5
MS-62	110	40					5
MS-60	60	30					4

■ **Key Identifier:** Strong remains of a second "O" mintmark, both inside and below the first, which was set too low.

■ **Comments:** Similar to the 1882-O VAM 7, the 1883-O VAM 4 is desirable as a dramatic "O/O" variety that can be found with reflective surfaces.

■ **Certified VAM 4:** 1,013 **PL:** 23 **DMPL:** 23

CC:	66P	66N	65PNA	Mult.		

VAMs: 3, 4 / **Large and Small "Dot" Varieties** / **PF:** 8
Ref: B (5576), FS ($1-1884-003 & $1-1884-004), V

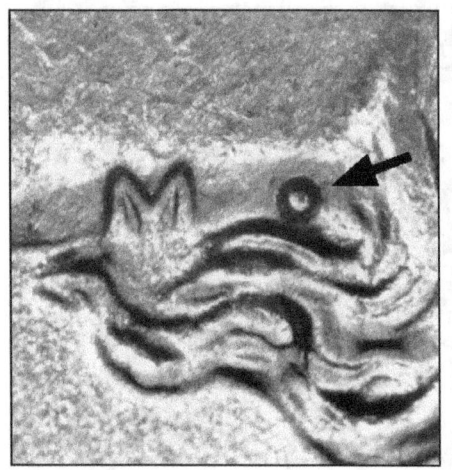 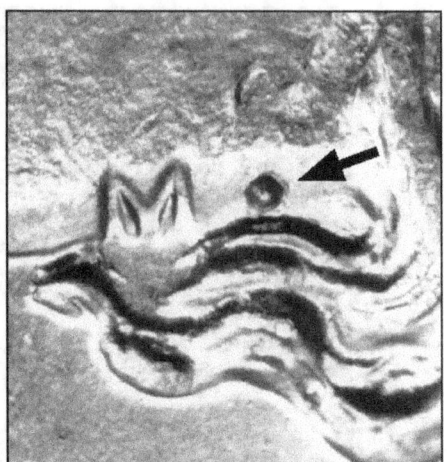

Placement of VAM 3 "Dot"   Placement of VAM 4 "Dot"

Grade	VAM 3/4	Com	PL	Com	DMPL	Com	RF
MS-65	600/NTH	300		500		4K	7+
MS-64	350/1400	65	400	100		675	7
MS-63	280	45	NTH	75	NTH	140	6
MS-62	150	40					5
MS-60	100	35					5
AU-50	60	18					5

■ **Key Identifiers:** Raised dot of metal to the right of Morgan's initial on Liberty's neck on the obverse, and to the left of the wreath bow on the reverse.

■ **Comments:** Though the dots on both VAMs look similar, the obverse dot on the VAM 4 is smaller and closer to the "M" than the dot on the VAM 3. VAMs 3 and 4 are about equally scarce.

■ **Certified VAM 3:** 312 **PL:** 10 **DMPL:** 2
■ **Certified VAM 4:** 352 **PL:** 14 **DMPL:** 5

CC: VAM 3	66[N]	66[N]	65[PNA]	Mult.		
VAM 4	66[P]	65[PNA]	Mult.			

VAM: 6 / **Repunched Mintmark** / **PF:** 7
Ref: Q, V

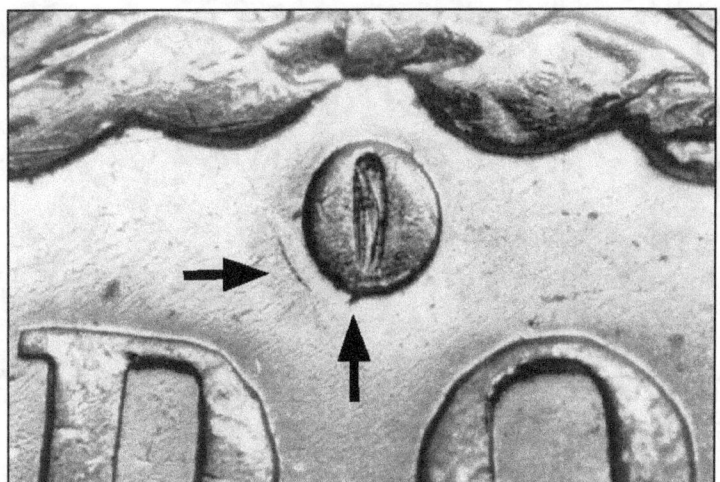

"O/O" mintmark

Grade	VAM 6	Com	PL	Com	DMPL	Com	RF
MS-66	NTH	400	NTH				8
MS-65	275	175	300	200	NTH	800	7
MS-64	175	60	200	85	400	300	6
MS-63	90	45	100	60	150	90	5
MS-62	75	40					5
MS-60	35	30					5

■ **Key Identifier:** Strong remains of a second "O" mintmark both inside and to the lower left outside of the mintmark.

■ **Comments:** Although scarce, when it is found the VAM 6 is often encountered in very high grades with reflective surfaces.

■ **Certified VAM 6:** 521 **PL:** 59 **DMPL:** 193

CC:	66PL[N]	66PL[P]	66[PNA]	Mult.		

VAMs: 6, 9 / **Repunched Mintmark** / **PF:** 6
Ref: Q, V

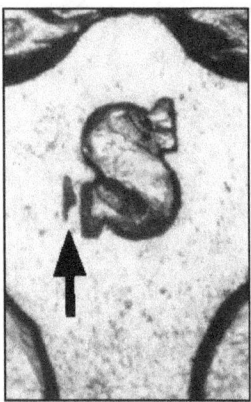 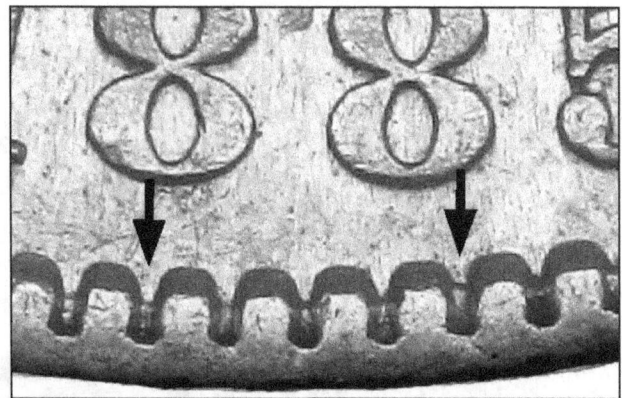

"S/S" mintmark　　　Repunched "8" in denticles

Grade	VAM 6/9	Com	PL	Com	DMPL	Com	RF
MS-65	NTH	6K	UNK		UNK		7/8
MS-64	NTH	1.7K					7/8
MS-63	825	275	NTH	4K			7/8
MS-62	600	250	NTH	675			6/7+
MS-60	400	200	NTH	300			6/7+
AU-50	150/?	125					6/7+

■ **Key Identifiers:** Clear remains of an original "S" visible at the bottom left of the mintmark. VAM 9 shows slight remnants of an "885" struck into the denticles.

■ **Comments:** Nice doubling on the bottom serif of the "S" makes the VAM 6 one of the top "S/S" varieties. VAM 9, a recent discovery, is much rarer than VAM 6. With few certified, and almost none traded, it is too early to determine the value of VAM 9, but it is likely to bring a substantial premium over an already scarce and underappreciated VAM 6.

■ **Certified VAM 6:** 138　**PL:** 2　**DMPL:** 0
■ **Certified VAM 9:** 1　**PL:** 0　**DMPL:** 0

CC: VAM 6	65P	65P	65P	64PNA	Mult.	
VAM 9	20A					

VAMs: 1A, 1A1, 21 (formerly 1B)
Obverse Die Gouge, Misplaced Date / PF: 6
Ref: V

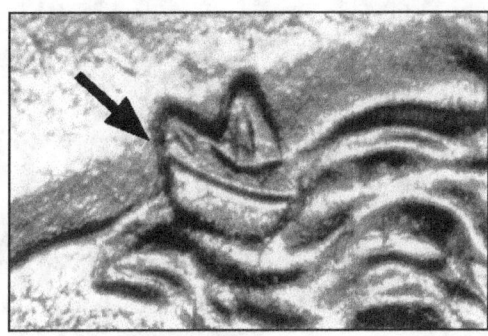

The 1A Line in "6"   The Line thru "M"

Grade	VAM 1A & 1A1/21	Com	PL	Com	DMPL	Com	RF
MS-66	450	325	UNK		UNK		7+/8
MS-65	250	140	NTH	200	NTH	1.1K	7/7
MS-64	180	60	NTH	100	NTH	350	6/6
MS-63	100	45	125	60	175	90	5/5
MS-62	75	40					5/5
MS-60	45	30					4/4

■ **Key Identifiers:** VAM 1A displays a line above the bowl of the "6". VAM 1A1 was struck from clashed dies, showing "In" and "st" from "In God we trust" on the obverse. VAM 21 shows a misplaced date (a portion of the number "8") through the letter "M".

■ **Comments:** None of these varieties is a major rarity, but all are interesting for their features. VAM 1A should not be confused with VAM 1A, Die Pair 2, a recently discovered variety that looks very similar.

■ **Certified VAMs 1A, 1A1:** 629 **PL:** 5 **DMPL:** 4
■ **Certified VAM 21:** 489 **PL:** 2 **DMPL:** 2

CC: VAMs 1A/1A1	66PN	Mult.			
VAM 21	66P	65PNA	Mult.		

VAM: 17 / **Doubled Die Reverse** / **PF:** 7
Ref: V

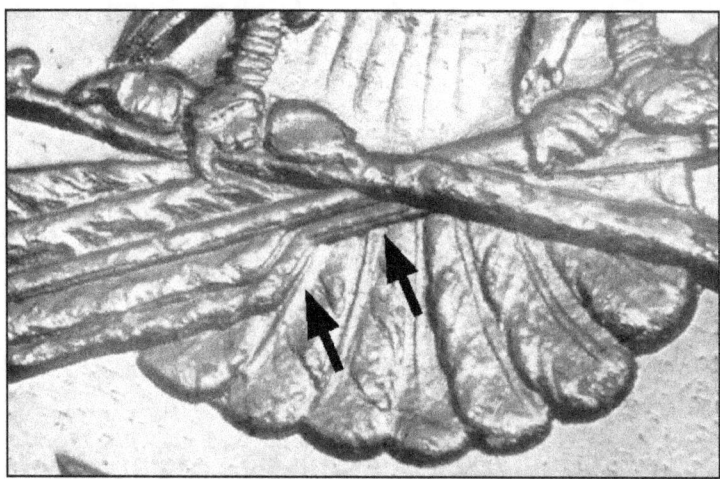

Doubled arrows

Grade	VAM 17	Com	PL	Com	DMPL	Com	RF
MS-66	500	325	NTH		NTH		6-
MS-65	300	140	NTH	200	NTH	1.1K	6-
MS-64	200	60	NTH	100	NTH	350	5+
MS-63	175	45	200	60	NTH	90	5
MS-62	125	40					5
MS-60	75	30					5

■ **Key Identifier:** The lower edges of the bottom arrows and the olive branch are clearly doubled.

■ **Comments:** Scarcer than the VAM Book suggests, the VAM 17 is gaining in popularity as it becomes more well-known.

■ **Certified VAM 17:** 511   **PL:** 22   **DMPL:** 9

CC:	67P	67N	67N	67N	66PLN	66PLA

VAM: 1A / **Clashed Die Reverse** / **PF:** 9
Ref: FS ($1-005.27) (FS-$1-1886o-001a), K, Q, V

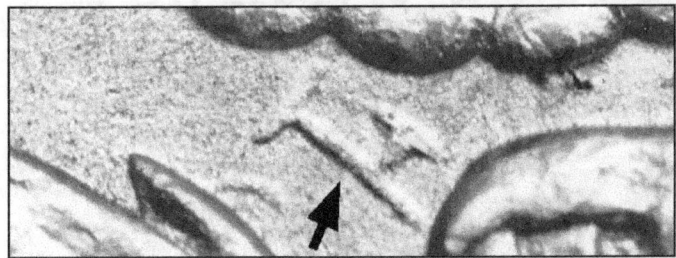

Clashed "E" of LIBERTY on the obverse die

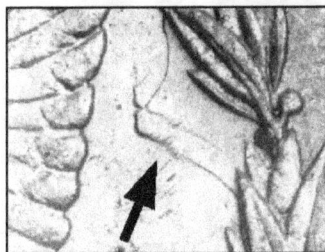

Two clashes inside
right reverse wreath

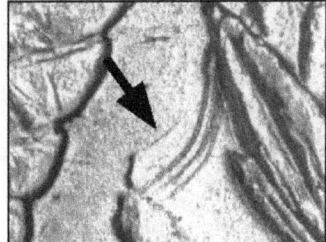

Seven clashes inside
right wreath

Grade	VAM 1A	Com	PL	Com	DMPL	Com	RF
MS-63	6.5K	3.3K	UNK		UNK		8
MS-62	2.3K	750					7
MS-60	1K	600					7
AU-58	535	200					7
AU-50	200	70					6
XF-40	110	30					5

■ **Key Identifier:** Clashed die with a strong "E" clash under the eagle's tailfeathers, to the left of the ribbon bow.

■ **Comments:** The VAM 1A is rare in Mint State and can be found with one, two or seven clashes on the reverse. The market currently treats the value of multiple clashes equally.

■ **Certified VAM 1A:** 703 **PL:** 2 **DMPL:** 0

CC:	63P	62PNA	Mult.			

VAM: 2 / **Repunched Mintmark** / **PF:** 6
Ref: B (5588), V

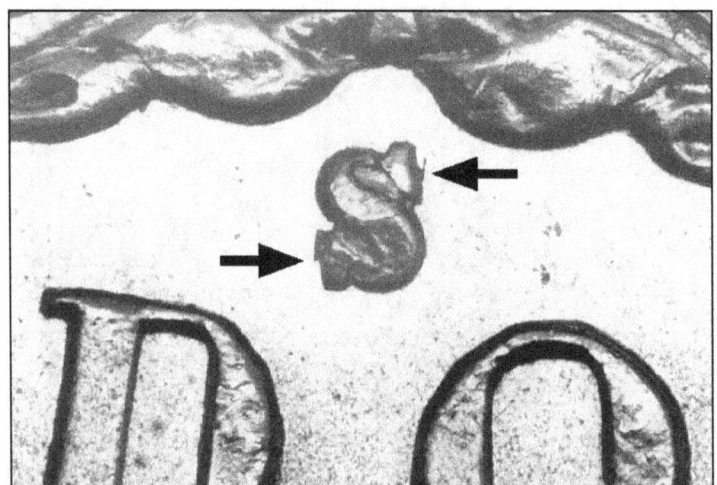

"S/S" mintmark

Grade	VAM 2	Com	PL	Com	DMPL	Com	RF
MS-65	NTH	2.9K	NTH	3500	NTH	24.5K	7
MS-64	NTH	700	1265+	900	NTH	7.4K	7
MS-63	600	450	NTH	500	NTH	1.9K	6
MS-62	500	350					6
MS-60	300	275					6
AU-50	175	150					5

■ **Key Identifier:** Part of an underlying "S" is visible in front of the top serif of the mintmark.

■ **Comments:** The VAM 2 is currently the only 1886-S variety worth a premium.

■ **Certified VAM 2:** 530   **PL:** 26   **DMPL:** 7

CC:	66P	66N	65DMA	65PLPNA	65PNA	Mult.

VAM: 1A / **Die Break Reverse** / **PF:** 10
Ref: V

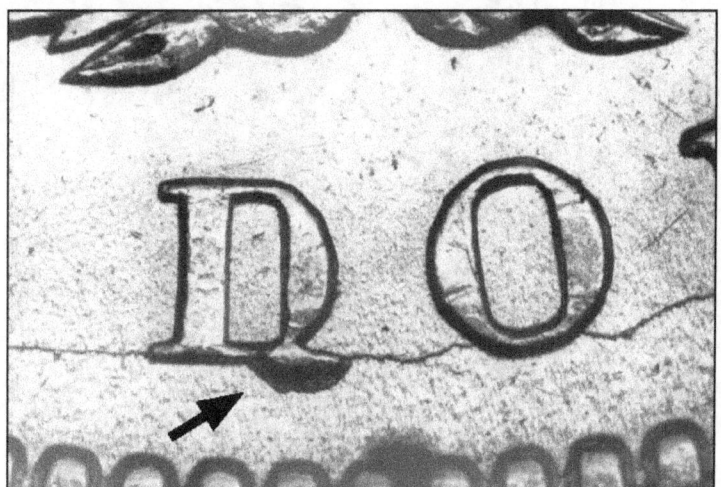

"D" with "Donkey Tail"

Grade	VAM 1A	Com	PL	Com	DMPL	Com	RF
MS-62	20K	35	UNK		UNK		8
MS-60	NTH	30					7
AU-58	1100	25					7
AU-50	750	20					6
XF-40	550	18					6
VF-30	300	17					6

■ **Key Identifier:** Die break at bottom right of the "D" in DOLLAR, forming what looks like a donkey tail.

■ **Comments:** Struck at the end of the die's production life, the VAM 1A is rare and in high demand. Early Die State specimens with just the die crack showing bring a significantly lower premium.

■ **Certified VAM 1A:** 196   **PL:** 0   **DMPL:** 0

CC:	62P	62N	62A	62A	61PN	Mult.

VAM: 2 / **Overdate** / **PF:** 10
Ref: B (5593), FS ($1-005.3) ($1-1887-002), Q, R, V

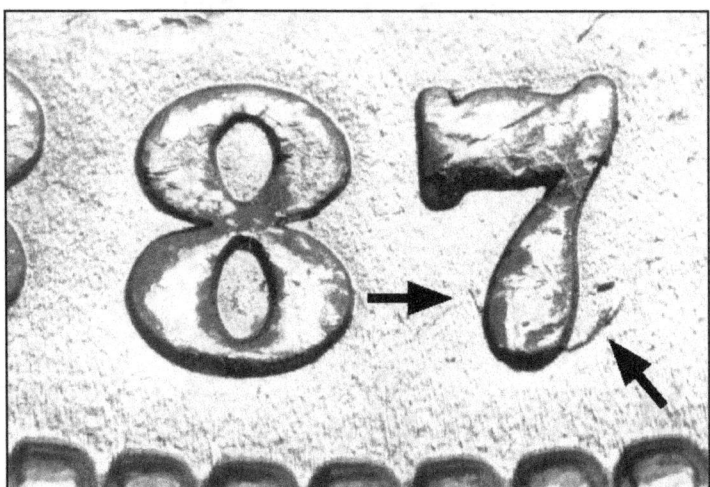

"7/6" overdate feature

Grade	VAM 2	Com	PL	Com	DMPL	Com	RF
MS66	16.1K	325	NTH		NTH		8
MS65	2.9K	150	4.3K	200	15K	1.05K	7
MS64	875	60	1.1K	85	4K	350	6
MS63	550	45	600	60	3.5K	90	5
MS60	210	30					5
AU50	200	20					4

■ **Key Identifier:** Bottom of the underlying "6" is visible as a curved line through the lower stem of the "7".

■ **Comments:** Discovered in the mid-1970s, its popularity has increased to the point at which it is now considered an integral part of a complete Morgan dollar set. Mint State specimens have recently surfaced.

■ **Certified VAM 2:** 2,181   **PL:** 442   **DMPL:** 27

CC:	66PL[P]	66PL[P]	66PL[N]	65DM[P]	65DM[P]	Mult.

VAM: 5 / **Repunched Date** / **PF:** 6
Ref: B (5594), V

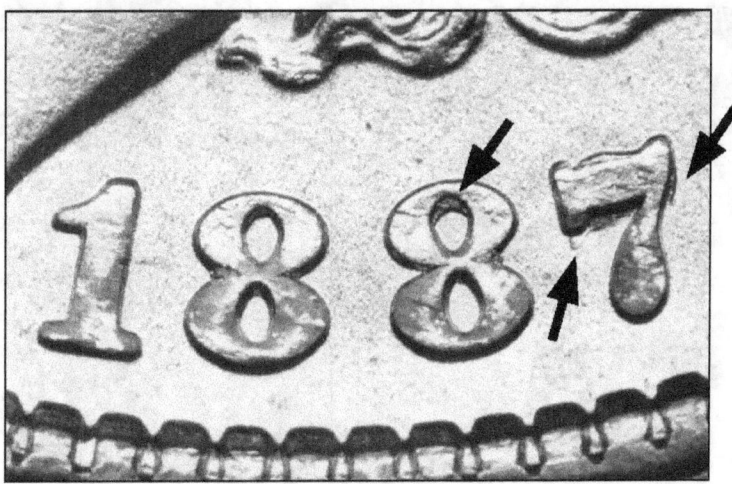

Doubled numerals in the date

Grade	VAM 5	Com	PL	Com	DMPL	Com	RF
MS-65	325	150	UNK		UNK		7
MS-64	170	60					6
MS-63	130	45					5
MS-62	95	40					5
MS-60	80	30					4
AU-50	45	20					4

■ **Key Identifier:** Remains of the "1887" underdate can be seen, particularly inside the top bowl of the second "8".

■ **Comments:** Surprisingly scarce, the VAM 5 is underappreciated by most collectors.

■ **Certified VAM 5:** 329   **PL:** 0   **DMPL:** 0

CC:	65P	65N	64PNA	Mult.		

VAMs: 12, 12A / **Doubled Die Obverse** / **PF:** 8
Ref: K, V

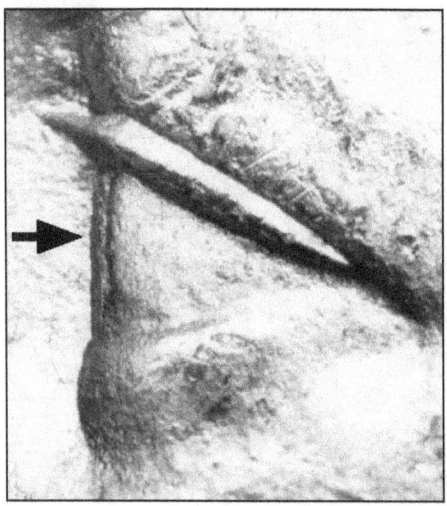

Doubled front of Liberty's eye

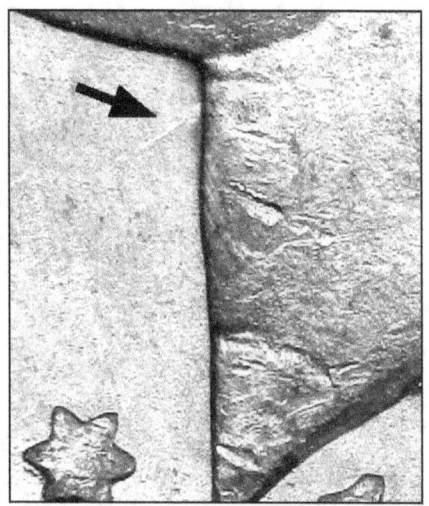

VAM 12A with die clash

Grade	VAM 12/ 12A	Com	PL	Com	DMPL	Com	RF
MS-67	NTH	750	UNK	1000	UNK		8
MS-66	450	325	NTH	450	NTH		7
MS-65	200	150	NTH	200	NTH	1.05K	7
MS-64	150	60	275	85	825	350	6
MS-63	125	45	175	60	280	90	5
MS-60	55	30					4

■ **Key Identifiers:** The vertical line marking the front of Liberty's eye is doubled with another line to the right of the first, resembling an alligator's eye. The word LIBERTY in the headband is also doubled, as are the tops of the letters in PLURIBUS.

■ **Comments:** Always popular because of its name, VAM 12 is a variety that you can likely find with a bit of searching. VAM 12A shows a line extending from Ms. Liberty's neck and a clashed "st" on the obverse from the "trust" on the reverse (see Kimpton, 2005).

■ **Certified VAMs 12, 12A:** 3,480 **PL:** 12 **DMPL:** 17

CC:	67PN	Mult.				

VAM: 2 / **Repunched Date** / **PF:** 8
Ref: B (5596), FS ($1-005.7) ($1-1887o-002), Q, V

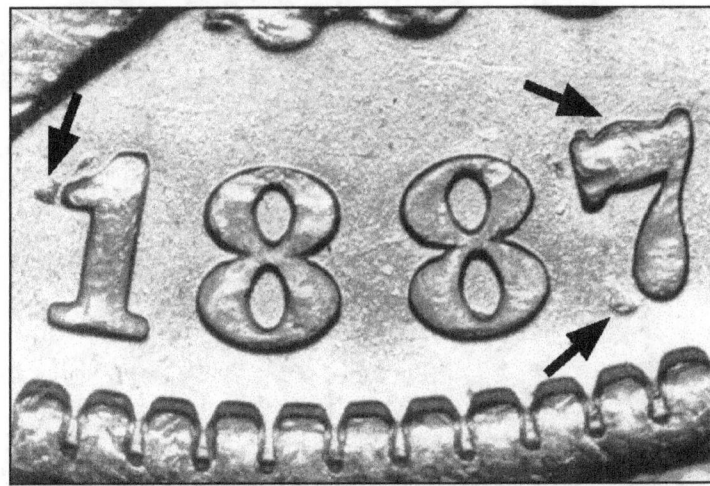

Numerals in the date show doubling and tripling.

Grade	VAM 2	Com	PL	Com	DMPL	Com	RF
MS-64	500	425	UNK		UNK	1.5K	8
MS-63	325	90	NTH		NTH	300	7
MS-62	175	75					6
MS-60	150	45					6
AU-58	125	30					5
AU-50	95	20					4

■ **Key Identifiers:** The remains of the original "1" and "7" in the date are shifted far to the left, with tripling visible on the "7".

■ **Comments:** Often confused with the VAM 3 "7/6" Overdate, the VAM 2 is scarce in its own right, particularly in high grades.

■ **Certified VAM 2:** 584 **PL:** 5 **DMPL:** 3

CC:	64ᴾᴺᴬ	Mult.				

VAM: 3 / **Overdate** / **PF:** 10
Ref: B (5597), FS ($1-005.5) ($1-1887o-003), Q, R, V

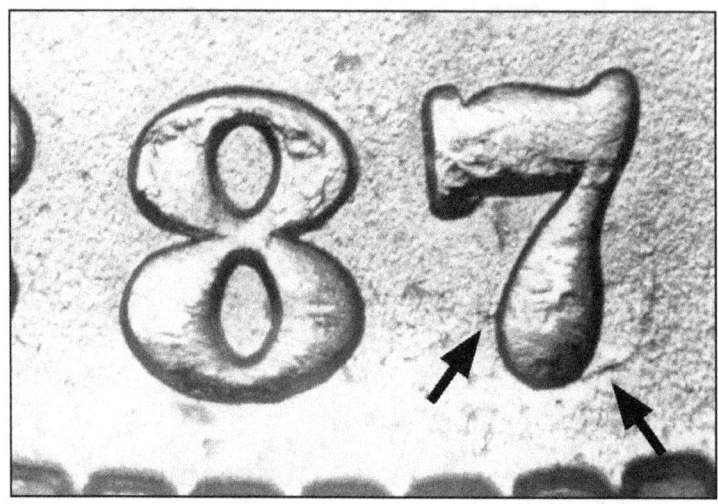

"7/6-O" overdate

Grade	VAM 3	Com	PL	Com	DMPL	Com	RF
MS-64	7500	425	UNK		UNK		7
MS-63	2100	90					6
MS-62	1100	75					6
MS-60	750	45					6
AU-58	275	30					6
AU-50	155	20					5

■ **Key Identifier:** The right outside curve of the underlying "6" is visible beneath the "7".

■ **Comments:** Discovered soon after the 1887 Philadelphia "7/6" Overdate, the O-Mint "7/6" in top grades is worth a huge premium.

■ **Certified VAM 3:** 1,202   **PL:** 0   **DMPL:** 0

CC:	64PNA	Mult.				

VAM: 5 / **Doubled Die Obverse** / **PF:** 7
Ref: V

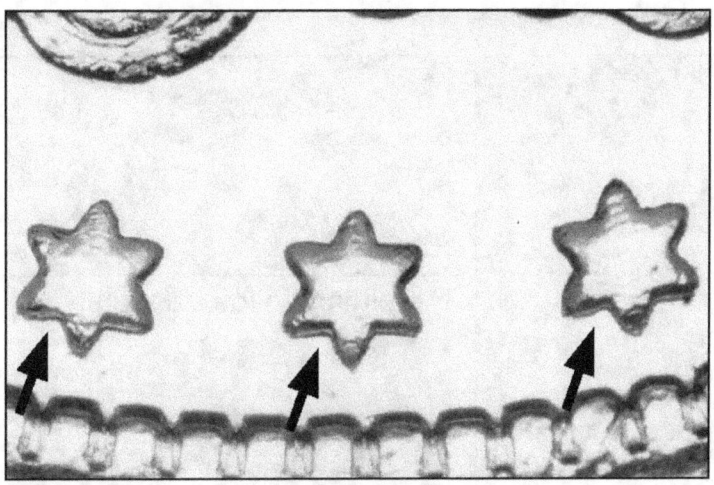

Doubled stars to the right of the date

Grade	VAM 5	Com	PL	Com	DMPL	Com	RF
MS-64	500	425	UNK		UNK		7
MS-63	170	90					7
MS-62	100	75					6
MS-60	95	45					5
AU-58	90	30					5
AU-50	70	20					5

■ **Key Identifier:** The stars to the left and right of the date exhibit clear doubling toward the rim.

■ **Comments:** The VAM 5 is infrequently encountered and often confused with other varieties. Even certified specimens that are attributed may be misattributed.

■ **Certified VAM 5:** 329 **PL:** 0 **DMPL:** 0

CC:	65P	65N	64PNA	Mult.		

VAMs: 22A (formerly VAM 22), 22B
Doubled Die Obverse/Pitted Die Reverse / PF: 8
Ref: K, Q, V

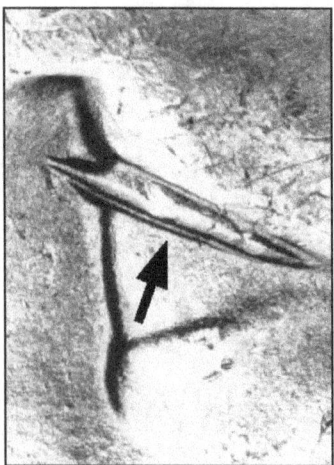

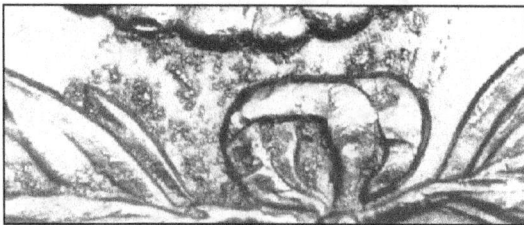

Die pitting on lower reverse

Doubled eyelid

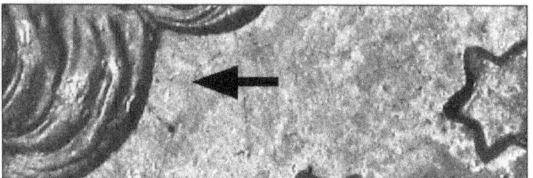

Clashed "T" on obverse of VAM 22B

Grade	VAM 22A/22B	Com	PL	Com	DMPL	Com	RF
MS-63	NTH	90					8
MS-62	875+	75					7
MS-60	300	45					7
AU-50	175	30					6+
XF-40	80	20					6
VF-30	50	18					6

■ **Key Identifiers:** The stars to the left of the date are doubled as is Liberty's upper eyelid. Strong pitting on reverse.

■ **Comments:** VAM 22A replaces the former VAM 1A and VAM 22. It is rare in Mint State and undervalued in all grades. VAM 22B shows a clashed "G" and "t" on the obverse from "In God we trust" on the reverse (see Kimpton, 2005). Currently, there is no apparent price difference between VAM 22A and VAM 22B.

■ **Certified VAMs 22A, 22B:** 177   **PL:** 0   **DMPL:** 0

CC:	63PNA	Mult.				

VAM: 2 / **Repunched Mintmark** / **PF:** 7
Ref: Q, V

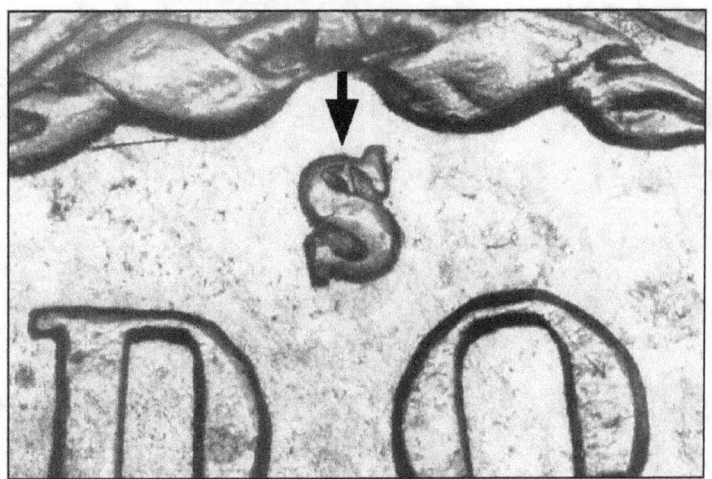

"S/S" mintmark

Grade	VAM 2	Com	PL	Com	DMPL	Com	RF
MS-66	NTH	8.5K					8
MS-65	NTH	2.7K	NTH	3.1K	25.3K	23.5K	7
MS-64	NTH	650	NTH	800	NTH	6.4K	7
MS-63	400	240	NTH	300	NTH	2.7K	6
MS-62	200	150					6
MS-60	140	95					5

■ **Key Identifiers:** The top serif of the underlying "S" is visible inside the top loop of the mintmark. Also shows die-damaged denticles below "87" in the date.

■ **Comments:** Although the VAM 2 is easily obtainable, it is nonetheless desirable for the clarity of its repunched mintmark.

■ **Certified VAM 2:** 363 **PL:** 15 **DMPL:** 16

CC:	66[N]	65[PN]	Mult.			

VAMs: 11, 11A / **Doubled Die Obverse** / **PF:** 6
Ref: V

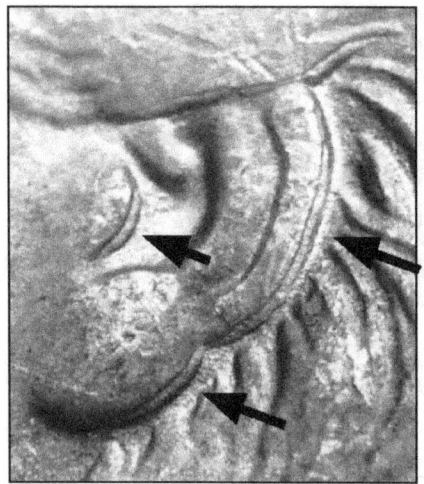

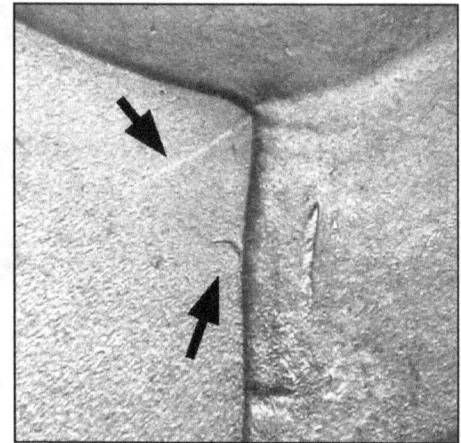

VAM 11A showing clash line
and small "n" by Liberty's neck

Obverse doubled ear

Grade	VAM 11/ 11A	Com	PL	Com	DMPL	Com	RF
MS-65	350	185	UNK		UNK		7+
MS-64	260	60					6
MS-63	140	45					5
MS-62	130	40					5
MS-60	50	35					4
AU-50	35	20					4

■ **Key Identifiers:** Liberty's ear is strongly doubled toward the left on the inside as well as on the outer edge. The strand of hair just above the ear is also doubled. VAM 11A shows a clashed "n" on the obverse from "In God we trust" on the reverse (refer to Kimpton, 2005).

■ **Comments:** The dramatic doubling makes this relatively scarce VAM quite popular.

■ **Certified VAMs 11, 11A:** 1,019   **PL:** 0   **DMPL:** 0

CC:	66ᴺ	65ᴾᴺᴬ	Mult.			

VAM: 1A / **Clashed Die Reverse** / **PF:** 8
Ref: FS ($1-1888o-001a), K, Q, V

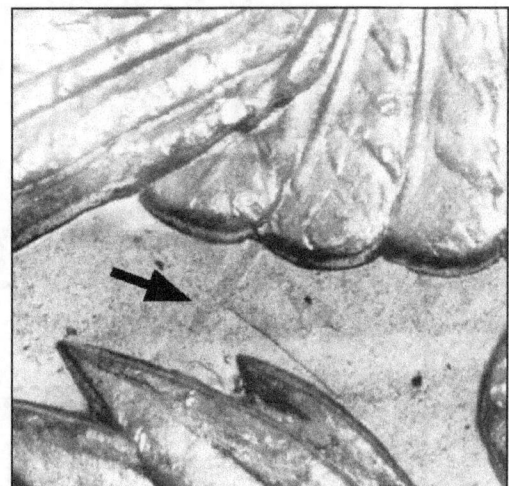

Obverse die break   Clashed "E" on reverse

Grade	VAM 1A	Com	PL	Com	DMPL	Com	RF
MS-65	NTH	550	UNK		UNK		8
MS-64	350	75					7
MS-63	225	45					7
MS-62	160	40					6
MS-61	150	35					6
MS-60	140	30					5

■ **Key Identifiers:** A partial "E" (two-thirds complete) is visible under the eagle's tailfeathers to the left of the ribbon bow. A large obverse die crack runs from the rim down through the "R" of PLURIBUS on later-die-state specimens.

■ **Comments:** Once thought to be quite rare, more Mint State specimens have surfaced than expected. John Roberts discovered the first known example of an "O"-mintmark clash on the obverse of this variety.

■ **Certified VAM 1A:** 634   **PL:** 0   **DMPL:** 0

CC:	65P	65P	64PNA	Mult.		

VAM: 1B LDS / **Die Break Obverse** / **PF:** 10
Ref: FS ($1-1888o-001b), Q, V

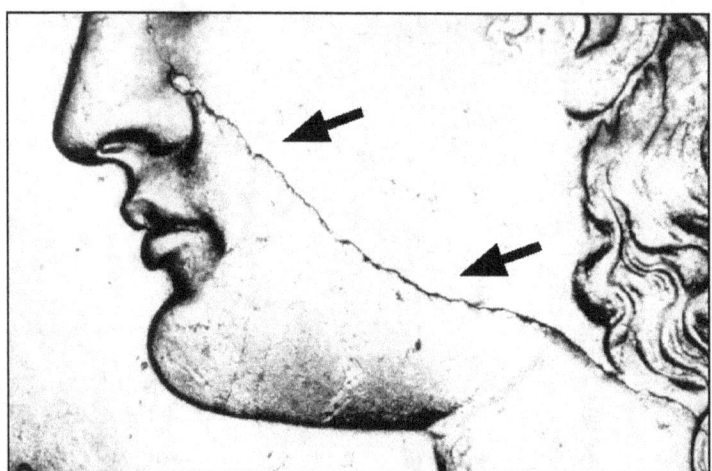

Die break across Liberty's cheek

Grade	VAM 1B	Com	PL	Com	DMPL	Com	RF
MS-64	9.5K	75	UNK		UNK		8
MS-63	8.9K	45					7
MS-62	5K	40					7
MS-61	3.5K	35					7
MS-60	2.5K	30					7
AU-50	NTH	20					6+

■ **Key Identifier:** A major die break runs from the rim, between the "E" and the "P" of PLURIBUS into the field, and down across Liberty's nose and cheek.

■ **Comments:** The VAM 1B is the most dramatic die break in the Morgan dollar series. The "Scarface" is rare in all grades and in great demand. It is rarely seen in Circulated grades, indicating that most surviving specimens were dispersed from the GSA hoard. Early Die State examples showing less of the die break bring *much* lower premiums than the Late Die State specimen seen here.

■ **Certified VAM 1B:** 156   **PL:** 0   **DMPL:** 0

CC:	64P	63PNA	Mult.			

VAM: 4 / **Doubled Die Obverse** / **PF:** 10
Ref: B (5603), FS ($1-006) ($1-1888o-002), Q, R, V

▶ Doubling on Ms. Liberty's nose, lips and chin

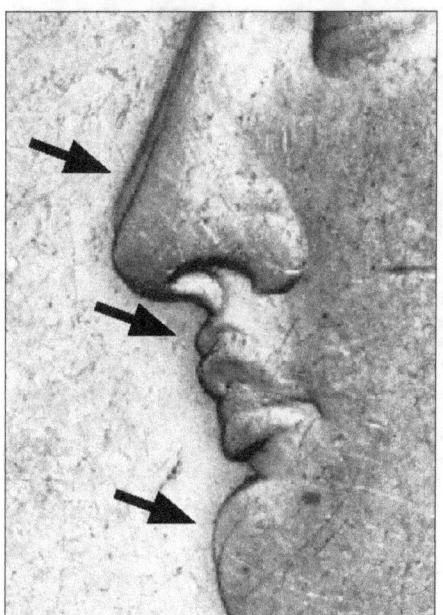

Grade	VAM 4	Com	PL	Com	DMPL	Com	RF
MS-61	12K+	35	UNK		UNK		8
AU-58	8K+	30			NTH*	50	7
AU-55	3.1K	25					7
AU-50	1.4K	20					6
XF-40	350	18					5
VF-30	250	17					4

■ **Key Identifier:** Liberty's profile is so strongly doubled that two complete sets of noses, lips and chins are clearly defined.

■ **Comments:** The whimsically named "Hot Lips" variety is the No. 1 doubled-die obverse in the Morgan dollar series. Only six Mint State specimens are known. All are low-grade Mint State with the Finest Known grading MS-61.

■ **Certified VAM 4:** 1,523   **PL:** 0   **DMPL:** 2

CC:	61P	61N	61N	61N	60DMP	60P

*Leroy Van Allen's PCGS MS-60 DMPL sold for $25.3K in 2008.

VAM: 9 / **Doubled Die Reverse** / **PF:** 7
Ref: B (5602), Q, V

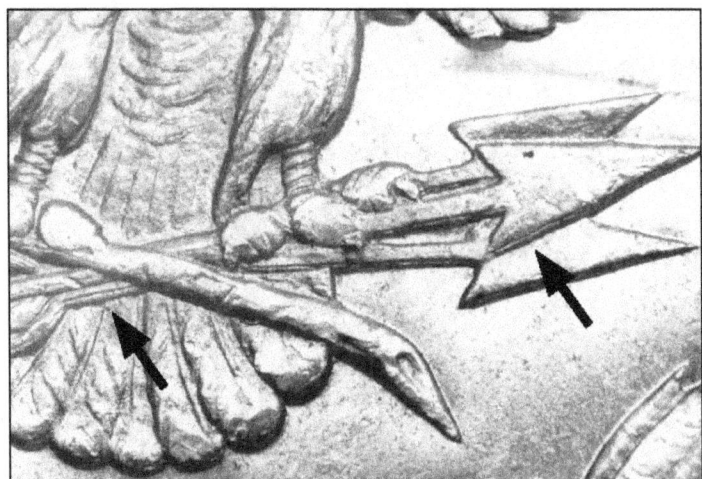

Doubled arrow shaft and arrowheads

Grade	VAM 9	Com	PL	Com	DMPL	Com	RF
MS-66	2.7K	2K					8
MS-65	750	550	950	650	NTH	2.4K	7
MS-64	325	75	500	90	750	400	6
MS-63	150	45	175	60	250	90	5
MS-62	100	40					5
MS-60	60	35					4

■ **Key Identifier:** The lower reverse, particularly the bottom of the arrow shafts and arrowheads, shows strong doubling.

■ **Comments:** Although not as rare as the VAM Book indicates, the VAM 9 is nevertheless desirable as a strong doubled die. VAM 9 also shows a misplaced date with "18-8" repunched into the denticles. This variety is also known with rotated dies.

■ **Certified VAM 9:** 757   **PL:** 41   **DMPL:** 39

CC:	66DM[N]	66[PN]	Mult.			

VAMs: 2, 5, 6, 17, 18, 21, 24, 34
Oval "O" Mintmark Varieties / PF: 8
Ref: D, FS ($1-1888o-301), Q, V

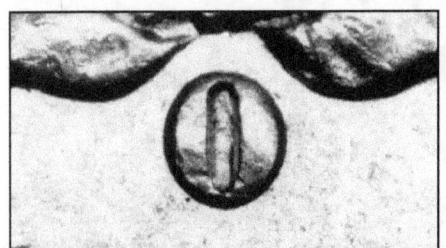

Scarce medium Oval "O"   Common medium Round "O"

Grade	VAMs/5 & 34	Com	PL	Com	DMPL	Com	RF
MS-64	NTH	75	UNK		UNK		8
MS-63	1.2K+	45					7
MS-60	450	40					6
AU-58	300	35					6
AU-50	250	20					6
XF-40	85/1K+	18					5/7+

■ **Key Identifier:** The mintmark is a medium-size oval rather than the much more common medium-size round "O".

■ **Comments:** All of the eight known 1888-O Oval "O" varieties are vastly underappreciated in relation to their rarity in Mint State. VAM 5 and the newly discovered VAM 34 are *ultra rare* in all grades. VAM 24 is rarer than VAMs 2, 6, 17, 18 and 21 Oval "O" varieties. There are no complete Mint State sets known, and only three complete sets of Circulated coins. For further information and images of the rare VAM 24 and *ultra rare* VAMs 5 and 34, refer to Van Allen Supplements, (2008). Pricing for VAMs 5 and 34 is substantially higher than for others. An Extra Fine of either would likely trade in excess of $1,000. (See page 7A.)

■ **Certified VAMs:** 576   **PL:** 0   **DMPL:** 0

CC: All Oval "O"s*	64P	64P	63PNA	Mult.		

*A combined census of the most common of the eight varieties

VAMs: 19A (formerly 5A), 19B, 22
Die Break Reverse / PF: 7
Ref: K, FS ($1-1889-019a & $1-1889-022), V

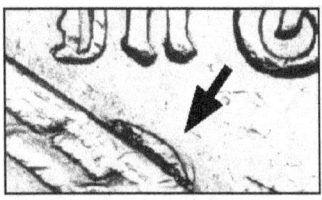

Die break above wing

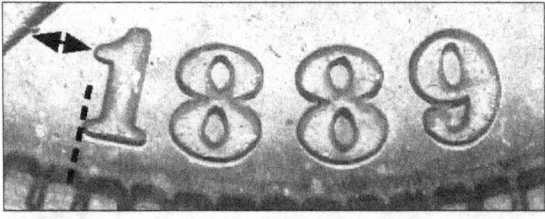

VAM 19A, and VAM 22 Far Date (below)

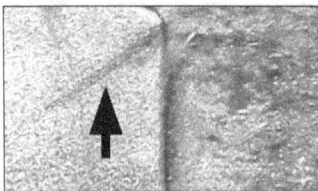

VAM 19B die clash
by Liberty's neck

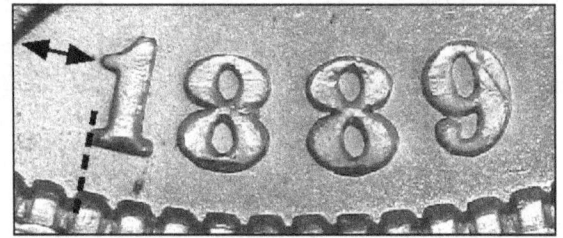

Grade	VAM 19A & 22	Com	PL	Com	DMPL	Com	RF
MS-65	550+	350					8
MS-64	400	60					7+
MS-63	375	45					6+
MS-62	200	40					6
MS-60	150	35					5
AU-50	85	20					5

■ **Key Identifier:** A die break in the form of raised metal is visible along the top edge of the eagle's right wing.

■ **Comments:** Created by a clash-damaged die, VAMs 19A and 22 are about equally scarce. VAM 22 is a far date – its date is farther from Ms. Liberty's neck than on VAM 19A. VAM 19B, a recent discovery, has a die clash line extending from Liberty's neck.

■ **Certified VAMs 19A, 19B:** 302   **PL:** 0   **DMPL:** 0
■ **Certified VAM 22:** 309   **PL:** 0   **DMPL:** 0

CC: VAMs 19A/19B	65PN	Mult.			
VAM 22	65P	Mult.			

VAMs: 1A1 (single clash), 1A2 (double clash)
Clashed Die Reverse / PF: 10
Ref: D, FS ($1-006.5) ($1-1889o-001a), K, Q, V

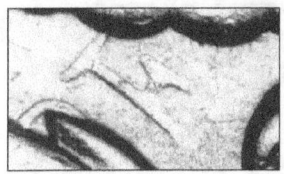

"E" on reverse

"O" mintmark clash on the obverse

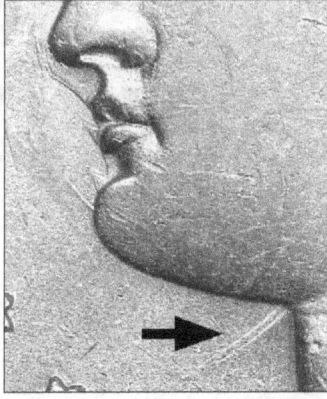

Double clash marks on the obverse

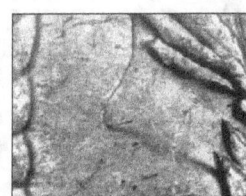

Single-clash 1A1

Double-clash 1A2

Grade	VAM 1A1/1A2	Com	PL	Com	DMPL	Com	RF
MS-61	NTH	140	UNK		UNK		8
MS-60	1K+	115			NTH		8
AU-58	900	75					7
AU-55	800	40					7
AU-50	750	30					6/8
XF-40	350/1K+	20					6/7+

■ **Key Identifiers:** Most of an "E" is visible underneath the eagle's tailfeathers to the left of the ribbon bow. Can be found with single and double clash marks, the double being *much* rarer.

■ **Comments:** Both are rare in all grades, with only five low-grade MS 1A1 varieties known. Kimpton (2005) dubbed VAM 1A2 the "King of Clashed Varieties," with its "O" mintmark and letters "G, t, r, d" from "In God we trust" clashed on the obverse.

■ **Certified VAM 1A1:** 130 **PL:** 0 **DMPL:** 1
■ **Certified VAM 1A2:** 7 **PL:** 0 **DMPL:** 0

CC: VAM 1A1	61A	61N	61S	60A	60A	58PNA
VAM 1A2	53N	50A	45A	45S	30A	12A

VAMs: 2, 2A (formerly VAM 17)
Oval "O" Mintmark Varieties / PF: 8
Ref: B (5606), Q, V

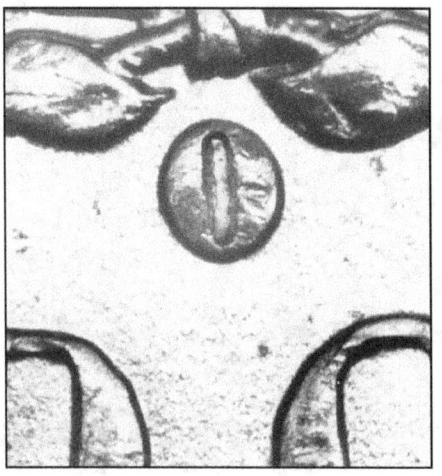

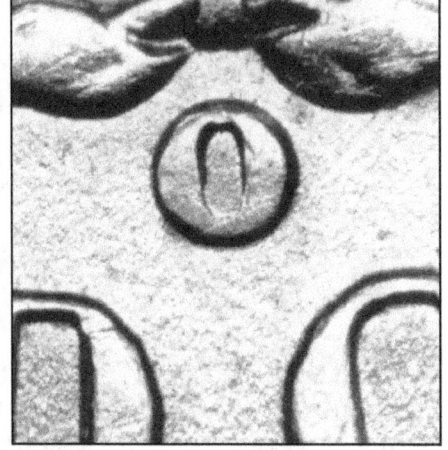

Scarce Oval "O" mintmark   Common round "O" mintmark

Grade	VAM 2/2A	Com	PL	Com	DMPL	Com	RF
MS-64	1.65K+	800	UNK		UNK		8
MS-63	NTH	375					7+
MS-62	1.5K	175					7+
MS-60	375	120					7
AU-58	325	50					6
AU-50	135	30					6

■ **Key Identifier:** The mintmark is a medium-size oval rather than the much more common medium-size round "O".

■ **Comments:** Only two Oval "O" varieties are known for this date, VAMs 2 and 2A, with the latter showing double clash lines extending from Ms. Liberty's neck. Both are highly desirable in Mint State. The census that follows is a compilation of both. VAM 17 was delisted, as it was found to be the same as VAM 2.

■ **Certified VAMs 2, 2A:** 727   **PL:** 0   **DMPL:** 0

CC:	64P	64P	62PNA	Mult.		

VAM: 6 / **Repunched Date** / **PF:** 7
Ref: V

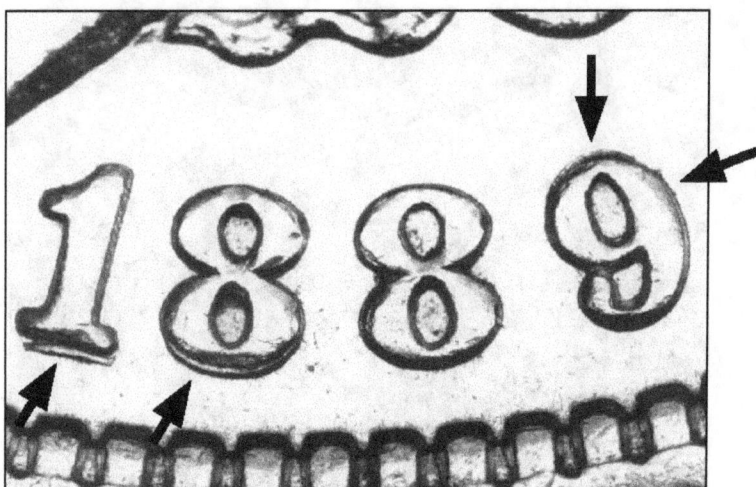

The doubled numerals of the date

Grade	VAM 6	Com	PL	Com	DMPL	Com	RF
MS-64	NTH	800					7
MS-63	400	375					7
MS-62	300	175					6
MS-60	200	120					6
AU-58	175	50					6
AU-50	145	30					5

■ **Key Identifier:** The first two numerals and the last numeral of the date ("18-9") are strongly doubled.

■ **Comments:** One of the most dramatic Morgan dollar repunched dates, and vastly underappreciated.

■ **Certified VAM 6:** 198   **PL:** 0   **DMPL:** 0

CC:	66P	64PNA	Mult.			

VAM: 4 / **Die Gouge on Reverse** / **PF:** 10
Ref: B (5597), F, FS ($1-007) ($1-1890cc-004), Q, V

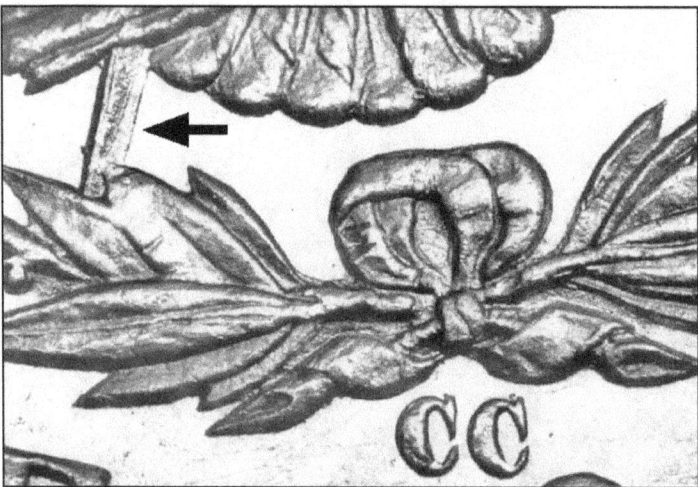

Die gouge to the left of the eagle's tailfeathers

Grade	VAM 4	Com	PL	Com	DMPL	Com	RF
MS-65	13.2K	5.5K	UNK		UNK	14.5K	8
MS-64	4.2K	1.5K	NTH		8K	3K	7
MS-63	2.5K	735	5.7K	900		1.4K	7
MS-62	2K	500					6
MS-60	1.5K	380					5
AU-50	750	200					5

■ **Key Identifier:** A spectacular die gouge runs from the junction of the arrow feathers and the eagle's tailfeathers to the wreath below.

■ **Comments:** A classic eyeball-noticeable variety that is a perennial favorite.

■ **Certified VAM 4:** 626   **PL:** 8   **DMPL:** 17

CC:	65^N	64DM^{PN}	Mult.			

VAMs: 2, 2A, 2B / **Doubled Die Obverse** / PF: 8/10
Ref: K, Q, V

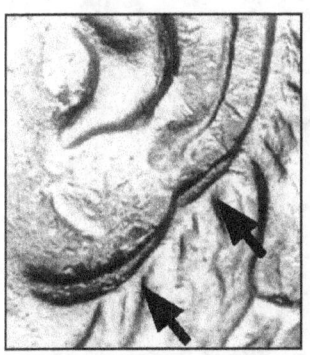 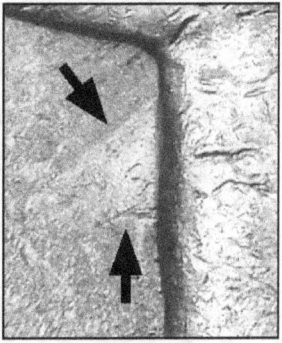 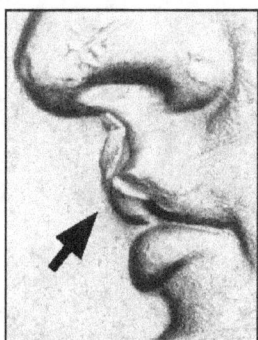

Doubled ear feature   VAM 2B clash mark   VAM 2A

Grade	VAM 2 & 2B/2A	Com	PL	Com	DMPL	Com	RF 2 & 2B/2A
MS-64	NTH	700	UNK		UNK	6.5K	7
MS-63	250	155	NTH	500	NTH	1.9K	6
MS-60	125/2.5K	45					6/8
AU-50	95/750	30					6/7
XF-40	50/600	20					5/7
VF-30	20/550	18					4/7

■ **Key Identifiers:** Liberty's ear shows strong doubling on the bottom edge, as well as halfway up the back. VAM 2A shows a "moustache"-like die break next to Ms. Liberty's lip, while VAM 2B has an incuse "n" clash in the field next to Liberty's neck.

■ **Comments:** The rare Late Die State of this variety, which commands a substantial premium, exhibits a die break above Liberty's lip, called the "moustache" variety. The Finest Known of this LDS is an MS-60. An *ultra rare* earlier die state "moustache" is known with about half the moustache. It too commands a substantial premium, although lower than that of the LDS.

■ **Certified VAMs 2, 2B:** 791 **PL:** 10 **DMPL:** 14
■ **Certified VAM 2A:** 93 **PL:** 0 **DMPL:** 0

CC: VAMs 2/2B	66PL[N]	66PL[N]	66PL[N]	65[P]	64DM[P]	64DM[A]
VAM 2A	60[S]	58[NA]	Mult.			

VAM: 3 / **Die Gouge on Reverse** / **PF:** 7
Ref: B (5624), Q, V

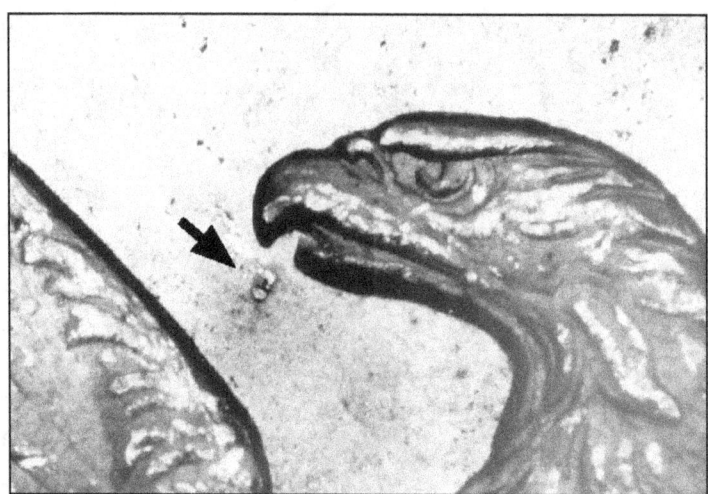

Reverse die gouge

Grade	VAM 3	Com	PL	Com	DMPL	Com	RF
MS-65	8.3K	8.3K	3.7K	3.7K	28.5K	28.5K	7
MS-64	1.2K	1.2K	1K	1K	4.8K	4.8K	6
MS-63	300	300	700	700	2.1K	2.1K	5
MS-62	225	225					4
MS-61	200	200					4
MS-60	190	190					4

■ **Key Identifier:** Whimsically named the "Spitting Eagle," the die gouge in front of the eagle's beak lends its name to the variety.

■ **Comments:** Heavily promoted, the VAM 3 is **NOT RARE**, but is actually one of the most common of all the 1890-CC varieties! While popular, we recommend that you acquire as close to the common price as possible.

■ **Certified VAM 3:** 3,614   **PL:** 39   **DMPL:** 39

CC:	66P	66N	65PNA	Mult.		

VAMs: 1A1, 1A2, 1A3 / **Clashed Die Reverse** / **PF:** 9
Ref: K, FS ($1-1891o-001a), V

  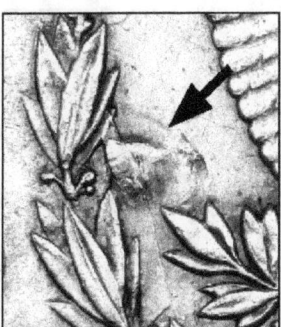

Clashed "E" by bow   Clash on 1A1   Die break on 1A3

Grade	VAM 1A1	Com	PL	Com	DMPL	Com	RF
MS-63	1K+	285	UNK		UNK		8
MS-62	750	175					7+
MS-61	450	125					7+
MS-60	400+	115					7+
AU-50	250	35					6
XF-40	120	20					5

■ **Key Identifiers:** A strong "E" sits under the eagle's tailfeathers to the left of the ribbon bow. Portions of "B" and "R" from LIBERTY may also be seen. VAM 1A2, an even later die state, also shows the incuse image of Liberty's eye socket inside the lower reverse right wreath. VAM 1A3 shows a die break near the left side of the wreath. This is the latest die state currently known.

■ **Comments:** VAM 1A1 exhibits the most complete "E" of any clashed reverse variety, and is *ultra rare* in BU; less than 10 Uncirculated specimens have been confirmed. According to Kimpton (2005), a clashed "O" mintmark can be seen on the obverse as well as a "D" from DOLLAR on the reverse. The VLDS VAM 1A3 is the rarest and most desirable die state. A rare and desirable *Hot 50* weak "E" – VAM 3A – is also known (refer to Oxman, 2008).

■ **Certified VAM 1A1*:** 470 **PL:** 0 **DMPL:** 0

CC*:	63A	62P	62N	62A	61PA	Mult.

*Pricing, condition census data for 1A2 / 1A3 are not currently known.

VAM: 3 / **Doubled Die Obverse** / **PF:** 7
Ref: V

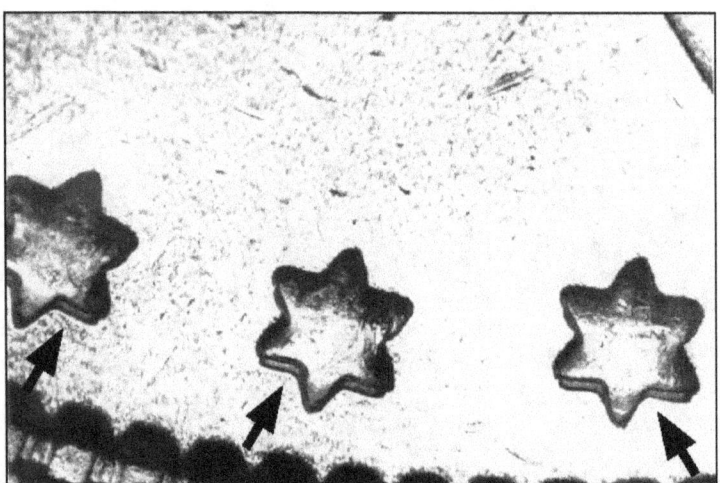

Doubled left stars

Grade	VAM 3	Com	PL	Com	DMPL	Com	RF
MS-64	NTH	250	UNK		UNK		7
MS-63	375	110					7
MS-62	135	75					7
MS-60	100	50					7
AU-50	80	30					6
XF-40	30	18					6

■ **Key Identifier:** Stars to the left of the date are doubled toward the rim.

■ **Comments:** The VAM 3 is the top 1891-S variety and is underappreciated, given its rarity.

■ **Certified VAM 3:** 211 **PL:** 0 **DMPL:** 0

CC:	64PN	Mult.			

VAM: 5 / **Doubled Die Obverse** / **PF:** 7
Ref: Q, V

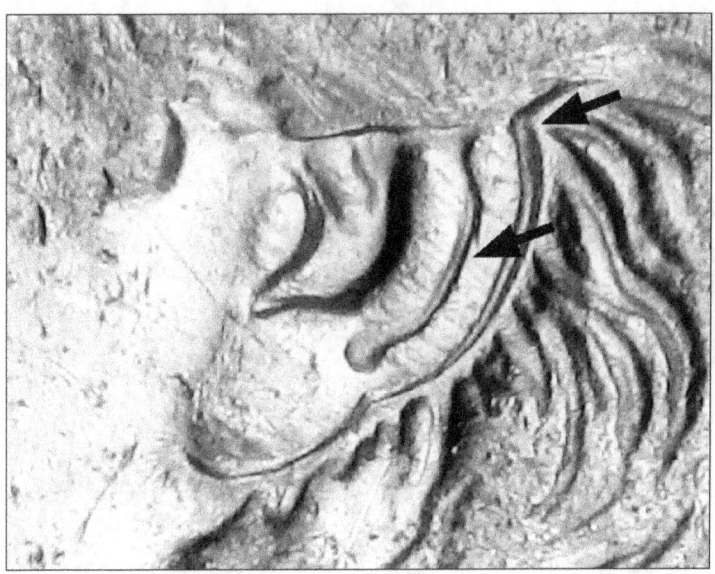

Doubling on Liberty's ear along the outer edges

Grade	VAM 5	Com	PL	Com	DMPL	Com	RF
MS-63	NTH	265	NTH		NTH		8
MS-62	220	175					7
MS-60	175	130					7
AU-58	125	85					6
AU-50	85	60					6
XF-40	60	35					5

■ **Key Identifiers:** Liberty's ear is doubled along the upper outside edge, as well as on the left inside.

■ **Comments:** The typical VAM 5 is weakly struck around Liberty's ear, making attribution difficult. Well-struck specimens are worth a premium.

■ **Certified VAM 5:** 315   **PL:** 0   **DMPL:** 0

CC:	64DM^P	64^P	64^P	64^P	64^P	63^A

VAM: 2 / **Repunched Date** / **PF:** 8
Ref: B (5628), Q, V

Obverse doubled date

Grade	VAM 2	Com	PL	Com	DMPL	Com	RF
AU-58	NTH	7.8K		UNK		UNK	7+
AU-55	NTH	2.5K					7
AU-50	NTH	1.6K					7
XF-45	1.27K	375					6+
XF-40	450	310					6+
VF-30	250	120					5

■ **Key Identifier:** All the numerals of the date are doubled, with the top inside of the "8" most prominent.

■ **Comments:** Only one Mint State specimen has come to light, and even in Circulated grades the VAM 2 is very scarce. Rare and desirable in grades of XF/AU and better.

■ **Certified VAM 2:** 164　**PL:** 0　**DMPL:** 1

CC:	61DMᴾ	58ᴾᴺᴬ	Mult.			

VAM: 4 / **Doubled Die Obverse** / **PF:** 7
Ref: V

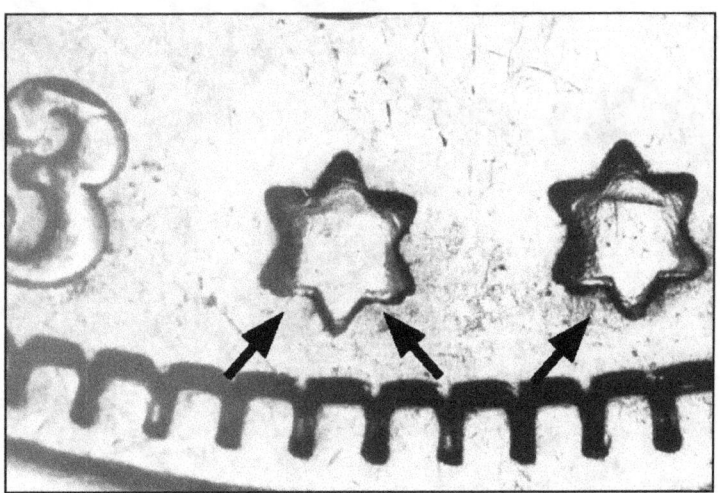

Obverse doubled stars

Grade	VAM 4	Com	PL	Com	DMPL	Com	RF
MS-63	NTH	1.1K	UNK		UNK		8
MS-62	975	750					7
MS-60	800	625					7
AU-58	500	400					6+
AU-50	425	320					6
XF-40	350	250					6

■ **Key Identifier:** All of the obverse stars on both sides of the date are doubled toward the rim.

■ **Comments:** This is considered to be the top 1893-P variety and is rare in BU condition.

■ **Certified VAM 4:** 701 **PL:** 7 **DMPL:** 0

CC:	64P	63PNA	Mult.			

VAM: 4 / **Repunched Mintmark** / **PF:** 7
Ref: B (5640), Q, V

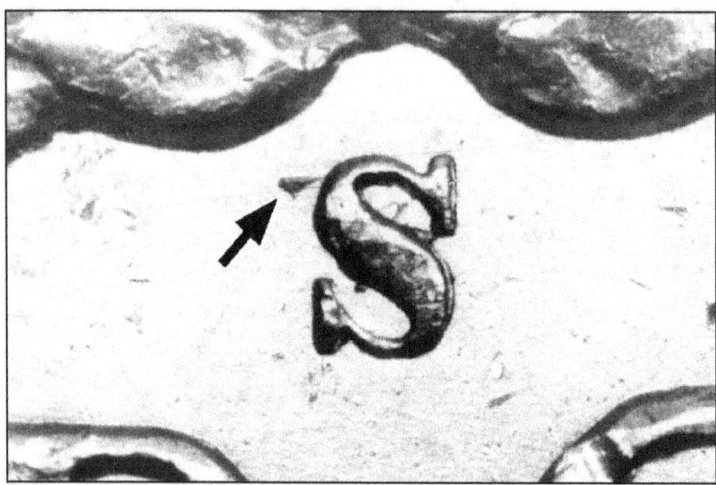

1895-S "S/Horizontal S"

Grade	VAM 4	Com	PL	Com	DMPL	Com	RF
MS-64	NTH	7.8K	NTH	9K	NTH	17K	7+
MS-63	6.5K	5.7K	7.5K	6.5K	NTH	9K	7
MS-60	4.5K	3.4K					7
AU-58	3.5K	2.5K					6
AU-50	2.5K	1.8K					6
XF-40	1.5K	1K					6

■ **Key Identifier:** A small triangular area of raised metal is visible to the top left of the mintmark, which represents the serif of a horizontally punched "S".

■ **Comments:** The VAM 4 is usually found with Proof-like surfaces, and is the only "S/Horizontal S" Morgan dollar variety. VAM 4 should not be confused with the *Hot 50* VAM 3, another rare "S/S" variety (refer to Oxman, 2008).

■ **Certified VAM 4:** 156   **PL:** 28   **DMPL:** 15

CC:	66P	65DMA	65DMA	64DMA	64DMA	64PLPNA

VAM: 4 / **Doubled Die Obverse** / **PF:** 7
Ref: B (5643), V

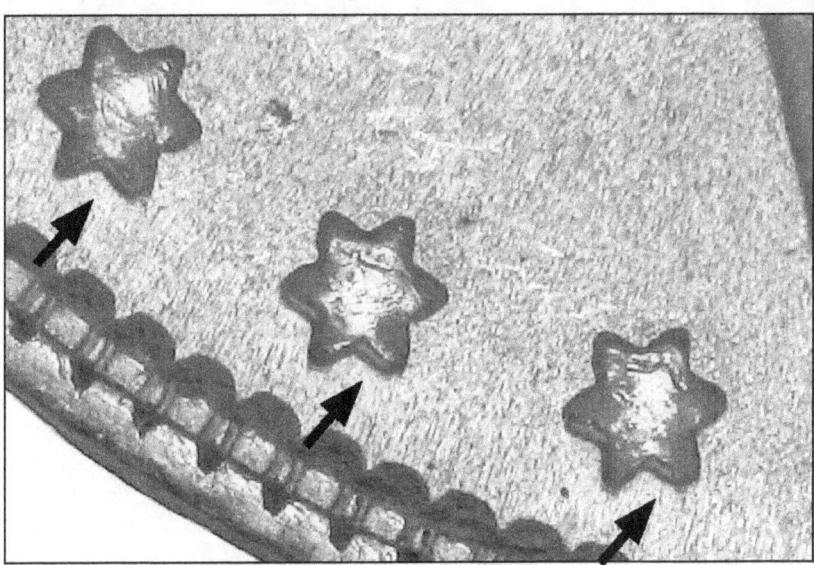

Obverse doubled stars

Grade	VAM 4	Com	PL	Com	DMPL	Com	RF
MS-65	400	175	UNK		UNK		8
MS-64	225	60	NTH	90	NTH	300	7
MS-63	185	45	NTH	65	NTH	90	6+
MS-62	125	40					6
MS-60	65	35					5
AU-50	40	20					5

■ **Key Identifier:** All the stars to the left and right of the date are doubled toward the rim.

■ **Comments:** Much scarcer than generally realized, the VAM 4 is the only catalogued 1896-P doubled die with doubled stars and a doubled eye.

■ **Certified VAM 4:** 317   **PL:** 3   **DMPL:** 3

CC:	66P	65PNA	Mult.			

VAM: 19 / **Misplaced Date** / **PF:** 7
Ref: V

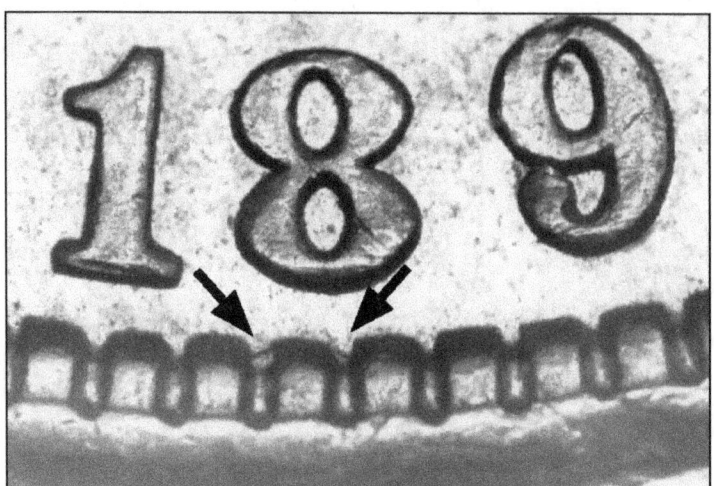

The "8" in the denticles

Grade	VAM 19	Com	PL	Com	DMPL	Com	RF
MS-65	300	175	UNK		UNK		7
MS-64	115	60	NTH	90	NTH	300	6
MS-63	100	45	NTH	65	NTH	90	6
MS-62	80	40					5
MS-60	70	35					4
AU-50	30	20					4

■ **Key Identifier:** The curved top of another "8" is visible in the denticles, directly under the "8" in the date.

■ **Comments:** VAM 19 was discovered a decade ago and is now one of many Morgan dollar varieties to show a misplaced numeral in the denticles.

■ **Certified VAM 19:** 358   **PL:** 4   **DMPL:** 5

CC:	66P	65PNA	Mult.			

VAM: 4 / **Mintmark Variety-type** / **PF:** 10
Ref: B (5648), D, FS ($1-008) ($1-1896o-004), Q, V, V2

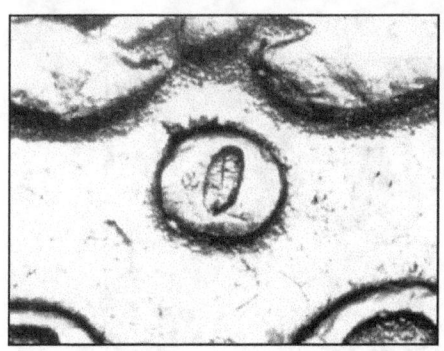

The Micro "o" mintmark

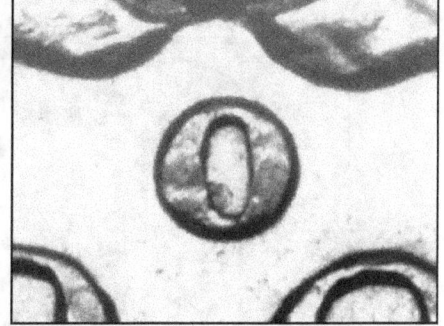

The normal "O" mintmark

Grade	VAM 4	Com	PL	Com	DMPL	Com	RF
AU-58	NTH		UNK		UNK		8
AU-50	NTH						7
XF-40	3000						7
VF-30	900						7
F-15	800						7
VG-8	250						7

■ **Key Identifiers:** The mintmark, always tilted to the right, is a Micro "o" rather than the much more common medium-size "O". Same reverse as the 1900-O and 1902-O Micro "o"s.

■ **Comments:** *Ultra rare* in all grades above Fine, the VAM 4 (like all post-1900 Micro "o" varieties) is both rare and highly desirable. Likely made at a private mint and often found well-Circulated in low grades, VAM 4 may have been a contemporary counterfeit that circulated along with other silver dollars without notice. No longer certified by major grading services, VAM 4 is still a variety cherished by collectors. A more detailed history of this is given by Fey (2008) and Van Allen (2005).

■ **Certified VAM 4:** No longer certified.

CC:	58N	55A	50A	50A	45PA	Mult.

VAM: 6A (VAM 1A does not exist)
Pitted Reverse Die / PF: 7
Ref: V

Pitting on lower reverse

Grade	VAM 6A	Com	PL	Com	DMPL	Com	RF
MS-66	NTH	1K	UNK		UNK		7+
MS-65	350	300					7
MS-64	150	60					6+
MS-63	140	45					5
MS-60	65	35					5
AU-50	45	18					4

■ **Key Identifier:** The wreath to the left of the ribbon, and the areas around it, show dramatic pitting.

■ **Comments:** VAM 1A is now believed not to exist, as all specimens seen are VAM 6A (the same reverse with date set to the left).

■ **Certified VAM 6A:** 1,135 **PL:** 0 **DMPL:** 0

CC:	66PN	Mult.				

VAMs: 4, 5, 6, 31, 32 / **Mintmark Variety-type** / **PF:** 10
Ref: B (5660), D, FS ($1-1899o-501), Q, V, V3

◀ VAM 4, normal date placement

▶ VAM 6, near date placement

▲ Note alignment with denticle. ▲

▶ Micro "o" mintmark

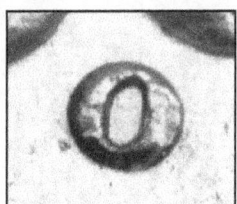

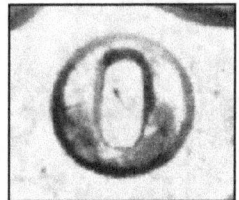

◀ Normal medium "O"

Grade	VAMs	Com	PL	Com	DMPL	Com	RF
MS-65	NTH	175	UNK		UNK		8
MS-63	2.4K+	45					7
MS-62	1.5K	40					7
MS-60	500	35					7
AU-50	180	18					6
XF-40	135	17					5

■ **Key Identifiers:** Identification can be made by date and mintmark positions, die lines and die cracks.

■ **Comments:** All varieties are rare in BU. VAM 32 appears to be the rarest of all the 1899-O Micro "o" varieties. Unlike the 1896-O, 1900-O and 1902-O Micro "o" varieties, there is no question that the 1899-O Micro "o"s were struck at the U.S. Mint. A detailed population and additional images are provided on pages 9A-10A.

■ **Certified VAMs:** 1,356 **PL:** 1 **DMPL:** 1

CC:	65P	65P	64PN	Mult.		

VAM: 7 / **Repunched Date** / **PF:** 7
Ref: V

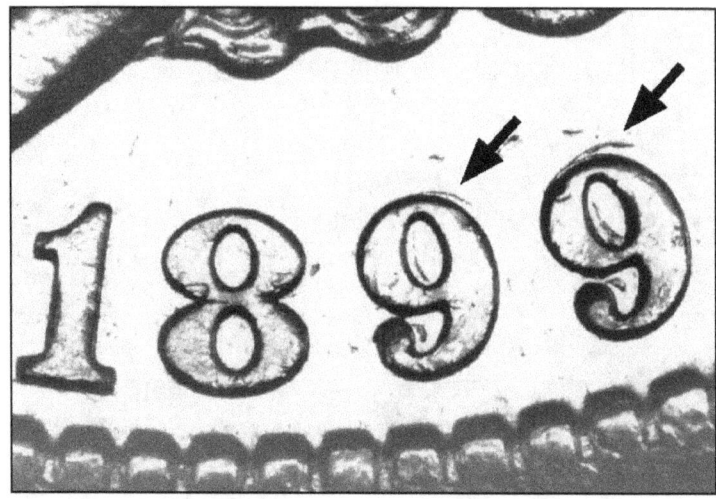

The doubled date

Grade	VAM 7	Com	PL	Com	DMPL	Com	RF
MS-65	NTH	1.8K	UNK		UNK		7
MS-64	NTH	700	NTH	800			6
MS-63	475	400	NTH	500			6
MS-62	375	325					6
MS-60	350	270					5
AU-50	175	100					5

■ **Key Identifier:** An arc trails off the top of each "9", showing the uneffaced remains of a date punched higher.

■ **Comments:** As a strongly doubled date, VAM 7 is both dramatic and popular.

■ **Certified VAM 7:** 336   **PL:** 0   **DMPL:** 0

CC:	67N	66P	65PNA	Mult.		

VAMs: 11, 24 / **Doubled Die Reverse** / **PF:** 8
Ref: B (5667), D, V

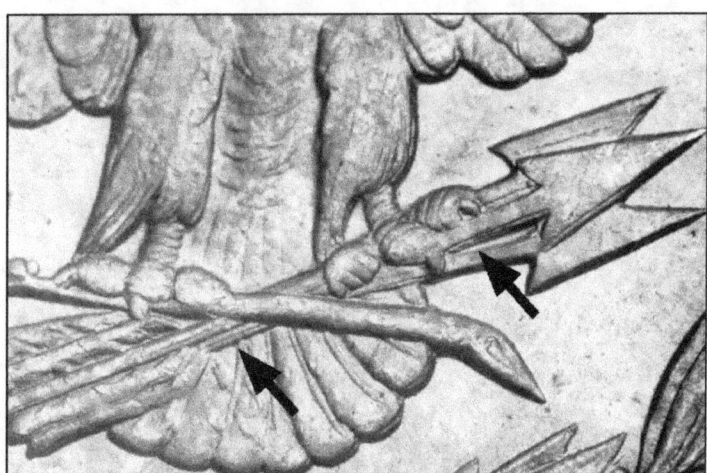

Doubled arrows on the reverse

Grade	VAM 11/24	Com	PL	Com	DMPL	Com	RF
MS-65	500	185	UNK		UNK		7/8
MS-64	200	60					6/7
MS-63	180	45					6/7
MS-62	150	40					6/7
MS-61	125	37					5/6
MS-60	115	35					5/6

■ **Key Identifiers:** The eagle and most of the design features around it have dramatic doubling. VAM 24 shows multiple punching on the stars to the right of the date and an "alligator eye."

■ **Comments:** Even though VAM 24 was discovered after VAM 11, VAM 11 appears to be the rarer of the two varieties, although both varieties are currently priced the same. Many older coins attributed as VAM 11 are likely to be VAM 24.

■ **Certified VAM 11:** 494 **PL:** 1 **DMPL:** 0
■ **Certified VAM 24:** 573 **PL:** 0 **DMPL:** 0

CC: VAM 11	65^N	65NA	Mult.		
VAM 24	66^P	66^P	65^{PN}	Mult.	

VAM: 5 / **Mintmark Variety-type** / **PF:** 10
Ref: B (5669), FS ($1-009) ($1-1900o-005), V2

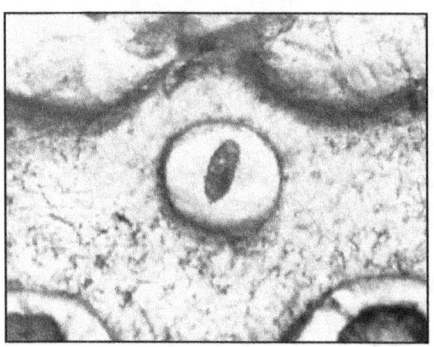 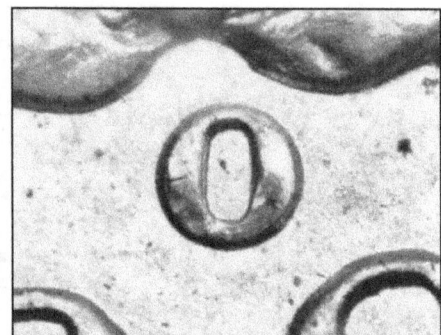

Micro "o" reverse   Medium "O" reverse

Grade	VAM 5	Com	PL	Com	DMPL	Com	RF
AU-58	NTH	25	UNK		UNK		8
AU-50	5K	20					7+
XF-40	3.5K	18					7+
VF-30	2.6K	17					7
F-15	400	16.5					7
VG-8	250	16.5					7

■ **Key Identifiers:** The mintmark, always tilted to the right, is a Micro "o" rather than the usual medium-size "O". Same reverse as the 1896-O and 1902-O Micro "o" Morgans.

■ **Comments:** *Ultra rare* in all grades above Fine, the VAM 5 (like the 1896-O and 1902-O Micro "o" varieties) is both rare and highly desirable. Likely made at a private mint and often found well-Circulated. VAM 5 may have been a contemporary counterfeit that circulated along with other silver dollars without notice. No longer certified by major grading services, VAM 5 is still a variety cherished by collectors. A more detailed history is given by Fey (2008) and Van Allen (2005).

■ **Certified VAM 5:** No longer certified.

CC:	58A	53P	53S	50A	Mult.	

VAMs: 15, 15A / **Doubled Die Obverse** / **PF:** 7
Ref: V

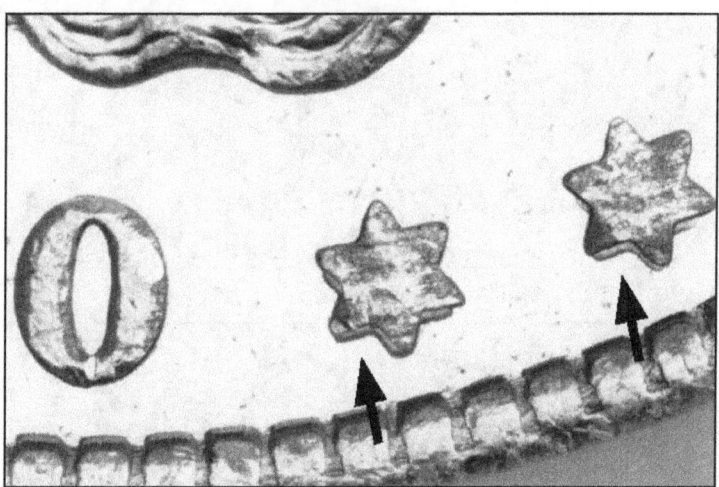

Doubled stars to the right of the date

Grade	VAM 15/15A	Com	PL	Com	DMPL	Com	RF
MS-65	425	175	600	250	UNK	5K	7
MS-64	200	60	350	100	850	725	6
MS-63	160	45	250	75	500	350	6
MS-62	75	40					5
MS-60	50	35					5
AU-50	25	18					4

■ **Key Identifiers:** The stars to the right of the date exhibit the strongest doubling of any post-1878 Morgan dollar. VAM 15A shows a partial incuse "n" from "In" on the reverse in the field next to Liberty's neck.

■ **Comments:** When found, the VAM 15 is often quite attractive and is frequently seen with reflective surfaces.

■ **Certified VAMs 15, 15A:** 729 **PL:** 26 **DMPL:** 4

CC:	66PNA	Mult.				

VAM: 29A / **Obverse Die Break** / **PF:** 10
Ref: FS ($1-1900o-029a), Q, V

Rare Late Die State of VAM 29A

The common die cracks of VAM 41A

Grade	VAM 29A	Com	PL	Com	DMPL	Com	RF
MS-62	NTH	40	UNK		UNK		8
MS-61	NTH	37					7+
AU-58	1.68K+	30					7+
AU-50	750	18					7
XF-40	500	16.5					7
VF-30	250	16.5					6+

■ **Key Identifier:** A spectacular die break runs from the denticles under the "Vee" of Liberty's neck through the "190" of the date.

■ **Comments:** The late stage of this die break is one of the most prominent breaks on any Morgan dollar and is very rare. This should not be confused with VAM 41A, which shows similar die cracks but not die breaks (i.e., raised metal on the surface of the coin). To differentiate, ensure that the die break starts at the denticles as shown above and follows exactly the same path.

■ **Certified VAM 29A:** 217   **PL:** 0   **DMPL:** 0

CC:	64A	63P	62P	62N	61N	61N

VAM: 9 / **Over-mintmark** / **PF:** 10
Ref: B (5671), FS ($1-1900o-501/009.5), H2, Q, V

 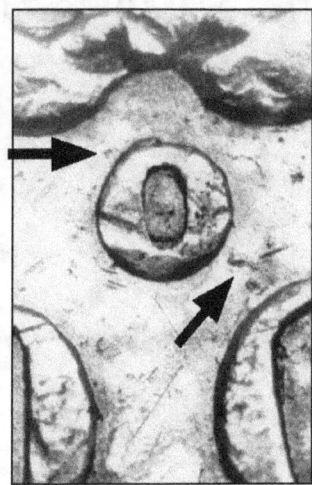

Doubled "00" in the date   The "O/CC" mintmark

Grade	VAM 9	Com	PL	Com	DMPL	Com	RF
MS-64	8.5K	60	UNK		UNK		8
MS-63	2.75K	45					8
MS-60	1.5K	35					8
AU-50	600	20					7
XF-40	350	18					7
VF-30	150	16.5					6+

■ **Key Identifiers:** The bottom of an underlying "C" is visible to the right of the "O" mintmark and is disconnected from it. The top inside of the zeros in the date are doubled.

■ **Comments:** VAM 9 is a key "O/CC" variety, and is highly prized by specialists. Further information about "O/CC" varieties is provided on pages 11A-12A.

■ **Certified VAM 9:** 128   **PL:** 0   **DMPL:** 0

CC:	64P	64N	64N	64N	64A	62P

VAMs: 7, 7A, 8, 8A, 8B, 10, 10A, 11, 12
Over-mintmarks / PF: 10
Ref: B (5671), FS ($1-009.5) ($1-1900o-501), Q, V

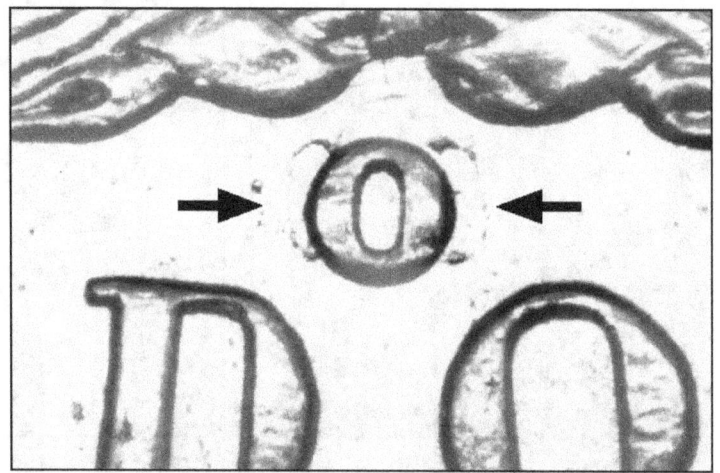

Example of the "O/CC" reverse (VAM 12)

Grade	VAMs	Com	PL	Com	DMPL	Com	RF
MS-65	2K	175	UNK		UNK		7
MS-64	1K	60					6
MS-63	750	45					5
MS-62	475	40					5
MS-61	350	37					5
MS-60	280	35					5

■ **Key Identifier:** The remains of an underlying "CC" are visible around the "O" mintmark.

■ **Comments:** All of the "O/CC" varieties tend to be priced approximately the same, except VAMs 7, 7A and 9, and the clashed varieties 8A, 8B and 10A identified by Kimpton (2005). For information about VAMs 7, 7A and 9, see pages 11A-12A. VAMs 7 and 7A are covered in Van Allen (2008).

■ **Certified VAMs:** 7,826   **PL:** 0   **DMPL:** 0

CC: All O/CC Vars.	66ᴾ	Mult.				

VAM: 3 / **Doubled Die Reverse** / **PF:** 10
Ref: B (5680), FS ($1-010) ($1-1901-003), R, V

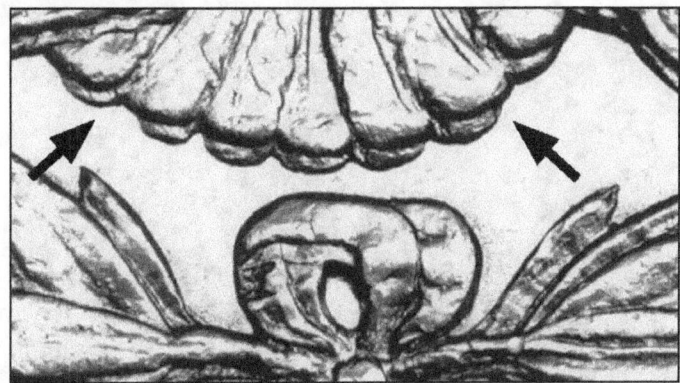

Doubled tailfeathers on reverse

Grade	VAM 3	Com	PL	Com	DMPL	Com	RF
MS-61	19K+	3K	UNK		UNK		8
MS-60	10K	2K					8
AU-58	5.5K	1K					7
AU-50	3.7K	320					7
XF-40	1.25K	95					6
VF-30	750	45					6

■ **Key Identifier:** Two complete sets of the eagle's tailfeathers are visible as a result of a misaligned hubbing toward 12 o'clock.

■ **Comments:** Because of its dramatic variety features, its popularity as a classic Red Book variety, and its rarity, the VAM 3 is on everyone's "Top Ten" list.

■ **Certified VAM 3:** 289 **PL:** 0 **DMPL:** 0

CC:	62[N]	61[A]	58[PNA]	Mult.		

1902-P Doubled Ear

VAM: 4 / **Doubled Die Obverse** / **PF:** 9
Ref: V

Doubled ear

Grade	VAM 4	Com	PL	Com	DMPL	Com	RF
MS-64	NTH	135	UNK	250	NTH	9.5K	8
MS-63	3.5K+	40	NTH	180	NTH	6K	8
MS-60	750+	25					7
AU-50	500	18					7
XF-40	250	16.5					6+
VF-30	175	16.5					6

■ **Key Identifiers:** Liberty's ear shows strong doubling along the back outer edge.

■ **Comments:** VAM 4 is rare and desirable and is considered the key 1902-P variety. This variety is *ultra rare* in Mint State.

■ **Certified VAM 4:** 108   **PL:** 2   **DMPL:** 1

CC:	65PLP	65N	64DMA	64A	63PLA	63PNA

VAM: 3 / **Mintmark Variety-type** / **PF:** 10
Ref: B (5690), D, FS ($1-011) ($1-1902o-003), Q, V2

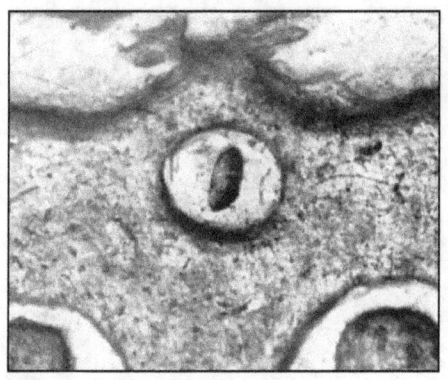 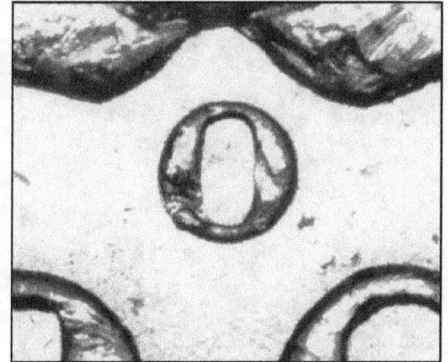

Micro "o" mintmark   Normal medium "O" mintmark

Grade	VAM 3	Com	PL	Com	DMPL	Com	RF
AU-53	NTH		UNK		UNK		8
AU-50	5.1K						7+
XF-40	4K						7+
VF-30	3K						7
F-15	450						7
VG	300						7

■ **Key Identifiers:** The mintmark, always tilted to the right, is a Micro "o" rather than the usual medium-size "O". Same reverse as the 1896-O and 1900-O Micro "o" Morgans.

■ **Comments:** *Ultra rare* in all grades above Fine, the VAM 3 (like the 1896-O and 1900-O Micro "o" varieties) is both rare and highly desirable. Likely made at a private mint and often found well-Circulated. VAM 3 may have been a contemporary counterfeit that circulated along with other silver dollars without notice. No longer certified by major grading services, VAM 3 is still a variety cherished by collectors. A more detailed history is given by Fey (2008) and Van Allen (2005).

■ **Certified VAM 3:** No longer certified.

CC:	55[A]	53[N]	50[P]	50[A]	50[A]	50[S]

VAM: 2 / **Mintmark Variety-type** / **PF:** 10
Ref: B (5697), FS ($1-1903s-002/011.5), Q, V

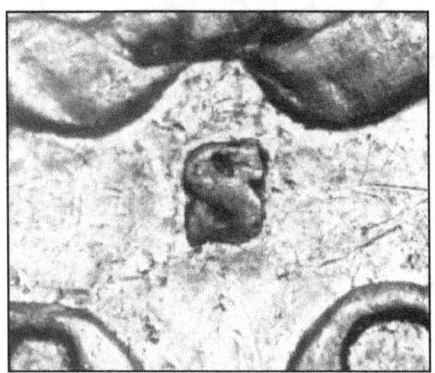

Small "s" mintmark

Normal large "S" mintmark

Grade	VAM 2	Com	PL	Com	DMPL	Com	RF
MS-62	21.8K	4.25K	UNK		UNK		8
MS-60	15K	3.6K					8
AU-58	13.9K	2K					7+
AU-50	3.7K	1.7K					7
XF-40	2.9K	340					6
VF-30	700	185					5

■ **Key Identifier:** The mintmark is a small, rounded "s" rather than the usual large "S".

■ **Comments:** This particular small "s" is unique to one Morgan dollar die in 1903, and is thought to have been intended only for use on Barber quarters. This variety has become highly popular. Only one Mint State specimen is known, which places heavy demand on AU-58 certified coins.

■ **Certified VAM 2:** 373　**PL:** 0　**DMPL:** 0

CC:	62N	58P	58P	58N	58N	55PNA

VAM: 41 (formerly 1A) / **Pitted Die Reverse** / **PF:** 7
Ref: V

Pitting around the ribbon bow

Grade	VAM 41	Com	PL	Com	DMPL	Com	RF
MS-65	500	140	UNK	475	NTH	9K	7
MS-64	170	38	NTH	75	NTH	7.2K	6
MS-63	150	29	NTH	50	NTH	1.6K	5
MS-62	125	20					5
MS-60	90	18					4
AU-50	50	16					4

■ **Key Identifier:** The wreath to the left of the ribbon bow on the reverse shows dramatic pitting, as does the area around it.

■ **Comments:** Often referred to as a "rusted die," the reverse of the VAM 41 is one of the most extreme cases of pitting of any silver dollar. There are others listed in the *Hit List 40* and *Hot 50* by Jeff Oxman.

■ **Certified VAM 41:** 431   **PL:** 0   **DMPL:** 0

CC:	65DM^P	65DM^A	65^P	65^P	65^P	64^{PNA}

VAMs: 4, 13, 13A, 25, 25A, 26, 26A, 27, 27A, 28, 28A, 29, 29A, 44

"Infrequent Reeding" Varieties / PF: 7

Ref: B (5705), V3

Wide (left) vs. normal reeding

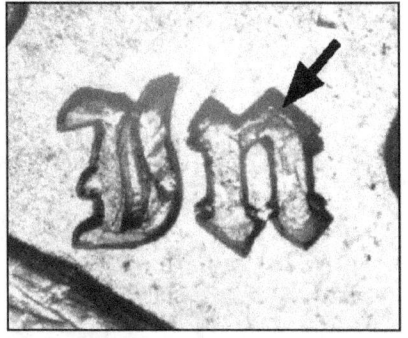

Doubling on "n" of VAM 4

Grade	IR VAMs/44	Com	PL	Com	DMPL	Com	RF
MS-65	NTH	140	UNK	475	NTH	9K	7
MS-64	200	38	NTH	75	NTH	7.2K	7
MS-63	160	29	NTH	50	NTH	1.6K	6
MS-62	95	20					6
MS-60	65	18					5
AU-50	40/>1K+	16					5/8

■ **Key Identifiers:** On all 1921-P Wide Reeding varieties, the edge reeds number only 157, as opposed to the normal reed count of 177 to 194 reeds for the rest of the Morgan dollar series. VAM 4 shows a nice doubled "n" from "In God we trust."

■ **Comments:** VAM 4 is one of the most popular of the various Wide Reeding varieties and exhibits a clearly doubled "n" in the word "In." The rarest and most desirable is VAM 44, the first reported D^2 reverse with infrequent reeding. Because of VAM 44, only one or two complete Infrequent Reeding (IR) sets are known. Further information about all IR varieties is provided on pages 13A-14A, and in Van Allen (2007).

■ **Certified IR VAMs:** 1,386   **PL:** 4   **DMPL:** 1

CC: All Varieties	65P	65P	65N	64PNA	Mult.	

VAM: 1A / **Filled Die Reverse** / **PF:** 9
Ref: V

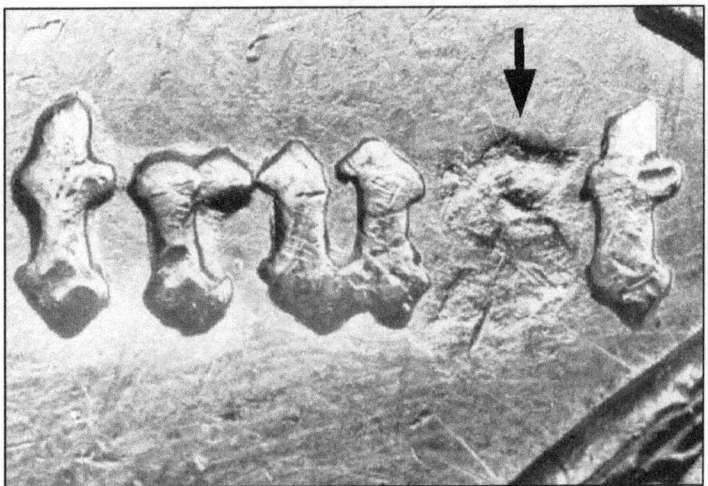

"Tru-t" in the motto

Grade	VAM 1A	Com	PL	Com	DMPL	Com	RF
MS-64	NTH	130	NTH	750	NTH	8K	7+
MS-63	1.2K+	60	NTH	400	NTH	1.9K	7
MS-62	450	50					6
MS-61	425	40					6
MS-60	400	38					6
AU-50	350	17					5

■ **Key Identifier:** The "s" in "trust" is filled on the reverse die, resulting in "tru-t."

■ **Comments:** The VAM 1A is one of the few spectacular filled-die varieties in the Morgan dollar series.

■ **Certified VAM 1A:** 147   **PL:** 0   **DMPL:** 0

CC:	65P	65P	65P	65DMN	64PNA	Mult.

TOP 100
Morgan Dollar Varieties

APPENDIX A

1878-S B¹ REVERSES

I t is not possible in a book of this size to show images of all pick-up points for all varieties. However, the table at right, which includes the Condition Census, population and estimated overall rarity for each 1878-S B¹ reverse, will help you determine your coin's rarity. For additional images, refer to *A Decade of Top 100 Insights* by Michael S. Fey (2008) and *Long Nock: A Guide to the 1878-S B¹ Reverse Varieties* by John Roberts (2008). Prices for the rarer varieties or those in higher grades will vary considerably from the value guidelines given on page 23. For example, VAMs 60, 62 and 72 are considerably rarer than VAMs 26 through 59 and typically trade for substantial premiums. VAM 72, although a fairly recent discovery, appears to be the key to the series. With only four specimens currently known, the demand for this variety exceeds supply. You can expect spirited bidding for this variety among 1878-S B1 reverse collectors.

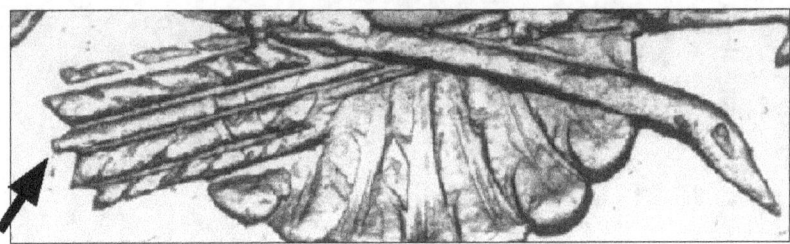

B¹ reverse with its long center arrow shaft

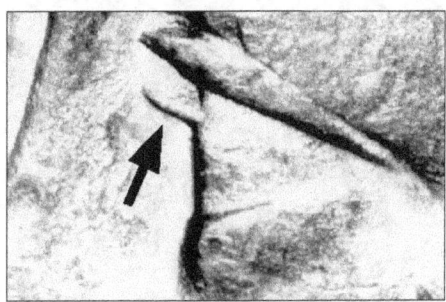

VAM 58 obverse with eye spike

Condition Census for the 1878-S B¹ Reverse Varieties

Date/VAM	Finest top six known certified specimens						PL	DMPL	POP*	Rarity**
1878-S V26	N53	P50	A50	A50	A50	P45	0	0	77	R-7-
1878-S V27	N64	A55	A55	A55	A55	A55	0	0	133	R-6+
1878-S V56	N63	A63	P55	A55	A50	A50	0	0	71	R-7-
1878-S V57	A61	PA58	Mult.				0	0	111	R-6+
1878-S V58	A53	P50	A50	PA45	Mult.		0	0	69	R-7
1878-S V59	N55	A55	A55	A55	P53	P50	0	0	34	R-7
1878-S V60	N63	A62DM	A50	PA45	Mult.		0	1	13	R-7+
1878-S V62	P53	A50	N45	P20	A20	PA15	0	0	13	R-7+
1878-S V72	N58	A20	P15	A8			0	0	4	R-8

N=NGC   A=ANACS   P=PCGS   *POP: Combined population   **Rarity: Est. overall rarity

Total certified=653 (includes certified 1878-S B¹ reverses not attributed)

3A

1879-S "REVERSE OF '78"

The 1879-S "Reverse of '78" warrants a separate book, and David Wang's *Guide to the 1879-S Reverse of 1878 Morgan Silver Dollars* is the first and best reference on the subject. With recent discoveries of VAMs 34B, 56 (perhaps a 56A, if one includes a die break across Ms. Liberty's cap), 66 and 67, both Wang and Leroy Van Allen have added pages of new information and defining images on the subject. Opposite is a breakdown of the current Condition Census, population and estimate of rarity by variety.

Prices for the rarer varieties or those in higher grades will vary considerably from the pricing guidelines for common varieties given on page 25. For example, VAMs 6, 23, 34A and 51 are recognized as rarer than the series as a whole and command additional premiums. VAMs 34B, 56, 66 and 67 are considerably rarer than the series generally and will trade for substantial premiums. There are currently no complete sets known in any grade! The demand for these varieties exceeds supply. You can expect spirited bidding for these varieties among 1879-S "Reverse of '78" collectors.

1879-S "Reverse of '78" Parallel Arrow Feather

Condition Census for the 1879-S "Reverse of '78" Varieties

Date/VAM	Finest top six known certified specimens						PL	DMPL	POP*	RF**
1879-S R'78	N66PL	P66	P66	N65DM	N65PL	N65PL	188	15	3620	R-5
VAM 4	P64	P64	N64	PNA63	Mult.		0	0	48	R-5
VAM 6	PNA62	Mult.					0	0	36	R-6+
VAM 9	P66	P65	PNA64				0	0	198	R-5
VAM 23	A63	P62	A62	A62	A61		0	0	21	R-7
VAM 25	PA62	Mult.					0	0	36	R-6
VAM 34	N62	A62	P58	P50	A50	P45	0	0	38	R-5+
VAM 34A	P62	P58	N58	A58	N55	A53	0	0	28	R-6+
VAM 34B	A53	A45	A45	A20			0	0	4	R-8
VAM 35	P64	N64	A63	PNA62	Mult.		0	0	40	R-5
VAM 39	P65	PNA64	Mult.				0	0	135	R-5

*Combined population **Est. overall rarity A=ANACS N=NGC P=PCGS   **Continued on next page...**

Condition Census for the 1879-S "Reverse of '78" Varieties

Date/VAM	Finest top six known certified specimens					PL	DMPL	POP*	RF**
VAM 42	A64	PNA 63	Mult.			0	0	93	R-5
VAM 43	P64	PNA63	Mult.			0	0	30	R-5
VAM 46	P64	PNA 63	Mult.			0	0	64	R-5
VAM 50	A55	N50	A50	PNA45	Mult.	0	0	21	R-7
VAM 51	P64PL	P63PL	N63PL	P63	A62	4	0	16	R-7
VAM 52	N64PL	P64	PNA63	Mult.		3	0	44	R-5+
VAM 56/56A	S50PL	S30	S20	S12	S12	1	0	5	R-8
VAM 66	S45	S20	S12			0	0	3	R-8
VAM 67***	Raw XF					0	0	1	R-8

*Combined population   **Est. overall rarity   ***Recent discovery   A=ANACS   N=NGC   P=PCGS   S=SEGS

1888 Oval "O" Varieties

The reader is referred to images by Leroy Van Allen in VAM Book Supplements for the 1888-O Oval "O" Morgans. VAMs 2, 6, 17, 18 and 21 currently command equal premiums, whereas VAM 24 can command an additional premium of about 25% in AU or better. Mint State 1888-O VAM 5s have traded hands privately in excess of $4,000, whereas Circulated specimens of VAMs 5 and 34 have traded hands for $1,000 or more. There is currently great demand for both varieties.

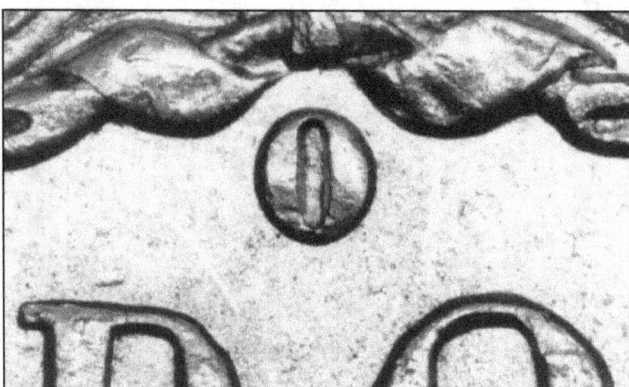

Scarce medium Oval "O"

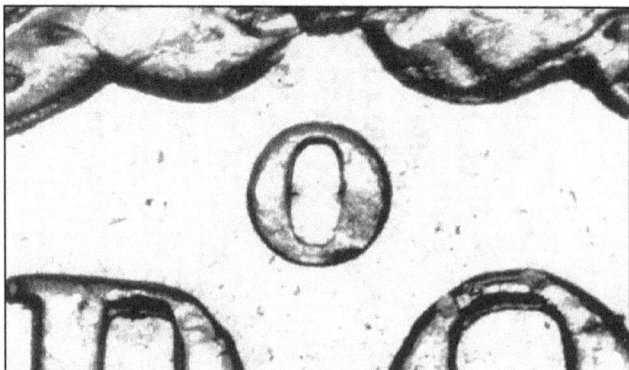

Common medium round "O"

Condition Census for the 1888-O Oval "O" Varieties (Oct. 2008)

Date/VAM	Finest six known certified specimens						PL	DMPL	POP*	RF**
1888-O V2	P64	P64	PA63	Mult.			1	0	164	R-6
1888-O V5	P63	A61	P60	P58	AU55	A53	0	0	13	R-7+
1888-O V6	P63	A63	A62	P61	N55	A55	0	0	86	R-7-
1888-O V17	A63	PNA58	Mult.				0	0	165	R-6
1888-O V18	N62	P60	A58	PNA55	Mult.		0	0	41	R-7-
1888-O V21	A63	P61	A61	PN58	Mult.		0	0	75	R-7-
1888-O V24	A58	P55	A55	A55	A53	A53	0	0	42	R-7
1888-O V34***	P61	P55	P45	Raw XF			0	0	5	R-8

*Combined population   **Overall Rarity   ***Recent discovery   A=ANACS   N=NGC   P=PCGS

1899 MICRO "o" VARIETIES

Pricing for VAMs 4, 6 and 31 are about the same. VAM 5 commands a 25% higher premium, and VAM 32 is the rarest of the 1899 Micro "o" varieties and commands a 50% or higher premium. (See page 87.)

VAM 4	VAM 31
Tilted Micro "o" with die cracks in "ED" of UNITED and "OF" on later die states.	Slightly tilted Micro "o" with die cracks at the top of "TED" and a prominent die scratch by the eagle's right leg.

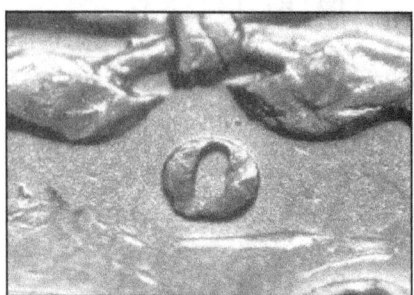

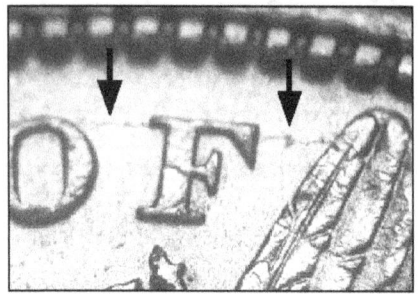

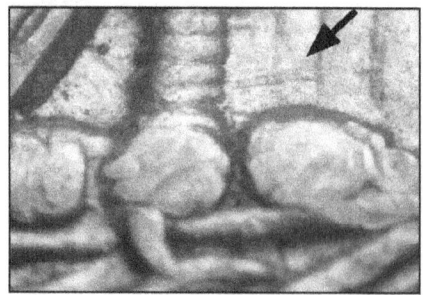

10A VAM 32

Tilted Micro "o" slightly left of ribbon bow (see lines). Die cracks in "TED" of UNITED and STATES OF.

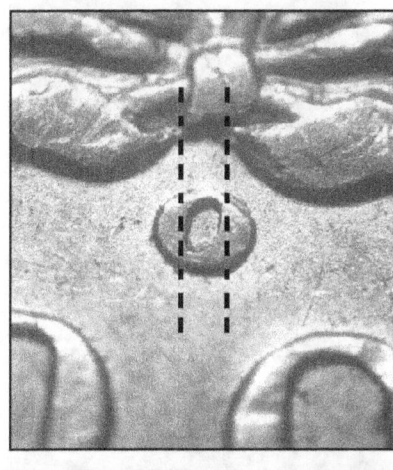

Condition Census for the 1899-O Micro "o" Varieties (Oct. 2008)

Date/VAM	Finest six known certified specimens						PL	DMPL	POP*	RF**
1899-O V4	P65	P64	N64	A64	PA63	Mult.	1	0	325	R-6-
1899-O V5	P65	P64DM	I64	PN63	Mult.		0	1	232	R-6
1899-O V6	P64	P63	P63	N63	A63	PNA62	0	0	469	R-6-
1899-O V31	P64	N64	P63	P63	PA62	Mult.	0	0	257	R-6
1899-O V32	A61	A61	P60	N60	PNA58	Mult.	0	0	73	R-7

*Combined population   **Overall Rarity   A=ANACS   I=PCI   N=NGC   P=PCGS

1900 "O/CC" VARIETIES

All the 1900 "O/CC" varieties tend to be priced equally, except for VAMs 7, 7A, and 9. The later die state of VAM 7 is VAM 7A, which can be identified by a small blob of metal above the "9" in the date. VAMs 8B and 10B are relatively recent clashed die varieties described by Kimpton (2005). Populations of these are too new to determine rarity. VAMs 7 and 7A, as pictured by Leroy Van Allen in his VAM Book Supplements for 1900 "O/CC" Morgans, are well recognized rare die varieties and bring premiums as high as the *Top 100* VAM 9 in corresponding grades. While populations of the VAM 7 and 7A have not been followed as closely as VAM 9, we feel these varieties will remain both rare and desirable.

We don't know of any complete Mint State sets of the 1900 "O/CC" varieties, and assume several Circulated sets may exist. Completion of either a Circulated or Mint State "O/CC" set is attainable and would make for a significant and worthy accomplishment.

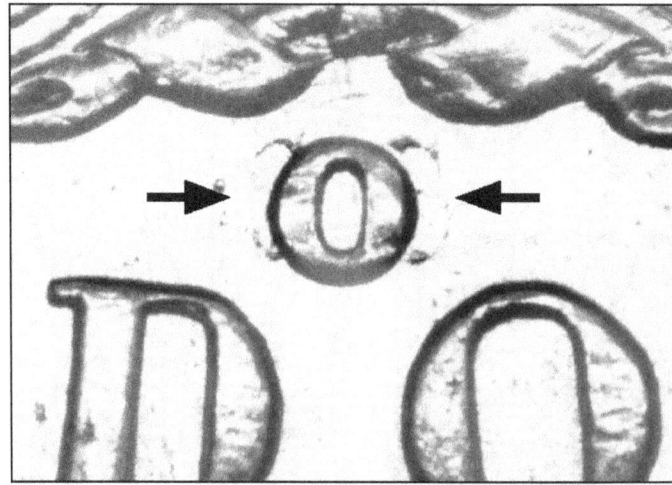

VAM 12 "O/CC" reverse

Condition Census for the 1900 O/CC Varieties

Date/VAM	Finest six known certified specimens						PL	DMPL	POP*	RF**
1900 O/CCs	PN67	PN66	Mult.				0	0	6271^	R-4
VAM 7	A64	N63	A63	N62	N62	PA55	0	0	22	R-7
VAM 7A	A58	N55	P53	A53	PN50	Mult.	0	0	41	R-7
VAM 8	P65	N65	PNA64	Mult.			0	0	170	R-4
VAM 8A	PN65	Mult.					0	0	237	R-4
VAM 8B***	A62	A62	NA61				0	0	19	R-6
VAM 9	P64	N64	N64	N64	A64	P62	0	0	128	R-6+
VAM 10	P65	PA64	Mult.				0	0	105	R-4
VAM 10A****	A64	A63	Mult.				0	0	31	R-5
VAM 11	P66	P66	PNA65	Mult.			0	0	591	R-4
VAM 12	P66	P66	P66	PNA65	Mult.		0	0	211	R-4

*Combined population   **Est. overall rarity   A=ANACS   N=NGC   P=PCGS
***PCGS does not recognize this VAM   ****Neither PCGS nor NGC recognize this VAM

1921 Wide Reeding VAMs

All 1921 Wide Reeding varieties are priced equally, except for VAM 44. VAM 44 appears to be *ultra rare* and is the only known Wide Reeding variety with a D^2 reverse (16 berries on the reverse) as compared to the D^1 reverse normally found on Wide Reeding specimens (with 17 berries). As such, only two specimens are currently known. One traded hands for more than $1,000.

VAM 25A is a recent die-state discovery, with oblong die gouges near the denticles above the first "S" in STATES. Its population has not yet been fully recognized. We believe more will surface as collectors attribute their varieties. Van Allen published the *1921P Infrequently Reeded or Wide Reeding Morgan Dollar Attribution Guide*, the ultimate guide to attributing the Wide Reeding varieties, in 2005.

Thus far, only two Circulated sets of the 1921 Wide Reeding varieties are possible, placing very high demand on the VAM 44 in order for collectors to assemble a complete set.

Wide reeding (left) and normal reeding

Condition Census for the 1921 Wide Reeding Varieties

Date/VAM	Finest six known certified specimens						PL	DMPL	POP*	RF**
1921 WRD	P65	NA64	P65	PNA64	N65	Mult.	4	1	889	R-5
VAM 4	NA64	Mult.					0	0	91	R-6
VAM 13	A64	A63PL	A63	Mult.			1	0	106	R-5
VAM 25	A63	A63	A62	Mult.			0	0	30	R-5
VAM 25A	A63	A60	A55				0	0	3	R-7
VAM 26	A64	A64	A63	Mult.			0	0	75	R-5
VAM 27	A64	A63	A63	A62	Mult.		0	0	10	R-6
VAM 27A	A64	A64	A64	A64	A63	Mult.	0	0	83	R-5
VAM 28	A63	A63	A62	Mult.			0	0	66	R-5
VAM 29	A64	A63	A63	A62	A62	A61	0	0	31	R-5+
VAM 44***	P58	Raw AU					0	0	2	R-8

*Combined population **Est. overall rarity ***Recent discovery A=ANACS I-ICGS N=NGC P=PCGS

Note: Only ANACS recognizes all the different Wide Reed varieties; NGC recognizes VAM 4.

"ROTATES"

By Michael S. Fey

A dearly departed VAM friend, Terry Armstrong, fondly referred to coins having a rotated reverse as "rotates." Pick up any nice "rotates" lately?

Advanced Morgan and Peace dollar collectors who have been searching through thousands of silver dollars over the years know one thing for sure: "Rotated Reverse" Morgan and Peace dollars are rarely encountered. If and when you're lucky enough to see one, there's only one way to describe it: "Wow!" It's this "Wow!" factor that makes me love them and has caused me to further explore the rotated dies market, which so far as I can tell is still in the "Wild Wild West" stage of pricing and development.

What we know

"Rotates," rotated reverses, or more accurately "rotated dies" are caused by either the hammer or anvil die – or both – rotating clockwise or counterclockwise relative to the upside-down "coin turn" (180-degree difference; ↑↓) normally seen on coins. A "medal turn" (↑↑), for example, would normally have an obverse and reverse aligned in the same direction.

I interviewed noted error coin specialists David Camire of Numismatic Conservation Services (NCS), Fred Weinberg of Fred Weinberg & Co., Rich Schemmer of Rich Schemmer Error Coins, and Ron Landis, formerly of the Gallery Mint, who has working experience with a coin press used to strike Morgan and Peace dollars. Here's what I learned about how rotated dies may have occurred.

Human error: Morgan and Peace silver dollar dies were aligned by eye using pencil marks, so human error (or intent) may have caused the rotated dies we see today. Later, notching or flattening one side of the die by grinding so that the die pair would only fit in a "coin turn" position was employed to

16A

minimize the chance for error. As Morgan and Peace dollar dies are rarely seen today, it's not clear when or if the practice of flattening dies was used in minting silver dollars.

Loose mounting screws: If the three to four mounting screws holding the obverse or reverse dies were loose, the dies could be free to move during striking.

Broken die holder: If the die holder broke, new mounting screws could be drilled as a temporary holder until a new die holder could be manufactured and installed. This assumes that there were no other die holders on hand, or the Mint was trying to cut costs by attempting to re-use the existing broken die holder.

Broken bolster plate: The bolster plate also held the die in place, and if broken could be temporarily held in place by drilling new holes and adding three or four set screws until a new one was installed.

Dollars struck under conditions described in these last three scenarios could exhibit fixed rotations or variable degrees of rotations, depending on how freely the dies rotated during the intense physical action of striking coins at 150 tons of pressure. Regardless of the cause, the result can be a VAM variety with an infinite number of possible rotations, or a dollar that some collectors refer to as a collectable "error" coin.

What we see

Fast forward 130 years since the first Morgan was struck and we're still trying to understand whether specific VAM varieties resulted from fixed rotated dies or from different rotations. What makes this such a difficult question to answer is that (1) Collectors have not used a consistent standard to report the degree of rotation on specific varieties, and (2) collectors, dealers, and some grading services don't accurately measure and report rotated dies on an accepted Morgan and Peace dollar standard. I hope this will change.

The older approach to measuring rotated dies was based

on a clock (i.e., circle) having 360 degrees. Thus, a coin having a reported 270-degree rotation would be the same today as if one or both dies only rotated a mere 90 degrees counter-clockwise from the other. Collectors mostly eyeball rotations, so that a 75-degree rotation may encompass anything from 50 degrees to 90 degrees or more. Further, at what point does a collector know what is defined as 0 degrees on the obverse and exactly where to measure the angle on the reverse?

Leroy Van Allen established the "market standard" with the development of his Rota Flip™ die rotation guide in 1991 and his publication, *Rotated Die Coin Measurements*, to show precisely how to obtain an accurate measurement (available for $19.95 + $2 S&H at Leroy Van Allen, P.O. Box 196, Sidney, OH 45365; see pages 26B-27B.) It's a "must buy" with copious illustrations that will help you accurately measure rotated dies on a wide range of coin types. His standard is based on a clockwise and counterclockwise measurement that never exceeds 180 degrees. Accurate measurement of these rotations otherwise is not intuitive, and is not as easy as you may think!

Rotated dies population

The best statistical information we have about rotated dies comes from the ANACS population report. A review of data from March 2002 indicated that approximately 91 Mint State and 22 Circulated (113 total) Morgan dollars of varying dates and degrees of rotation were certified. Similarly, only 13 Mint State and 3 Circulated (16) Peace dollars were certified. Even if we increased these numbers severalfold to account for the unreported rotated dollars graded by other services, I would estimate that perhaps less than a few thousand of the approximate 500 million Morgan and Peace dollars remaining in the marketplace exhibit rotated dies. The point is, as a class, all Morgan and Peace dollar rotated dies are rare in any grade, and more so in Mint State. When one considers the population of specific dates, rotations and VAM

18A Desirable Regions for Rotated Dies on Morgans

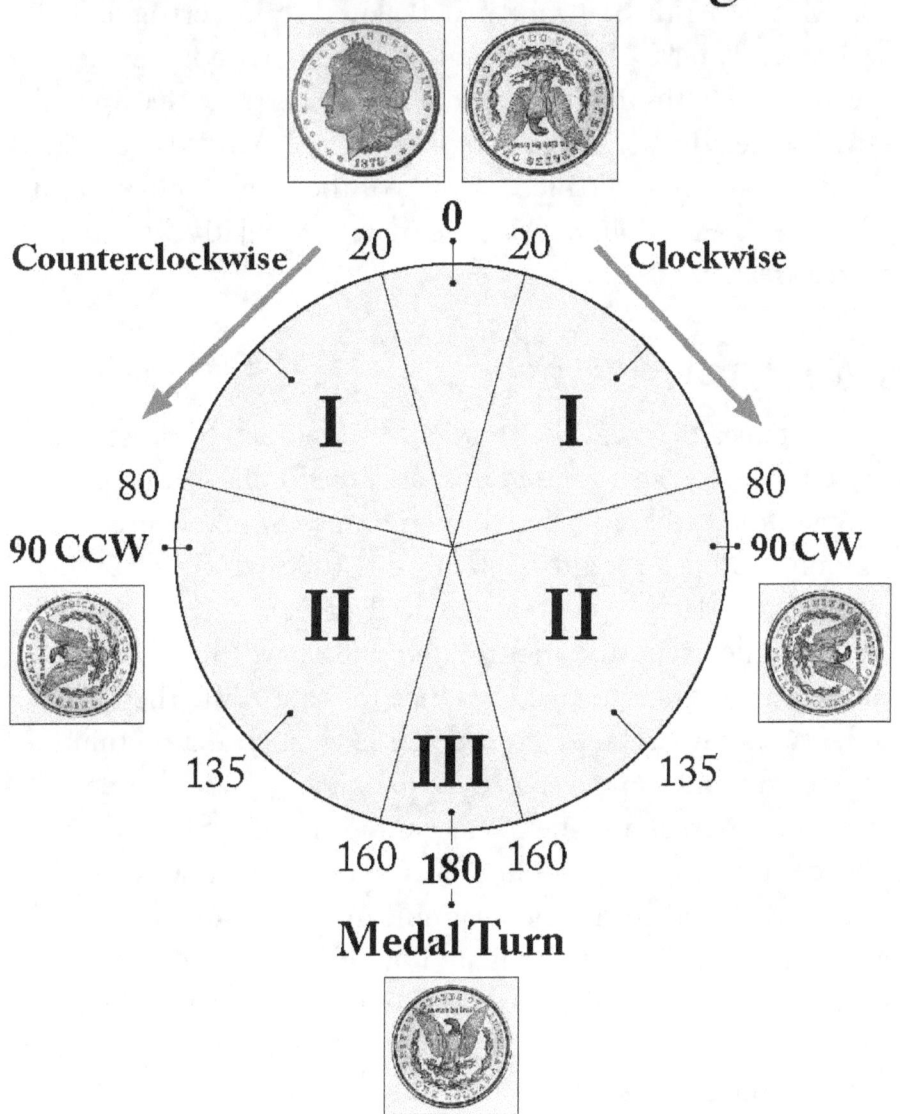

No Premium: 0 degrees +/- 20 degrees

Region I: 20 degrees to 79 degrees

Region II: 80 degrees to 159 degrees (where II is more desirable than I)

Region III: 160 +/- 20 degrees (The Best!)

varieties of rotated dollars, they only get rarer.

The most common rotated Morgan dollar is the 1878-CC with 67 Mint State and 5 Circulated coins certified. That's nearly 64% of all the rotated dollars graded. Next is the 1886-O with only 8 Circulated coins certified, leaving all others as relatively much rarer. Similarly, 11 Mint State 1923 Peace dollars were certified, or 69% of the total population of all rotated Peace dollars. All other dates are relatively much more rare.

Desirable rotates

Opposite is a diagram that Jeff and I developed to illustrate desirable regions for rotated dies on silver dollars. It is broken down into several regions: No premium (0 +/- 20 degrees), Region I (20 to 79 degrees), Region II (80 to 160 degrees), and Region III (160 degrees +/- 20 degrees).

Van Allen reported that rotated dollars within +/- 15 degrees are within normal tolerance for the Mint. Therefore, to be sure that a rotated silver dollar is worthy of a premium, we recommend using a slightly expanded 0 +/- 20 degree rotation region as a "little or no premium" zone. Silver dollars rotated in Region I at +/-20 to 79 degrees are a marvel to behold and should command a significant premium. However, an even greater "Wow!" is elicited by coins at 90 degrees or more (+/- 80 to 159 degrees) clockwise or counterclockwise (Region II). These should command an even greater premium. Perhaps the greatest "Wow!"– and rarer yet – occurs with coins at 180 +/- 20 degrees (Region III). These silver dollar rotated dies should command the highest premium.

Rotated dies price guide

As mentioned earlier, pricing of rotated dies has been like the Wild Wild West, perhaps because up until now there hasn't been a value guide. I've been monitoring prices of rotated dollars on eBay for several years. I've seen Mint State 1878-CCs offered for a "Buy It Now" price of $2,500, while others have sold for about $250. I've seen AU 1923 Peace dollars trade for well over $300, while Mint State coins bring $250 or less. The accompanying "Morgan & Peace Dollar Rotated Dies Price Guide" is an attempt to estimate values based on rarity, grade and desirable region of rotation. It doesn't include price estimates for coins in Region III, which at this time are considered *ultra rare*, but it takes into account a 25-50% additional premium for coins at exactly 90 degrees clockwise or counterclockwise rotation. It's just a starting place in a collecting area that will undoubtedly change rapidly over time.

Supply and demand will ultimately dictate the pricing of various rotated dollars. Since rotated die collectors will tend to collect more than just one date, one degree of rotation, and perhaps more than one grade of these dollars as they acquire nicer specimens, it would only take about 50-100 collectors, certainly far less than the readers of this publication, to buy the entire population of all rotated silver dollars estimated to exist! So, expect these coins to rise significantly in value over time. Enjoy!

For More Information

Fackelman, Jay. *Rotated Die Coin Census (RDCS)*; 1999. Information: www.RotatedDies.com. Contact: RotatedDies@hotmail.com.

Oxman, Jeff. "The Nature of Rotated Dies," *Sovereign Entities (SEGS)*, Volume 3, No. 1, 2001.

Van Allen, Leroy. *Rotated Die Coin Measurements. Rota Flip*™; 1999. Contact: vams@woh.rr.com.

Morgan & Peace Dollar Rotated Dies Price Guide

Morgan Dollars

Rotated Reverse	Reg.	F/VF	Com	XF	Com	AU	Com	60	Com	62	Com	63	Com	64	Com
1878-CC VAM 22	I	150	50	200	52	250	75	300	150	350	160	400	175	750	285
May not exist	II	200	50	225	52	250	75	400	150	500	160	750	175	1000	285
1879-O VAM ?*	I														
May not exist	II														
1882 VAM 1*	I	200	11	225	13	300	15	400	20	450	25				
May not exist	II														
1883-O VAM 1	I	100	11	175	13	275	15	300	20	400	24	NTH	27	NTH	36
May not exist	II														
1886-O VAM 4, 11	I	150	11	300	14	450	60	750	315	NTH	1000	NTH	1850	NTH	5500
May not exist	II														
1887 VAM 27	I	150	11	225	13	300	15	400	20	450	24	NTH	27	NTH	36
	II	175	11	275	13	350	15	450	20	500	24	NTH	27	NTH	36
1888-O VAM 9	I	100	12	175	13	275	15	300	21	350	26	450	30	1000	41
	II	125	12	200	13	300	15	350	21	400	26	500	30	1500	41
1889 VAM 18A	I	100	11	125	13	175	15	250	20	400	25	450	29	1000	39
May not exist	II														

*Reported, not verified   Attributed with assistance from Leroy Van Allen, 3/18/09   Continued on next page...

Morgan & Peace Dollar Rotated Dies Price Guide

Morgan Dollars, continued

Rotated Reverse	Reg.	F/VF	Com	XF	Com	AU	Com	60-1	Com	62	Com	63	Com	64	Com
1889-O VAM 1, 3, 9	I	125	11	250	14	300	23	350	100	NTH	175	NTH	245	NTH	420
	II	150	11	275	14	350	23	450	100	NTH	175	NTH	245	NTH	420
1890-O VAM 8, 23	I	175	11	275	14	350	18	400	37	NTH	50	NTH	65	NTH	135
May not exist	II														
1891-O VAM 8	I	125	11	250	14	300	26	350	100	NTH	150	NTH	195	NTH	425
	II	150	11	275	14	350	26	450	100	NTH	150	NTH	195	NTH	425
1894-O VAM 6A	I	200	25	300	40	400	120	500	385	NTH	1000	NTH	2300	NTH	5000
May not exist	II														
1899-O VAM ?*	I														
May not exist	II														
1901-O VAM 46	I	125	11	150	13	200	15	250	23	NTH	25	NTH	29	NTH	38
May not exist	II														
1904-O VAM 13, 18, 40	I	125	11	150	14	200	15	250	21	NTH	25	NTH	28	NTH	36
	II	150	11	175	14	225	15	275	21	NTH	25	NTH	28	NTH	36
1921 VAM 45	I	125	8	150	8	200	9	250	13	350	16	450	19	NTH	26
May not exist	II														

Morgan Dollars

Rotated Reverse	Reg.	F/VF	Com	XF	Com	AU	Com	60-1	Com	62	Com	63	Com	64	Com
1921-D VAM 1	I	150	8	175	9	225	10	275	30	NTH	35	NTH	37	NTH	74
May not exist	II														

Peace Dollars

Rotated Reverse	Reg.	F/VF	Com	XF	Com	AU	Com	60-1	Com	62	Com	63	Com	64	Com
1921 VAM 1, 2BA, ?	I	125	7.5	175	8	275	9	300	12	400	17	500	20	NTH	28
	II	150	7.5	200	8	300	9	350	12	450	17	550	20	NTH	28
1922-D VAM 2	I	150	7.5	150	8	200	9	250	18	350	25	450	35	NTH	60
	II	175	7.5	175	8	225	9	275	18	400	25	500	35	NTH	60
1923 VAM 1	I	100	7.5	150	8	200	9	250	12	350	17	450	20	NTH	27
	II	125	7.5	175	8	225	9	275	12	375	17	500	20	NTH	27
1924 VAM 1*	I	150	7.5	250	8	300	9	350	12	500	17	NTH	20	NTH	27
	II														
1927-D VAM ?*	I	150	7.5	150	8	200	9	250	18	350	25	450	35	NTH	60
May not exist	II														

*Reported but not verified   Attributed with assistance from Leroy Van Allen, 3/18/09

TOP 100
Morgan Dollar Varieties

APPENDIX B

Rank Order of Top 100 DMPL Varieties

Combined number certified by PCGS, NGC and ANACS (MS only)

Date / VAM	DMPL	Date / VAM	DMPL
1878 V115	0	1879-S V9	0
1878 V171	0	1879-O V28	0
1878 V5	0	1879-S V25	0
1878 V198	0	1879-S V34A	0
1878-CC V6	0	1879-S V35	0
1878-CC V18	0	1879-S V52	0
1878-CC V24	0	1879-S V56 (56A)	0
1878-S V26	0	1879-S V66	0
1878-S V27	0	1879-S V67	0
1878-S V56	0	1880 V1A	0
1878-S V57	0	1880 V23	0
1878-S V58	0	1880 V6	0
1878-S V59	0	1880 V7	0
1878-S V62	0	1880 V8	0
1878-S V72	0	1880-O V43	0
1878 V14-11	0	1880-O V48	0
1878 V203/203A	0	1880-O V49	0
1878 V220	0	1880-O V6	0
1878 V223	0	1882 O/S V3,4,5	0
1879-S V23	0	1882 O/S V3 EDS	0
1879-S V34	0	1883 V10	0
1879-S V34B	0	1885-S V6	0
1879-S V39	0	1885-S V9	0
1879-S V4	0	1886-O V1A	0
1879-S V42	0	1887-O V22A/22B	0
1879-S V43	0	1887-O V3	0
1879-S V46	0	1887-O V5	0
1879-S V50	0	1887 V1A	0
1879-S V51	0	1887 V5	0
1879-S V6	0	1888-O V17	0

Date / VAM	DMPL
1888-O V18	0
1888-O V1A	0
1888-O V1B LDS	0
1888-O V2	0
1888-O V21	0
1888-O V24	0
1888-O V34	0
1888-O V5	0
1888-O V6	0
1888 V11/11A	0
1889-O V1A2	0
1889-O V2/2A(17)	0
1889-O V6	0
1889 V19A/19B	0
1889 V22	0
1891-O V1A/1A2	0
1891-O V1A3	0
1891-S V3	0
1891 V2A	0
1892-O V7	0
1893 V4	0
1897 V6A	0
1899-O V31	0
1899-O V32	0
1899-O V4	0
1899-O V6	0
1899-S V7	0
1900 O/CC V10	0
1900 O/CC V10A	0
1900 O/CC V11	0
1900 O/CC V12	0
1900 O/CC V7	0
1900 O/CC V7A	0
1900 O/CC V8	0
1900 O/CC V8A	0
1900 O/CC V8B	0

Date / VAM	DMPL
1900 O/CC V9	0
1900 O/CCs	0
1900-O V29A	0
1900 V11	0
1900 V24	0
1901 V3	0
1903-S V2	0
1921 V13	0
1921 V25	0
1921 V25A	0
1921 V27	0
1921 V27A	0
1921 V28	0
1921 V29	0
1921 V4	0
1921 V44	0
1921-D V1A	0
1921 V41(1A)	0
1921 V26	0
1878-S B1 Rev.	1
1878 V117	1
1878-S V60	1
1879-O V4	1
1882 O/S V4 EDS	1
1889-O V1A1	1
1892-S V2	1
1899-O V5	1
1902 V4	1
1921 WRD	1
1878 V45	2
1880 V9	2
1884 V3	2
1886 V21 (1B)	2
1888-O V4	2
1878 V44/44A	3
1880-O V5	3

Date / VAM	DMPL
1880-S V10	3
1882 O/O V7	3
1887-O V2	3
1896 V4	3
1882 O/S V5 EDS	4
1886 V1A1	4
1880-O V6A/6C	5
1884 V4	5
1896 V19	5
1878 V100A & B	6
1878 V141/141A	7
1878 V9	7
1886-S V2	7
1886 V17	9
1891 V2/2B	14
1879-S R'78	15
1895-S V4	15
1887-S V2	16
1887 V12/12A	17
1890-CC V4	17
1878 V70	19
1878 V15	23
1883 O/O V4	23
1887 V2	27

Date / VAM	DMPL
1878 V32	29
1878 V41/41B	30
1880-CC V4	31
1888-O V9	39
1891-CC V3	39
1880-CC V5	42
1880-CC V6	42
1878-CC V11	50
1880-O V4	50
1879-CC V3	51
1880-S V9	55
1878 V23	78
1880-S V8	86
1884 O/O V6	193

Date / VAM	DMPL
*1896-O V4	Rare
*1900-O V5	Rare
*1902-O V3	Rare

*Not certified; there are no known specimens with DMPL surfaces.

Rank Order of Top 100 Proof-like Varieties

Combined number certified by PCGS, NGC and ANACS (MS only)

Date / VAM	PL	Date / VAM	PL
1878 V5	0	1880 V1A	0
1878-S V26	0	1880 V23	0
1878-S V27	0	1880 V6	0
1878-S V56	0	1880 V7	0
1878-S V57	0	1880 V8	0
1878-S V58	0	1880 V9	0
1878-S V59	0	1880-O V49	0
1878-S V60	0	1882 O/S V3,4,5	0
1878-S V62	0	1882 O/S V3 EDS	0
1878-S V72	0	1882 O/S V4 EDS	0
1878 V14-11	0	1883 V10	0
1878 V203/203A	0	1885-S V9	0
1878 V220	0	1887-O V22A/22B	0
1879-S V23	0	1887-O V5	0
1879-S V34	0	1887 V1A	0
1879-S V34B	0	1887 V5	0
1879-S V39	0	1888-O V17	0
1879-S V4	0	1888-O V18	0
1879-S V42	0	1888-O V1A	0
1879-S V43	0	1888-O V1B LDS	0
1879-S V46	0	1888-O V21	0
1879-S V50	0	1888-O V24	0
1879-S V6	0	1888-O V34	0
1879-S V9	0	1888-O V4	0
1879-O V28	0	1888-O V5	0
1879-S V25	0	1888-O V6	0
1879-S V34A	0	1888 V11/11A	0
1879-S V35	0	1889-O V1A1	0
1879-S V66	0	1889-O V1A2	0
1879-S V67	0	1889-O V2/2A(17)	0

Date / VAM	PL	Date / VAM	PL
1889-O V6	0	1921 V44	0
1889 V19A/19B	0	1921-D V1A	0
1889 V22	0	1921 V41(1A)	0
1891-O V1A/1A2	0	1921 V26	0
1891-O V1A3	0	1878-S B1 Rev.	1
1891-S V3	0	1878 V115	1
1891 V2A	0	1878 V117	1
1892-O V7	0	1878 V198	1
1892-S V2	0	1878 V223	1
1897 V6A	0	1879-S V56 (56A)	1
1899-O V31	0	1880-O V43	1
1899-O V32	0	1880-O V6	1
1899-O V5	0	1880-S V10	1
1899-O V6	0	1888-S V2	1
1900 O/CC V10	0	1899-O V4	1
1900 O/CC V10A	0	1900 V11	1
1900 O/CC V11	0	1921 V13	1
1900 O/CC V12	0	1878 V9	2
1900 O/CC V7	0	1885-S V6	2
1900 O/CC V7A	0	1886-O V1A	2
1900 O/CC V8	0	1886 V21 (1B)	2
1900 O/CC V8A	0	1887-O V3	2
1900 O/CC V8B	0	1902 V4	2
1900 O/CC V9	0	1878 V141/141A	3
1900 O/CCs	0	1879-O V4	3
1900-O V29A	0	1879-S V52	3
1900 V24	0	1896 V4	3
1901 V3	0	1879-S V51	4
1903-S V2	0	1880-O V48	4
1921 V25	0	1882 O/S V5 EDS	4
1921 V25A	0	1896 V19	4
1921 V27	0	1921 WRD	4
1921 V27A	0	1878-CC V24	5
1921 V28	0	1886 V1A1	5
1921 V29	0	1887-O V2	5
1921 V4	0	1878-CC V6	6

Date / VAM	PL
1893 V4	7
1882 O/O V7	8
1890-CC V4	8
1884 V3	10
1891 V2/2B	10
1899-S V7	10
1878 V44/44A	12
1878 V100A & B	12
1880-O V6A/6C	12
1887 V12/12A	12
1884 V4	14
1887-S V2	15
1878 V45	17
1878-CC V18	17
1880-O V5	19
1886 V17	22
1883 O/O V4	23
1878 V41/41B	24
1886-S V2	26
1878 V171	28
1895-S V4	28
1878 V32	29
1880-O V4	38
1891-CC V3	39

Date / VAM	PL
1880-CC V4	41
1888-O V9	41
1878 V15	44
1880-CC V6	51
1884 O/O V6	59
1878-CC V11	68
1878 V70	69
1880-S V8	76
1880-S V9	78
1880-CC V5	98
1879-CC V3	107
1878 V23	111
1879-S R'78	188
1887 V2	442

*1896-O V4	Rare
*1900-O V5	Rare
*1902-O V3	Rare

*Not certified; there are no known specimens with PL surfaces.

THE AUTHORS

Michael Fey

While most collectors and dealers know of Dr. Fey's expertise in advanced silver dollar collecting and investing, few know that he has comparable expertise in nearly all U.S. coinage types, in all types of Canadian and Maritime Province coins, in 20th century Philippine and Mexican types, and in working with clients of his Rare Coin Investments (RCI) business on a wide range of  numismatic investment properties. Dr. Fey was second under bidder on the Walter J. Childs specimen of the 1804 silver dollar (1999), generally thought to be the Finest Known example of the "King" of all U.S. coins.

Dr. Fey is a professional member of all the most recognized grading services (PCGS, NGC, NCS, ANACS and others), and at times has been engaged as a consultant. He maintains memberships in dozens of numismatic specialty organizations, and has published extensively on new variety discoveries in U.S. and foreign coins (see references at www.rcicoins.com). He currently publishes a quarterly newsletter, *Top 100 Insights and Value Guide*, with current trading values used by *Coin World* and *Numismatic News* and published in *COINage* magazine. He has given dozens of numismatic talks in public venues and has taught advanced courses at American Numismatic Association (ANA) summer conferences. His books, *The Top 100 Morgan Dollar Varieties: The VAM Keys*, co-authored with Jeff Oxman, and *A Decade of Top 100 Insights*, have become ground-breaking books and necessary references for advanced silver dollar collecting. He also assisted several other authors with editing and publishing their numismatic reference books. Dr. Fey has conducted numerous Spring and Fall *Ultra Rarity* Auctions through RCI, and has brought consignors record prices for their rare die varieties and collections.

Dr. Fey has donated much of his time to the coin collecting hobby. He is a past member of the ANA Board of Governors (2005-2007), served on several ANA committees by presidential appointment, and currently serves on the ANA Consumer Protection and Mediation committees. He is also a member of the ANA Advisory Board and is a member of the founding Board of the Society of Silver Dollar Collectors (SSDC). He served as president of the New Jersey Numismatic Society (2002), and is currently serving the Combined Organizations of Numismatic Error Collectors of America (CONECA) as Attributor of Trade, Morgan and Peace silver dollar varieties.

The hobby has recognized Dr. Fey's efforts in numismatics with an ANA Glen B. Smedley award, three ANA Presidential Awards, The National Silver Dollar Roundtable Presidential Award and the New Jersey Numismatic Society Charles F. Nettleship Award, as well as dozens of certificates and awards for speaking and teaching engagements.

Dr. Fey was a founder and president of New Life Health Products Corp., was awarded two patents and a trademark for a drug he developed to help people quit smoking, and received grants from the National Heart, Lung and Blood Institute. He was founder and chairman of Venture Match of New Jersey and a founder and board member of the Venture Association of New Jersey, two not-for profit organizations, and was a director of the Rutgers University Technical Assistance Program.

He was director of the Food Division of Radiation Technology, Inc., and was a Technical Brand Manager for the Proctor & Gamble Company.

Dr. Fey received a Ph.D. (1980) from Cornell University,

an M.S. from Louisiana State University (1976), a B.S. from St. John's University (1972), and had MBA coursework from Xavier University. He served his country as a Vietnam era officer in the U.S. Army Chemical Corp.

Jeff Oxman

Jeff Oxman, whose collecting interests have spanned almost five decades, is today a respected author, researcher, lecturer and collector. For the past 25 years his primary focus has been Morgan and Peace dollars, where he has devoted his energies to discovering, writing about, and attributing the more than 3,000 known die varieties. As a result of his research, Oxman is often called upon for his silver dollar ex-

pertise, and his consulting resumé includes all of the top numismatic trade newspapers and grading services.

A turning point in his numismatic career, as well as in the hobby's approach to collecting U.S. silver dollars, came in 1988, when he and a handful of other silver dollar specialists banded together to form the Society of Silver Dollar Collectors (SSDC). Oxman was its Founding President, and the SSDC, which is still catering to the interests of Morgan and Peace dollar variety specialists, remains at the forefront of U.S. silver dollar collecting.

Oxman's writing talents have been showcased on a number of occasions as guest columnist for the Collectors' Clearinghouse pages in *Coin World*, as well as co-commentator for a front-page feature about silver dollars in the *Coin Dealer Newsletter* (*Greysheet*). In addition, he has contributed articles for most of the club publications where he is a member, including a VAM article in the April 2000 issue of the ANA

Numismatist. Oxman has also served as Editor for several numismatic publications, including the *NASC Quarterly* and the *SSDC Research Journal.*

Jeff Oxman has been asked to contribute to a number of books about U.S. silver dollars, including writing a chapter in *The Comprehensive U.S. Silver Dollar Encyclopedia* by John Highfill, who received the NLG Extraordinary Merit Award for his work. Oxman also contributed extensively to Q. David Bowers' award-winning two-volume reference set, *Silver Dollars & Trade Dollars of the United States, A Complete Encyclopedia.* In fact, Oxman is involved in many, if not most, of the upcoming projects concentrating on the subject of U.S. silver dollars.

With the release of *The Top 100 Morgan Dollar Varieties* in 1997, Oxman and co-writer, Michael Fey, took VAMs to the vanguard of U.S. silver dollar collecting. The concept was to focus on the 100 key die varieties in the Morgan dollar series, and the impact was immediate. Now, thousands of hobbyists are enjoying the exciting specialty of VAM collecting, and it is, in fact, one of the "hottest" areas of the current coin market.

In 1998 Oxman began writing a series of attribution guides for silver dollar enthusiasts. His first release, with co-writer Les Hartnett, was entitled *The Morgan Dollar 8-TF Attribution Guide.* It sold out in three weeks! This was followed by *The Morgan Dollar 7/8-TF Attribution Guide,* which is now in its third printing. And in 1999, Oxman and Chicago computer programmer John Baumgart broke new ground by developing a series of CD-ROMs which spotlight various VAM sets, including *The 8-TF Attribution Wizard,* *The Top 100 Attribution Wizard,* *The Hot 50 Attribution Wizard,* and *The Top 50 Peace dollar Attribution Wizard.* Together, these titles introduced numismatists to the amazing cutting-edge technology of computer-assisted attributions.

In 2000, Oxman released *Hot 50 Morgan Dollar Varieties,* which presented "fifty exciting new varieties that supplement the *Top 100* listings. The *Top 100* and *Hot 50* monikers immediately caught on and are now accepted as an integral part of Morgan dollar collecting.

Oxman's next effort was the best-selling *Top 50 Peace Dollar Varieties*, written with co-author, Dr. David Close. Released in June 2002, this book represents the first published volume devoted exclusively to U.S. Peace dollars. And after only three months, the book went into its second printing.

As a reflection of his extensive contributions to the field of U.S. silver dollars, the National Silver Dollar Roundtable (NSDR) honored Oxman with its Man of the Year award in 1997. He later became President of the organization, and at the 2002 F.U.N. convention in Florida, Oxman's name was added to a very select group of 11 other well-known luminaries who, over the past 20 years, had received the NSDR Lifetime Achievement Award.

Oxman currently is serving a two-year term as president of the NSDC, and he remains active in a number of local, regional and national clubs as a frequent guest speaker. In addition, Oxman has developed a popular VAM auction site, VAMQUEST.com, which provides a two-way market for VAM collectors to buy and sell rare varieties.

What makes this busy specialist tick? For Jeff Oxman, it's the thrill and excitement of what he calls the "variety revolution." Like other specialists, Oxman believes that the varieties of every coin series represent one of the last true frontiers of numismatics, and now his efforts are focused on keeping Morgan and Peace dollars at the leading edge of that revolution.

ABOUT THE TOP 100

The organized collecting of Morgan dollar varieties reached a new level in 1965 with the publication of Leroy Van Allen's original volume, *Morgan and Peace Dollar Varieties*. About 100 major die varieties, estimated mintages and value estimates were listed. As the popularity of various varieties increased and information about the rarity of others evolved over the years, Jeff Oxman, executive director of the Society of Silver Dollar Collectors, published the "Value-Guide and Checklist for Morgan Dollar Varieties," which spanned three issues of the *SSDC Journal* – Winter/Spring 1993 (Vol. 5/6, No. 4/1), Summer 1993 (Vol. 6, No.2), and Winter/Spring 1994 issues (Vol. 7, No. 1).

In 1995, a survey was taken to determine the *Top 100* Morgans by calculating the number of pieces in the collections of SSDC members, as well as the coins' grades. That data, combined with statistics from ANACS, NGC and PCGS population reports, resulted in the first Condition Census of the six Finest Known coins, which was reported in the first edition of the *Top 100* book.

The *Top 100*, as determined by the authors in the first edition in 1997, represented both popular Morgan dollar varieties listed in the current price guides and collected by Morgan enthusiasts, and the evolution of the previous 30 years of collecting experience in rare and desirable Morgan varieties.

Selecting the *Top 100* was not an easy process. Judgments were made taking into account both popularity and rarity. Other rare Morgan dollar varieties may have been excellent candidates for the *Top 100*, but may not have been as popular as one of the more plentiful varieties that had made the first *Top 100* list. Many new books have since been published, such as Jeff Oxman's *Hot 50* and *Hit List 40*, David Wang's *Guide to 1879-S Reverse of 1878 Morgan Silver Dollars*, and Mark Kimpton's *Elite Clashed Morgan Dollars*, all of which added new and interesting die varieties to collect.

Over the past decade since the *Top 100* was published, Dr. Fey has written a quarterly newsletter, the *Top 100 Insights and Value Guide*, which follows new discoveries and developments in the *Top 100* as well as other die varieties, and current pricing trends. Many new *Top 100* silver dollars joined the *Top 100* listing as a result of either a new obverse or reverse being discovered paired with the interesting variety feature that made the variety a *Top 100* coin in the first place. The only new variety that was added by the authors was the 1878 8-TF VAM 14.11, which replaced the 8-TF VAM 11, now believed to be a VAM listing error, and thought not to exist.

In addition, the authors have now expanded classes of *Top 100* varieties to include all of the different VAMS that could be collected to complete the set for that variety.

As your collecting interest in varieties grows, you will be making decisions on which other varieties you wish to collect. There will, of course, be new discoveries of interesting rare die varieties, and only time will tell which of them will ultimately become the rarest and most popular.

Tell Us About Your New Finds

In order to present an accurate picture of the rarity, popularity and value of the *Top 100* Morgans for future publications, we encourage you to send information about your finds to: Michael S. Fey, Ph.D., RCI, P.O. Box C, Ironia, NJ 07845; e-mail address: feyms@aol.com.

If you would like to receive a response, please include a self-addressed, stamped envelope. Provide the date, mintmark, variety and grade, and include the certification service, assigned grade, and slab number (if available), along with your telephone number.

If you choose to send coins to RCI, please ship them via insured, registered mail and include a self-addressed, pre-paid, insured and registered return envelope for returning them.

Coins may also be sent to Leroy Van Allen for review and possible VAM assignment. Send these to: Leroy Van Allen, P.O. Box 196, Sidney, OH 45365.

Be sure to ship your coins via insured, registered mail, and include a self-addresed, pre-paid, insured and registered return envelope or payment to cover the out-of-pocket expense. Also, please add $5 per coin for attribution review.

THE TOP 100 CHECKLIST

✓	Date	VAM	Description
	1878-P	5	Doubled "RIB" obverse
	1878-P	9	"First Morgan Dollar"
	1878-P	9A	"First Morgan Dollar" with clash
	1878-P	14.11	"Wild Eye Spikes" / A^1c reverse
	1878-P	15	Key II / I obverse + A^1e reverse
	1878-P	23	Doubled lips and profile
	1878-P	32	Three extra tailfeathers
	1878-P	41	Most complete "7/7" tailfeathers
	1878-P	41B	Clashed VAM 41
	1878-P	44	Tripled obv. "blossoms & leaves"
	1878-P	44A	Clashed VAM 44
	1878-P	45	Talons and legs doubled to the left
	1878-P	70	7-TF B^1 reverse doubled "RIB"
	1878-P	100-1	Type I obverse/B^2 reverse
	1878-P	100-2	Type I obverse/Different reverse
	1878-P	115	Tripled obverse/B^2a reverse
	1878-P	198	Tripled obverse/B^2f reverse
	1878-P	117	Tripled obverse star/B^2b reverse
	1878-P	141	Tripled obverse star/B^2c reverse
	1878-P	141A	Clashed tripled obv. star/B^2c rev.
	1878-P	171	Tripled "R"
	1878-P	203	Short wheat leaf with "Rev. of '78"
	1878-P	203A	Short wheat leaf with clash
	1878-P	220	Tripled "R" with "Rev. of '79"
	1878-P	223	Washed-out "L" with "Rev. of '79"
	1878-CC	6	Doubled obv./CC touches wreath

✓	Date	VAM	Description
	1878-CC	11	Lines in eagle's wing reverse
	1878-CC	18	Doubled obverse/CC chips
	1878-CC	24	Doubled obverse/CC left
	1878-CC	24A	Doubled obverse/CC left with clash
	1878-S	26	Eye chips/B^1 reverse
	1878-S	27	Broken "D"/B^1 reverse
	1878-S	56	Double eye spikes/B^1 reverse
	1878-S	57	Eye chips/B^1 reverse
	1878-S	58	Big eye spike/B^1 reverse
	1878-S	59	No eye spike/B^1 reverse
	1878-S	60	Rare first B^1 reverse
	1878-S	62	Very rare/B^1 reverse
	1878-S	72	*Ultra rare* B^1 reverse
	1879-O	4	"O/Horizontal O"
	1879-O	28	Doubled 7/"O/Horizontal O"
	1879-S	4	Reverse of '78
	1879-S	6	Reverse of '78
	1879-S	9	Reverse of '78
	1879-S	23	Reverse of '78
	1879-S	25	Reverse of '78
	1879-S	34	Reverse of '78
	1879-S	34A	Reverse of '78
	1879-S	34B	Reverse of '78
	1879-S	35	Reverse of '78
	1879-S	39	Reverse of '78
	1879-S	42	Reverse of '78
	1879-S	43	Reverse of '78
	1879-S	46	Reverse of '78
	1879-S	50	Reverse of '78

18B

✓	Date	VAM	Description
	1879-S	51	Reverse of '78
	1879-S	52	Reverse of '78
	1879-S	56 (56A)	Reverse of '78
	1879-S	66	Reverse of '78
	1879-S	67	Reverse of '78
	1879-CC	3	"Capped Die" CC
	1880-P	1A	Knobbed "8"
	1880-P	6	"8/7" "Spikes" overdate
	1880-P	7	"8/7" "Crossbar" overdate
	1880-P	8	"8/7" "Ears" overdate
	1880-P	9	"8/7" "Stem" overdate
	1880-P	23	"80/79" overdate
	1880-CC	4	"80/79" obverse/Reverse '78
	1880-CC	5	High "8/7" obverse/Reverse '79
	1880-CC	6	Low "8/7" obverse/Reverse '79
	1880-O	4	"80/79" "Crossbar" overdate
	1880-O	5	"8/7" "Crossbar" overdate
	1880-O	6	"Ear" overdate
	1880-O	6A	"8/7" "Ear" overdate
	1880-O	6C	"8/7" "Ear" overdate clashed
	1880-O	43	Doubled ear
	1880-O	48	"Hangnail" reverse
	1880-O	49	"8/7" "Ear/Hangnail" overdate
	1880-S	8	"80/79" diagonal overdate/Med. "S"
	1880-S	9	"80/79" diagonal overdate/Lg. "S"
	1880-S	10	"8/7" "Crossbar" overdate
	1882-O	3	"O/S" flush mintmark
	1882-O	3A	"O/S" flush mintmark with clash
	1882-O	3 EDS	"O/S" flush mintmark EDS

✓	Date	VAM	Description
	1882-O	4	"O/S" depressed mintmark
	1882-O	4 EDS	"O/S" depressed mintmark EDS
	1882-O	5	"O/S" broken mintmark
	1882-O	5 EDS	"O/S" broken mintmark EDS
	1882-O	7	"O/O" mintmark
	1883-P	10	Sextupled obverse stars
	1883-O	4	"O/O" mintmark
	1884-P	3	Large "dot"
	1884-P	4	Small "dot"
	1884-O	6	"O/O" mintmark
	1885-S	6	"S/S" mintmark
	1885-S	9	"S/S" mintmark w/misplaced date
	1886-P	1A	Line in "6"
	1886-P	1A1	Line in "6" with clashed dies
	1886-P	21	Misplaced date
	1886-P	17	Doubled arrows
	1886-O	1A	"E" on reverse
	1886-S	2	"S/S" mintmark
	1887-P	1A	"Donkey Tail"
	1887-P	2	"7/6" overdate
	1887-P	5	Doubled date
	1887-P	12	"Alligator Eye"
	1887-P	12A	Clashed "Alligator Eye"
	1887-O	2	Doubled date
	1887-O	3	"7/6" overdate
	1887-O	5	Doubled stars
	1887-O	22A	Pitted reverse
	1887-O	22B	Clashed pitted reverse

✓	Date	VAM	Description
	1887-S	2	"S/S" mintmark
	1888-P	11	Doubled ear
	1888-P	11A	Clashed doubled ear
	1888-O	1A	"E" on reverse
	1888-O	1B LDS	"Scarface" variety
	1888-O	4	"Hot Lips" variety
	1888-O	9	Doubled arrows
	1888-O	2	Oval "O" mintmark
	1888-O	5	Oval "O" mintmark
	1888-O	6	Oval "O" mintmark
	1888-O	17	Oval "O" mintmark
	1888-O	18	Oval "O" mintmark
	1888-O	21	Oval "O" mintmark
	1888-O	24	Oval "O" mintmark
	1888-O	34	Oval "O" mintmark
	1889-P	19A	"Barwing"
	1889-P	19B	Clashed "Barwing"
	1889-P	22	Near date "Barwing"
	1889-O	1A1	Single clash/"E" on reverse
	1889-O	1A2	Double clash/"E" on reverse
	1889-O	2	Oval "O" mintmark
	1889-O	2A	Oval "O" mintmark
	1889-O	6	Doubled date
	1890-CC	4	"Tailbar" variety
	1891-P	2	Doubled ear
	1891-P	2A	Doubled ear and "moustache"
	1891-P	2B	Clashed doubled ear
	1891-CC	3	"Spitting Eagle" reverse
	1891-O	1A1	"E" on reverse

✓	Date	VAM	Description
	1891-O	1A2	LDS "E" on reverse
	1891-O	1A3	VLDS "E" on reverse
	1891-S	3	Doubled stars
	1892-O	5	Doubled ear
	1892-S	2	Doubled date
	1893-P	4	Doubled stars
	1895-S	4	"S/Horizontal S"
	1896-P	4	Doubled stars
	1896-P	19	"8" in denticles
	1896-O	4	Micro "o" mintmark
	1897-P	6A	Pitted reverse
	1899-O	4	Micro "o" mintmark
	1899-O	5	Micro "o" mintmark
	1899-O	6	Micro "o" mintmark
	1899-O	31	Micro "o" mintmark
	1899-O	32	Micro "o" mintmark
	1899-S	7	Doubled date
	1900-P	11	Doubled reverse
	1900-P	24	Multiple punched stars obverse
	1900-O	5	Micro "o" Mintmark
	1900-O	15	Doubled obverse stars
	1900-O	15A	Clashed doubled obverse stars
	1900-O	29A	Die break thru date
	1900-O	7	"O/CC" mintmark
	1900-O	7A	"O/CC" mintmark
	1900-O	8	"O/CC" mintmark
	1900-O	8A	"O/CC" mintmark
	1900-O	8B	"O/CC" mintmark
	1900-O	9	"O/CC" mintmark

✓	Date	VAM	Description
	1900-O	10	"O/CC" mintmark
	1900-O	10A	"O/CC" mintmark
	1900-O	11	"O/CC" mintmark
	1900-O	12	"O/CC" mintmark
	1901-P	3	"Shifted Eagle"
	1902-P	4	Doubled ear
	1902-O	3	Micro "o" mintmark
	1903-S	2	Small "s" mintmark
	1921-P	41	Pitted reverse
	1921-P	4	Wide reeding
	1921-P	13	Wide reeding
	1921-P	13A	Wide reeding
	1921-P	25	Wide reeding
	1921-P	25A	Wide reeding
	1921-P	26	Wide reeding
	1921-P	26A	Wide reeding
	1921-P	27	Wide reeding
	1921-P	27A	Wide reeding
	1921-P	28	Wide reeding
	1921-P	28A	Wide reeding
	1921-P	29	Wide reeding
	1921-P	29A	Wide reeding
	1921-P	44	Rare wide reeding
	1921-D	1A	"Tru-t" variety

Morgan Dollar Overlays for Die Clash Analysis 23B

Have your local copy shop print the top two images on transparency film for you.

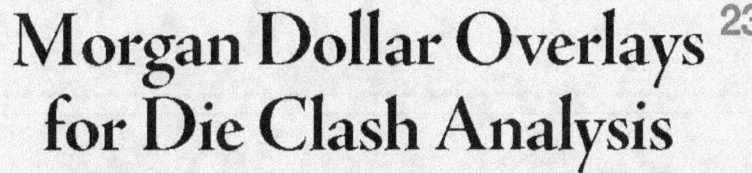

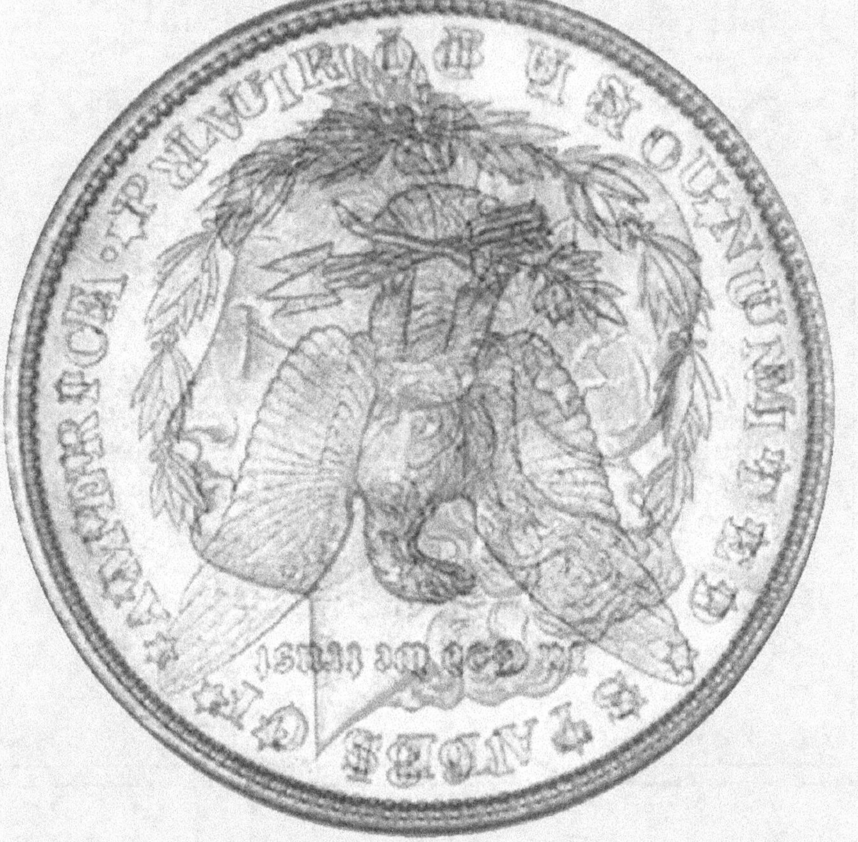

What the experts are saying about the Top 100

"An extremely important reference work that no Morgan dollar buyer should be without. With silver dollar variety collecting still in its infancy, I expect the field to expand dramatically in the years to come. Any collector or dealer who routinely uses this book gains a very worthwhile edge."

— Jim Halperin, Co-Chairman,
Heritage Auction Galleries (HA.com)

"No one is more responsible for the renewed — and rapidly growing — interest in VAMS than Michael Fey and Jeff Oxman. No one. That resurgence began with their landmark 1997 book, *Top 100*. This is the long-awaited and expanded update. The first one sold out quickly; I predict this one will sell out almost before the ink is dry."

— James Taylor, CEO & President, ANACS

"If the VAM Book is the foundation of dollar variety collecting, then *Top 100 Morgan Dollar Varieties: The VAM Keys* has been the cornerstone for the past decade. It provided the much-needed focus and architecture that allowed the hobby to head in new directions and reach unimaginable heights. This book will continue to be at the forefront of guiding and serving collectors and remains indispensable for their use."

— Leroy Van Allen

What the experts are saying about the Top 100

"In the dozen years since its debut, *The VAM Keys* book has revolutionized the collecting of Morgan Dollar varieties, taking this previously overlooked speciality into the mainstream. The number of collectors seeking *Top 100* VAMs has multiplied many times over. While their attribution is now much easier, the competition to locate unattributed rarities is far more keen due to this handy guide."

— David W. Lange, Research Director, NGC

"One of the perks of coin collecting is the thrill of the hunt and the exhilaration of the find... always has been, always will be. What better series than the Morgan Dollar to feed this habit? The newly revised, easy-to-read and comprehensive *Top 100* book you are holding in your hand will enable you to capitalize on the most important aspect of numismatics... having FUN. Enjoy!"

— Bill Fivaz

FURTHER REFERENCES

Please check Amazon Kindle for Michael S. Fey, Ph.D., and Leroy Van Allen & A. George Mall is publications. For hard copy print of books, please contact Dr. Fey at RCI, P.O. Box C, Ironia, N J 07845 or eMail: Feyms@aol.com.

Hard copy books are also available at *The Institute for Silver Dollar Education and Research*, at website: *Ilovesilverdollars.org* or by contacting Executive Director John Baumgart at John.Baum gart@comcast.net

Amazon Kindle

Fey, Michael S. 2019. *The Complete Virtual Guide to Pricing Your Morgan Silver Dollars*. 286 pp. RCI

Van Allen, Leroy, & A. George Mallis. 2023. *Part I or II or III of Three. Comprehensive Catalog and Encyclopedia or Morgan & Peace Dollars*. RCI Total 520 pp.

Leroy Van Allen. 2011. *Wonders of Morgan Dollars*. 139 pp. RCI

Leroy Van Allen. 2013. *Wonders of Peace Dollars*. 273 pp. RCI

Leroy Van Allen. 2006. *Morgan Dollars 8 & 7 Over 8 Tail Feather Story*. 52 pp. RCI

Leroy Van Allen. 2010. *1878 P 7 Tail Feather Morgan Dollar Attribution Guide*. 130 pp. RCI

Leroy Van Allen. 2006. *1878 S Morgan Dollar Attribution Guide*. 139 pp. RCI

Fey, Michael S. 2009 The Top 100 Morgan Dollar Varieties: The VAM Keys

FURTHER REFERENCES

Hard Copy Books

Fey, Michael S. 2019. The Top 100 Morgan Dollar Varieties: The VAM Keys. 286 pp. RCI

Fey, Michael S. 2008. *A Decade of Top 100 Insights*. RCI 174 pp.

Van Allen, Leroy. 1991. *RotaFlip Die Rotation Booklet and Guide*. 1991. RCI

Kimpton, M.D., Mark. 2005. *Elite Clashed Morgan Dollars*. RCI 160 pp

Van Allen, Leroy, & A. George Mallis. 2023. *Comprehensive Catalog and Encyclopedia or Morgan & Peace Dollars*. RCI Total 520 pp.

Van Allen, Leroy 2011. *Wonders of Morgan Dollars*. 139 pp. RCI

Van Allen, Leroy 2013. *Wonders of Peace Dollars*. 273 pp. RCI

Van Allen, Leroy 2006. *Morgan Dollars 8 & 7 Over 8 Tail Feather Story*. 52 pp. RCI

Van Allen, Leroy 2010. *1878 P 7 Tail Feather Morgan Dollar Attribution Guide*. 130 pp. RCI

Van Allen, Leroy 2006. *1878 S Morgan Dollar Attribution Guide*. 139 pp. RCI

Van Allen, Leroy 2013. *Die Gouges and Scratches Peace Dollar Attribution Guide. 109 pp* RCI

Van Allen, Leroy 2008. *1921 Scribbles Morgan Dollar Attribution Guide*. 234 pp. RCI

Van Allen, Leroy. 2013. *Misplaced Date Digits Morgan Dollar Attribution Guide*. 57 pp RCI

Van Allen, Leroy. 2017. *Dashed Under 8 Morgan Dollar Attribution Guide*. 53 pp. RCI

Van Allen, Leroy. 2009. *Overdates and Over Mint Marks of Morgan Dollar Attribution Guide*. 53 pp. RCI

Van Allen, Leroy. 2015. *Denticle & Die Impressions Morgan Dollar Attribution Guide*. 109 pp. RCI

Van Allen, Leroy. 2009. *1921 P Infrequently Reeded or Wide Reeding Morgan Dollar Attribution Guide*. 31 pp. RCI

Van Allen, Leroy. 2011 *Amazing Changing 1921 S VAM 1B Thorn Head Morgan Dollar*. 2011. 22 pp. RCI

Van Allen, Leroy. 2009. *1889 P Doubled Ear Morgan Dollar Attribution Guide*. 32 pp. RCI

Van Allen, Leroy. 2016. *Micro o and Other Counterfeit Morgan and Peace Dollars*. 191 pp RCI

Van Allen, Leroy. 2005. *Micro o Mint Mark on Morgan Dollars*. 32 pp. RCI

Van Allen, Leroy. 2005. *Die Markers for 1921 Morgan and Peace Proof Dollars*. 9 pp. RCI

Van Allen, Leroy and Baumgart, John. 1992-Date Various VAM Book Yearly Supplements. RCI

TOP 100
Morgan Dollar Varieties

"Fey and Oxman have significantly updated what is arguably the one 'must-have' book on Morgan Dollar varieties. Van Allen and Mallis painted the 'big picture,' but the *Top 100* brings many of its most interesting elements into the sharp focus they deserve."

— *John Roberts,*
Director of Attribution Services, ANACS

For as long as I can remember, I've carried a copy of *Top 100 Morgan Dollar Varieties* in my briefcase to every show I've attended. It gives a fellow like me who really isn't an expert in VAMs the knowledge I need about the best of the best. I'm elated to hear that there is now a new expanded edition!

— *Ken Potter,* Coin World *Columnist*

ISBN 978-0-9653645-5-3

90000

9 780965 364553